THE RISE OF THE NETWORKING REGION

The International Political Economy of New Regionalisms Series

The International Political Economy of New Regionalisms series presents innovative analyses of a range of novel regional relations and institutions. Going beyond established, formal, interstate economic organizations, this essential series provides informed interdisciplinary and international research and debate about myriad heterogeneous intermediate level interactions.

Reflective of its cosmopolitan and creative orientation, this series is developed by an international editorial team of established and emerging scholars in both the South and North. It reinforces ongoing networks of analysts in both academia and think-tanks as well as international agencies concerned with micro-, meso- and macro-level regionalisms.

Recent titles in the series (continued at the back of the book)

Shifting Geo-Economic Power of the Gulf
Oil, Finance and Institutions
Edited by Matteo Legrenzi and Bessma Momani

Building Regions
The Regionalization of the World Order
Luk Van Langenhove

National Solutions to Trans-Border Problems?
The Governance of Security and Risk in a Post-NAFTA North America
Edited by Isidro Morales

The Rise of the Networking Region

The Challenges of Regional Collaboration in a Globalized World

Edited by

HARALD BALDERSHEIM
University of Oslo, Norway

ARE VEGARD HAUG
University of Agder, Norway

MORTEN ØGÅRD
University of Agder, Norway

LONDON AND NEW YORK

First published 2011 by Ashgate Publishing

2 Park Square, Milton Park, Abingdon, Oxon OX14 4RN
711 Third Avenue, New York, NY 10017, USA

Routledge is an imprint of the Taylor & Francis Group, an informa business

First issued in paperback 2016

British Library Cataloguing in Publication Data
The rise of the networking region : the challenges of
  regional collaboration in a globalized world. -- (The
  international political economy of new regionalisms series)
  1. Scandinavia--Politics and government--1945-
  2. Interregionalism--Scandinavia.
  I. Series II. Baldersheim, Harald, 1944- III. Haug, Are
  Vegard. IV. Ogard, Morten.
  320.9'48'09051-dc22

Library of Congress Cataloging-in-Publication Data
Baldersheim, Harald, 1944-
  The rise of the networking region : the challenges of regional collaboration in a globalized world / by Harald Baldersheim, Are Vegard Haug, and Morten Xgerd.
    p. cm. -- (The international political economy of new regionalisms
series)
  Includes bibliographical references and index.
  ISBN 978-1-4094-2583-0 (hardback)
  1. Scandinavian cooperation. 2. Regionalism--Scandinavia. I. Haug, Are Vegard. II.
Xgerd, Morten. III. Title.
  JN7011.B35 2010
  303.48'248--dc22

2010052228

ISBN 978-1-4094-2583-0 (hbk)
ISBN 978-1-138-26132-7 (pbk)

Contents

List of Figures and Maps   *vii*
List of Tables   *ix*
Notes on Contributors   *xiii*
Preface   *xv*

1   The Rise of the Networking Region: The Challenges of
Regional Collaboration in a Globalized World   1
Harald Baldersheim and Morten Øgård

2   The Nordic Regions: Institutional Development and
Public Debate 1996–2009   13
Siv Sandberg

3   Knowledge Brokerage and Institutional Retooling:
Policy Preferences for Regional Development in a
Competitive World   23
Harald Baldersheim

4   Learning Ecologies: Capacity-Building in Nordic Regions and
Cities through Cross-Institutional and Cross-Border Cooperation   35
Harald Baldersheim and Morten Øgård

5   Regions in the European Architecture of Governance:
Towards Integrative Regionalism. The Attitudes of
Regional Policy-Makers   49
Harald Baldersheim

6   Transforming Governance in Cities and Regions in the
Nordic Countries: Adapting to "the New Citizen"?   65
Harald Baldersheim and Morten Øgård

7   Informatization of Political Roles and Communication Patterns:
Regional Advantages through Information and
Communication Technologies?   77
Are Vegard Haug

8   "The New Kid on the Block". Faroese Foreign Affairs –
        between Hierarchy and Network   95
        Joan Ólavsdóttir, Jens Christian Svabo Justinussen and
        Beinta í Jákupsstovu

9   Building Learning Ecologies: What Works and How?
        The Examples of the County Councils of Telemark and
        Aust-Agder (Norway)   115
        Jørgen Sande Lysa and Morten Øgård

10   International Cooperation of the New Danish Regions:
        Lifeline or Last Rites? The Case of Southern Denmark   133
        Niels Ejersbo

11   Cultural Policies as Development Strategies in Nordic Regions –
        A Comparison of Two Projects   141
        Aase Marthe J. Horrigmo

12   Conclusions: The Policy Nexus in Network Governance   165
        Harald Baldersheim, Are Vegard Haug and Morten Øgård

Bibliography   *171*
Index   *185*

List of Figures and Maps

Figures

1.1	Policy drives change: hypotheses	4
1.2	National contexts regarding the position of regions in the Nordic countries	7
1.3	The competitive environment of regions and cities: hypothesized collaborative inclinations	7

Maps

5.1	Nordic Cross-Border Cooperation Committes	53
5.2	Nordic Interreg III A/B Programme Areas	54
5.3	Nordic Regions Eligible for Support from Objective 1 and 2 Funds 2002–06	55

List of Tables

1.1   Survey data collected   9
1.A   Summary analysis of response rates and data attrition for
      city and regional councillors   12

2.1   The democratically elected regional levels in the
      Nordic countries at the beginning of the 2000s   15
2.2   The regional level in the Nordic countries 2010   20

3.1   Policy preferences of regional and urban politicians. Mean scores 1998
      and 2008   26
3.2   Policy options: who is in favour and who is against?
      Regression analysis   30
3.3   Policy options and cleavages: commentaries and summaries   31

4.1   Cross-border and cross-institutional involvement among
      Nordic regional and urban politicians 1998 and 2008.
      Mean scores (2008) and percentage "yes"   40
4.2   The usefulness of involvement in international networks
      according to the assessment of regional and urban politicians,
      and totals for 2008 and 1998   43
4.3   Determinants of network participation and satisfaction with
      outcomes. Regression analysis   45

5.1   Attitudes to cross-border and European governance.
      Survey of regional and urban elected representatives in
      Denmark, Finland, Norway, Sweden. 1998, 2008   59
5.2   Supporters and opponents of integrative and
      state-centred regionalism   63

6.1   Strategies and measures to enhance the responsiveness of local
      authorities, 1997/98–2007/08 (indices applied in surveys of
      Nordic cities and regions)   68
6.2   Nordic cities and regions: types of development initiatives by
      country, 1997/98–2007/08   70

6.3   Nordic cities only: types of development initiatives by
        country, 1997/98–2007/08   71
6.4   Correlation matrix for the indices of user orientation,
        market orientation, community involvement,
        transparency/information   73

7.1   General use of ICTs: Nordic city and regional politicians
        (average scores – typical month)   80
7.2   ICT and the role of the ombudsman: Nordic city and
        regional politicians (2008–09)   82
7.3   ICT and the role of *controller*: Nordic city and
        regional politicians (2008–09)   83
7.4   ICT and the role of *representative*: Nordic city and
        regional politicians (2008–09)   84
7.5   ICT and the role of *decision-maker*: Nordic city and
        regional politicians (2008–09)   85
7.6   ICT in the service of democracy – impacts on role components;
        summary: Nordic city and regional politicians   87
7.7   Regression analyses: ICT proficiency (use and experiences) and
        cross-institutional contact patterns. Nordic city and
        regional politicians (2006–08)   90
7.A   Operational definitions of the dependent and
        independent variables of Table 7.7   93

8.1   Faroese emissaries' responses to the question:
        "Do you mostly network with Danish actors?"   106
8.2   Faroese politicians' involvement in cross-border contacts
        compared to East Nordic regional and urban politicians   108
8.3   Overall satisfaction with international involvement:
        Faroese politicians compared to Nordic colleagues   108
8.4   Satisfaction with various regional/municipal collaborations:
        Faroese politicians compared to Nordic colleagues   109
8.5   Faroese politicians' views of European collaborations
        compared to other Nordic regional and urban politicians   110
8.6   "It is about time for each region to develop its
        own foreign policy"   110
8.7   "It is about time for each region to develop its own foreign policy".
        Respondents grouped according to their party's position on Faroese
        autonomy   111
8.8   "It is about time for each region to develop its
        own foreign policy"   112

9.1   Telemark County Council's international involvement
       ca. 2000–08   120
9.2   Aust-Agder County Council's international involvement
       ca. 2000–09   124
9.3   The learning ecologies of Telemark and
       Aust-Agder County Councils   130

Notes on Contributors

Harald Baldersheim is Professor in political science at the University of Oslo, Norway.

Niels Ejersbo is Associate Professor in political science at the University of Southern Denmark, Odense.

Are Vegard Haug is Associate Professor in political science and governance at the University of Agder, Norway.

Aase Marthe Horrigmo is a PhD student in political science and governance at the University of Agder, Norway.

Beinta í Jákupsstovu is Associate Professor in political science at Molde University College, Norway, and at the University of the Faroe Islands.

Joan Ólavsdóttir has a Masters in political science from the University of the Faroe Islands.

Siv Sandberg is Associate Professor in public administration at Abo Academy, Finland.

Jørgen Sande Lysa has a Masters in political science from the University of Oslo, Norway.

Jens Christian Svabo Justinussen is Assistant Professor in political science at the University of the Faroe Islands.

Morten Øgård is Associate Professor in political science and governance at the University of Agder, Norway.

Preface

This book is based on the project "The Emergence of the Networking Region", financed by a grant from the Nordic Council of Ministers through NORDREGIO, Stockholm. The project covers the four Nordic countries of Denmark, Finland, Norway and Sweden plus the Faroe Islands. The data include a survey of regional and urban politicians from all regions of the respective countries, surveys of institutional developments in regions and cities plus a series of case studies. The project is at times a reiteration of one carried out about 10 years ago entitled "The Nordic Countries in Europe of the Regions", conducted by Harald Baldersheim and Krister Ståhlberg. We would like to thank NORDREGIO for permission to use the maps printed in Chapter 5.

Harald Baldersheim, Are Vegard Haug and
Morten Øgård

Chapter 1

The Rise of the Networking Region: The Challenges of Regional Collaboration in a Globalized World

Harald Baldersheim and Morten Øgård

Regions as Development Agents in Network Society

The international arena can no longer be fully understood without paying attention to the role of regional networks. Regional networks are emerging at continental as well as at sub-national scales. Continental and sub-national networks are intertwined through processes of globalization. Globalization implies freer and faster transmission of people, capital and information across national borders. National as well as local developments are increasingly at the mercy of decisions taken in far-away places (Martin and Schumann 1996, Beck 1997, Østerud 1999). In attempts to regain some control over their destinies nation-states band together in large-scale regional alliances such as the European Union, the North American Free Trade Agreement, or the ASEAN. At the sub-national level, with similar aims, regions and cities form cross-border clubs with their counterparts in other countries (Hobbs 1994, Goldsmith and Klausen 1997, Baldersheim and Ståhlberg 1999). The emergence of regional networks can be seen as bits of a larger picture, as outlined by Manuel Castells (1996) in *The Rise of the Network Society*, closely intertwined with the arrival of digital information technologies, restructuring of processes of production, and footloose capitalism. However, a rather bleak picture of the policy space available to national and local policy-makers emerges out of Castells' account.

In this volume we seek to understand processes of region-building in a bottom-up perspective. First, we chart the extent of cross-border networking of sub-national regions in the Nordic countries. Second, we analyse how sub-national regions strive to acquire a voice in the wider architecture of European governance. Third, we highlight the role of *political actors* and their views on these processes. We pay attention, in particular, to their role as development agents and their policy preferences in this respect. We try to show that regional policy-makers may have more policy space available than that recognized by the account of Manuel Castells.

In so doing we have expanded the group of regional policy-makers to include also elected officers from the larger *cities* of the respective regions since regional development policies today are moving beyond a rural-urban dichotomy in the pursuit of regional competitiveness.[1]

The analyses presented in this book also have a longitudinal dimension. The analyses build on and update a data base established 1997/98 covering all Nordic regions and larger cities (Baldersheim, Sandberg, Ståhlberg and Øgård 2001). Thus, a central aim of the book is to chart the changes in networking activities and related development initiatives that have taken place over the last 10 years. In the subsequent chapters we argue that the regional networks of the Nordic countries have moved from a "euro-euphoric" to a policy-centred stage.

Theoretical Foundations: Policy-driven Regionalism

Regional attitudes condensed into the well-known slogan of "Europe of the Regions" were a point of departure for our former project, which sought to probe the reality of such attitudes in terms of collaborative patterns and policy preferences among regional actors in the Nordic countries. Theoretical inspiration was found in notions about the rise of regional identity politics (Keating and Loughlin 1997), the learning region (Lundvall 1992, Amin and Thrift 1994) and the emergence of a room for regions in European integration through multi-level governance (Marks et al. 1994, Magone 2003). The emergent vanguard regions were expected to exhibit a fusion of these features, demonstrated in a combination of regional pride, preferences for "soft" development policies and pro-EU attitudes. We did find a group of regions characterized by such features, but we also found marked contrasts and cleavages among Nordic regions in terms of policy preferences, network participation and attitudes to state intervention and European integration. Interestingly, the cleavage between "status-quo-oriented" and "vanguard" regions cut across traditional centre-periphery cleavages in the Nordic countries.

Ten years on, the institutional landscape has changed both at the European level and in the Nordic countries regarding the position of regions. The Committee of the Regions, for example, though demonstrating much vitality, has not attained the central position many of its champions hoped for (Magone 2003). Furthermore, the Eurpean Union has expanded eastwards to include 10 former Warsaw Pact countries; the objectives of the structural and cohesion funds have been adjusted accordingly to take account of new geopolitical realities, with consequences for the eligibility of Nordic regions with regard to support from these funds. Nordic

---

1   This is how the Nordic Council of Ministers presents today's approach to regional policy challenges, "From a previous focus on equalising 'rich' and 'poor' regions, regional policy in the Nordic countries has for a number of years been dominated by efforts aimed at growth, competitiveness, entrepreneurship and innovation. The perspective has been broadened and the policy now applies to largely the entire national territory. Urban areas and other growth hubs in the urban networks have gained importance". *Nordic regional policy cooperation programme 2009–2012*, p. 48, Nordic Council of Ministers, 2009.

regions have followed highly diverging trajectories: Norwegian counties have been shorn of important functions (e.g. hospitals), the developmental capacity of the five new Danish regions is uncertain, while the organization and implementation of Finish regional policies remain as fragmented as ever. Only Swedish regions may be said to have increased in stature over the last decade with large-scale regions established in Vestra Götaland and Skåne and interesting experiments in collaboration taking place in other counties (Baldersheim 2004, Sandberg 2005).

However, the Nordic countries also include "home rule" regions (Åland, Greenland, the Faroes) that deviate sharply from the normal structures of regional governance in their respective countries. How have these regions fared in the international climate of globalization during the last decade? Our volume covers one case, the Faroes Islands, located in the Atlantic Ocean between Scotland and Iceland, with aspiration towards nationhood and with a special status as regards the European Union.

Today, the debate on regional development policies are shaped by theories of the information society (Castells 1996, 2005), the role of "the creative class" (Florida 2002, 2005, Landry 2000), culturalist perspectives (Putnam 1993, 2001, Clark 2004, Chabal and Daloz 2005) and models of institutional dynamics (March and Olsen 1995, Stone 1989, Stoker and Mossberger 1994, Koppenjan and Erik-Hans Klijn 2004). Our project has been guided in particular by the latter approach while we also seek to integrate the former perspectives into our analytical strategies. Our overall approach is inspired by the devise "policy determines politics" originally formulated by Lowi (1964).

In our case this means that the emergence of new policy options for regional development are seen as creating pressures on existing institutional structures, driving a search for new organizational patterns better suited to the pursuit of the new policies. The present-day turmoil as regards regional governance in all of the Nordic countries may be taken as symptomatic for institutional patterns being out of sync with the requirements of new policies. The emergent trend of networking governance is the outward expression of the quest for new patterns of collaboration in order to accommodate new policies. New policies require new partners. Our main hypothesis is that the more regions make efforts in order to formulate and implement information society type of policies the more they will be involved in dense and far-flung networks. These networks may again result in new patterns of governance, as indicated by Figure 1.1.

The research strategy of the project has been to analyse the relationships outlined in Figure 1.1: how regional actors perceive and choose between new policy options; how the pursuit of new options drives the emergence of cross-border policy networks; and how and to what extent these policy networks result in new patterns of regional governance. The basic idea is that new policy options and new policy networks are expected to create pressures on existing patterns of governance. Regions may react differently to these pressures. Reactions may also involve conflicts regarding policy choices, network involvement and governance strategies. In fact, new agendas may entail new cleavages more difficult to bridge

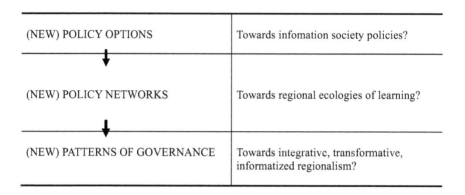

Figure 1.1   Policy drives change: hypotheses

than the those reflected by established party structures. Establised parties have grown out of conflicts typical of the industrial order (with echoes of earlier periods of nation-building). Information society may engender coflicts of a more post-materialist nature, related to identities, life styles or environmental issues.

First, regions are searching for appropriate *policies* in their capacities as development agents in information society. Policy measures developed for the industiral age have lost their relevance as labour intensive industries move to low-cost countries. Triple Helix is a designation in vogue since the 1990s to describe policy options to promote regional development initiatives in information society (Etzkowitz 2008). These options include close collaboration between research institutions, public authorities and business and industry. Practical expressions of such policies are the research parks that have sprouted on the outskirts of university campuses around Europe (Komninos 1992). In many cases the services provided directly by regions are reshaped to fit into the new policy concepts, especially in the field of culture and the environment. The attractiveness of regions hinges increasingly on urban and environmental qualities combined with well-developed digital infrastructure. Paradoxically, the endogenous model of development is dependent upon a capacity to learn from others, often from distant parts of the world.

Second, regions learn through participation in *policy networks*. A policy network is a collaborative arrangement among a group of regions focussing on a particular policy challenge, e.g. the touristic potential of costal regions or the digital infrastructure of peripheral regions. An *ecology of learning* designates the pattern of networks in which a region is involved. Policy networks may grow into ecologies of learning if there is a certain stability and cohesion to the patterns of networks. Through ecologies of learning regions are able to learn from and adapt to multi-facetted and changing environments. The term *ecology* of learning is intended to alert us to how regions adapt to an increasingly *competititve environment*. Regional geographers and economists have for some time been preoccupied with "the learning region", a term which denotes regions rich in mutually supportive inter-firm networks and also public-private partnerships (Morgan 1992, Amin and Thrift 1994, Simmie 1997, Boekema et al. 2000). What is lacking in these analyses, however, is an understanding of how *political actors* learn and change their policy preferences, including preferences for devleopment strategies. The concept of learning ecologies contributes to such an understanding.

Third, new policy options entail patterns of decision-making through *governance* structures. Governance refers to the organization of collective action without recourse to authoritative powers of hierarchy and command, or to situations in which those powers are distributed in ambiguous fashion (Peters and Pierre 2002). In such situations joint action relies largely on incentives and persuasion. The policy networks mentioned above are examples of embryonic governance patterns. The step from policy network to governance means to move from learning to collective action by developing joint decision-making procedures. In this project we have in particular sought to map the extent to which regional policy-makers advocate comprehensive roles for regions in European processes of decision-making as against those that think that regions should be limited to national roles or at most a role in established Nordic structures of collaboration. Policy-makers who advocate more influential roles for regions in European affairs are designated champions of *integrative regionalism.* The term integrative regionalism is coined to capture a role for regions *beyond* the one often outlined in accounts of regions in multi-level governance. The role of regions in multi-level governance has largely been portrayed as that of lobbying in Brussels (Marks et al. 1994). This is a role that regions increasingly took on during the 1990s as they established offices or other listening posts to gather information, monitor decision-making in EU institutions and collect as much money as possible from the structural and other EU funds. Such a role largely meant entering into a clientellistic relation to the Commision. Integrative regionalism is a movement to make regions institutionalized partners in decision-making at levels beyond the nation-state and especially in EU affairs.

Integrative regionalism is expected to have repercussions also for how regions relate to citizens and also for the roles of elected officers. New patterns of governance may entail pressures on the legitimacy of public authorities, requiring new *transformative strategies*, i.e. strategies intended to enhance citizen understanding of public action and trust in bodies of governance. As the role of regions as development agents is becoming more pronounced – in Norway and Denmark that of the service provider is actually reduced while Finnish regions were never really strong in this respect – strategies focussing on citizen involvement, dialogue and information may come more to the foreground. Is politics brought back in?

The roles of elected officers may also be put under pressure by new patterns of governance. Participation in joint decision-making across institutional borders as well as more demanding relations to citizens may require new political capacities. Can those requirements be met through informatization, i.e. putting digital resources at the disposal of elected representatives? The question can also be put the other way round: does informatization affect policy-makers' patterns of communication with citizens and across institutional borders?

A Comparative Framework of Analysis

The hypothesized developments outlined in Figure 1.1 are analysed in *a comparative framework* that highlights features of the national contexts in which regions are placed and also their spatial settings. The national contexts are defined through relationship to the EU (membership/non-membership) and the overall position of regions in the national political system. EU membership is expected to intensify exposure to international competition but also to open up policy opportunities, both of which are expected to augment regional activism. The position of regions is defined through the autonomy (range of functions) of regions; Swedish regions have been on the ascendancy in this regard, while Norwegian ones have become somewhat reduced and the Danish regions are hardly worthy of the name any more. Finnish regions remain in their limbo as advisory boards to strong national planning agencies (cf. Chapter 2 for further details). A greater range of functions means a greater range of responsibilities, which again presumably drives a search for new policy options and demands for more powers from the state. In Figure 1.2 the two features of the national contexts are combined, which yields four types of contexts: the weak outsider regions (Norway), the strong insider regions (Sweden) and weak insider regions (Finland and Denmark). The fourth position, strong outsider regions, is factually empty. Against this background, Norwegian and Swedish regions are expected to be the contrasts with regard to the developments pinpointed in Figure 1.1 while Denmark and Finland will occupy the middle ground.

The second feature of the comparative framework is that of geographic-institutional space. Regional policy-making takes place in a competitive environment composed of other regional policy-makers and also defined by their location on a centre-periphery dimension. Regions compete, first, in geographic space with other regions over attention and investments from national and international investors. Competition of this nature is structured mostly along a centre-periphery dimension. Regions with a central location can expect to be advantaged as locations for advanced industries, especially knowledge-intensive industries. Peripheral regions in Europe face an uphill struggle as labour-intensive industries move to low-cost locations.

Competition in institutional space is over the distribution of powers and functions in the public sector. Regions have often faced opposition particularly from cities, that resist the prospect of powerful regions. Traditionally, in the three Scandinavian countries, regions have been secondary authorities established for the aid of rural municipalities that were considered too weak to take on demanding tasks individually. Functions as comprehensive development agents were granted

EU membership		Regional autonomy	
		Weak(er*)	*Strong(er*)*
EU membership	*Out*	Norway	
	In	Denmark	Sweden
		Finland	

*indicates development over the last decade

Figure 1.2   National contexts regarding the position of regions in the Nordic countries

to regions only since the 1980s. However, many cities see themselves as the real development agents of their respective regions. Since the 2000s cities have been on the offensive, seeking to take back or at least enhance their capacities as development agents in their own right. Modern development concepts highlight attractive urban locations as the centrepieces of regional competitiveness (e.g. Dunford and Kafkalas 1992, Clark 2004b). Realizing such development concepts necessitates the cooperation of cities and regions but may be difficult to achieve when there are institutional borders that have to be bridged. As outlined in the next section on research design our data on regional policy-makers cover elected officers in cities as well as in regions, in order to analyse patterns of cleavage and cooperation between cities and regions.

Combining the two features yields the four-fold table in Figure 1.3.

Location[1]		Institution	
		City	*Region*
Location[1]	*Central*	Unwilling	Willing
	Peripheral	Willing	Willing

Figure 1.3   The competitive environment of regions and cities: hypothesized collaborative inclinations

[1]   Our notion of centrality builds on central place theory (Christaller 1933). Centrality is closely related to city size. Here, central regions are defined as regions with cities of at least 100,000 inhabitants; and accordingly, central cities are cities with at least 100,000 inhabitants.

For cooperation to take place both city and region have to be willing to enter into partnerships. Central cities are normally highly attractive locations and often do not have to make much efforts to attract new, advanced industries. Consequently, they have little incentive to join forces with regions and may feel they are better off on their own. Peripheral cities, on the other hand, are not the natural centres of gravity that central cities are. They may feel they may gain from joining forces with the surrounding region, especially when it comes to influencing national decisions on location of state investments.

Design and Data Collection

The units of analysis are Nordic regions (landsting, amt/new hospital and development regions, samkommuner and fylkeskommuner) and regional capitals (normally the largest cities in the regions). As mentioned above, the inclusion of cities in our research design reflects changes in regional policy orientation in the Nordic countries. The focus of regional development policy is no more exclusively on peripheral or backward regions but is framed as a part of national policies for development and competitiveness, in which strong regional centres – cities – are given a fundamental role so that a fusion of urban and regional development policies is under way. By comparing regions with the regional capitals we seek to assess to what extent such a policy focus is becoming a reality "on the ground" among policy-makers in regions and cities.

The data we have collected are a blend of case studies and surveys administered to policy-makers at the regional and urban levels in the Nordic countries of Denmark, Finland, Norway, Sweden and the Faroes. The following data have been collected: Surveys among city and regional *politicians* in Finland, Sweden, Denmark, Norway and the Faroes. The main focus was on network activities, development policies and international orientation; a further survey of *regions and cities* in Sweden, Denmark and Norway was also carried out, the main topic of which was strategic choices concerning organizational and management structures and processes (system capacity).

The response rate among politicians was substantially lower than what we experienced a decade ago. It varies from 58 per cent (Swedish regions) to 26 per cent (Finnish cities). The lower response rates might be a reflection of the turmoil and stress of structural reforms taking place in the Nordic countries at the time of data collection. Data attrition is analysed in detail in the Appendix to this chapter. The analysis demonstrates that the data is reasonably representative of the total population when broken down according to criteria of geography, political parties and gender. It should also be borne in mind that the aim was not to carry out a sample survey but to reach the total population of Nordic politicians of a certain category (members of the governing boards or committees of cities and regions). All cities and regions that we aimed for are covered. We therefore feel confident of the quality of the data when used for the analysis of

Table 1.1   Survey data collected

	System capacity survey		Survey among urban and regional politicians	
	Cities	*Regions*	*Cities*	*Regions*
Norway	Population 18 100 % N = 18	Population 18 100 % N = 18	Population 197 52 % N = 103	Population 189 55 % N = 103
Denmark*	Population 14 86 % N = 12	Population 5 100 % N = 5	Population 373 28 % N = 107	Population 200 50 % N = 100
Sweden	Population 22 64 % N = 14	Population 20 55 % N = 11	Population 304 38 % N = 115	Population 301 58 % N = 174
Finland	X	X	Population 230 26 % N = 59	Population 246 52 % N = 127
Faroes	X	X	Population 30 45 % N = 12	Population 42 50 % N = 24
N total	N = 44	N = 27	N = 396	N = 528

Note: * In Denmark the number of cities covered is larger than that of regions since we wanted to reach the same population of cities that was covered in our previous project of 1997/98

larger groups while in a number of cases analysis at the level of individual cities or regions cannot be done.

The collection of quantitative data was combined with case studies. The purpose of the case studies was in-depth analysis of the challenges of regional networking. The cases are the Faroes, South-Jutland in Denmark and the two south-east coast regions of Aust-Agder and Telemark in Norway plus the cities of Trollhättan in Sweden and Kristiansand in Norway.

Outline of the Book

We have through Figure 1.1 argued that such phenomena as globalization, European integration and technological innovation open up for new policy options that in the next round drive changes among regions and cities in the Nordic countries. To follow up this model, the report is divided into two parts. The research issues addressed in the first part are,

- Changes in policy choices and networking activities over the last 10 years;
- Emergent patterns of governance in cities and regions.

In the second part we bring in a qualitative approach to get a deeper understanding of the dynamics of networking activities among municipalities and regions. Here, we go into our third research question,

- The establishment and management of networks.

To set the scene Siv Sandberg in Chapter 2 outlines the institutional developments that have occurred at the regional level in the Nordic countries in the period of 1996–2009. The classical Nordic approaches to the institutional arrangement of the regional level seems to be dissolving and we see the rise of different models and understandings of how to best organize and develop regions.

What are the policy preferences of politicians for regional development in a competitive world? And have these preferences changed much over a 10-year period? Those are the questions that Baldersheim raises in Chapter 3. Baldersheim introduces the term *knowledge brokerage* to describe a central feature of the policy orientations of regional politicians. This orientation entails natural roles for politicians in their capacity as brokers between different socio-economic spheres.

In Chapter 4 Baldersheim and Øgård analyse why and how cities and regions engage in cross-border policy networks. A large proportion of politicians are involved in cross-border activities of one sort or another. Involvement goes beyond a small handful of top politicians; the pattern of involvement also demonstrates considerable stability over time. Through network involvement politicians establish a *learning ecology* that nurtures policy development in regions.

The findings reported by Baldersheim in Chapter 5 show that policy-makers in Nordic regions (including the main cities) are still, 10 years on, decidedly in favour of and prepared to take on extended roles in European structures of decision-making on behalf of their regions. Integrative regionalism is the dominant attitude.

A further aspect of governance is studied by Baldersheim and Øgård in Chapter 6: strategies of transformation, i.e. how cities and regions seek to enhance how they relate to citizens. The outcome is more complex governance structures that may enable cities and regions to deal more effectively with a more complex and dynamic environment.

Analysis of governance is taken one step further in Chapter 7 where Are Vegard Haug highlights how access to ICTs influences role formation among and communication patterns of politicians. The analysis is structured around the concept of *information ecology*, which identifies informational capacities as sources of political advantage.

Chapter 8 takes us from quantitative analysis of network patterns to the dynamics of networking in the European arena. In this chapter Joan Ólavsdóttir, Jens Svabo Justinussen and Beinta í Jákupsstovu seek to explain the formation of Faroese governmental bodies for foreign affairs and their capacities in the international political arena.

In Chapter 9 Sande Lysa and Øgård compare the international engagement of two county councils in Norway. They observe, first of all, that the two county councils are extensively involved in a variety of cross-border networks. Second, the back-office functions of network involvement are managed more professionally than before.

The Danish case is presented in Chapter 10 by Niels Ejersbo. The aim is to assess the effect of the structural reform in Denmark on regional internationalization strategies. It is a case study of the region of Southern Denmark. The region maintains international relations even after the reform.

In the last chapter, Aase Marthe Horrigmo adds an interesting new subject to our analysis of regional development strategies. Her interest is to study how culture can be used as a development strategy and she seeks to explain how two such radical innovations as "Film i Väst" and Quart Festivalen could emerge and become successes in two such initially unlikely places as Trollhättan and Kristiansand respectively.

Methodological Appendix

Table 1.A   Summary analysis of response rates and data attrition for city and regional councillors

	Regions/ cities	Gender	Party: pct SD of population and respondents		Party: pct largest non-socialist of population and respondents*	
	total response rates, pct.	female pct of population and respondents	regions	cities	regions	cities
Denmark	50/28	32/31	38/42	39/42	28/26	26/23
Finland	52/26	42/47	27/29	ND	21/19	ND
Norway	55/52	41/40	28/24	27/31	16/18	20/18
Sweden	58/38	44/42	40/36	38/30	20/21	23/21

Note: *Denmark: Venstre. Finland: Samlingspartiet. Norway: Høyre. Sweden: Moderaterna

Column 1: total response rates for regions and cities respectively. Cities have substantially lower response rates than regions in Denmark and Finland and somewhat lower rates in Sweden. Rates in Norway are almost equal for cites and regions. Consequently, the data set as a whole is somewhat skewed in favour of regions.

Column 2: Gives the proportion of female councillors in the population of councillors in the respective countries and the proportion of female councillors in the total responses. Respondents mirror the gender composition of their boards quite well.

Columns 3–4: Present the proportion of councillors of selected parties actually on the councils of regions and cities and the proportion of councillors of those parties among the respondents. Indicators are given for two parties (Social democrats and the largest non-socialist party of the respective countries). Overall, party composition of the respondent groups is satisfactory. The greatest deviation is that of social democrats in Swedish cities and regions, where the party is underrepresented among the respondents to the extent of six and eight percentage points respectively.

Chapter 2

The Nordic Regions:
Institutional Development and Public Debate
1996–2009

Siv Sandberg

Introduction

Traditionally, the regional administrative level in the Nordic countries has been a subject of political controversy. In unitary national states with strong local self-government, few functions or little popular support are left for what comes in between, the regional level (Baldersheim 1997, Nilsson 2007, Feltenius 2008). Furthermore, diverse and diffuse territorial divisions blur the totality of self-governed and state administrative regional bodies and distance them from ordinary citizens. It is not surprising that "sorting out the regional muddle" becomes part of any government's agenda, as has recently been the case in both Sweden and Finland (Dir 2004: 93, RP 59/2009). Right-wing political parties in Denmark, Norway and Sweden have had the abolition of the democratically-elected regional level as an item in their manifestos for decades. In Finland, it has never been possible to reach political agreement on establishing a self-governing regional level.

The middle of the 1990s witnessed a change in the climate of the discussion of regional levels. Finnish and Swedish membership of the EU in 1995 entailed a reorganization of regional politics and placed three of the Nordic countries in a political relationship where "Europe of the Regions" became a catchphrase and opinions concerning regions as independent political and economic actors gained a footing in the Finnish and Swedish debate. The results reported in this book follow up an earlier study of the position of regions in Denmark, Finland, Norway and Sweden. That study was conducted between 1996 and 2001, just after Finland and Sweden had joined the EU. By summing up many different findings and scattered signals, we concluded that the importance of the regional level in the Nordic countries seemed to be growing, even though the development was far from straightforward (Sandberg and Ståhlberg 2000, Baldersheim et al. 2001).

Only a few years later, at the beginning of the 2000s, the development observed around 1999 ended. Extensive reforms of public-sector structures and functions in Denmark, Finland and Norway went against the trends of the 1990s to strengthen the regional level (see for example *Indenrigs- og sundhetsministeriet 2004, RP 155/2006, St.Meld 12 2006–2007*). Instead, responsibilities were transferred from regionally elected bodies to state-owned professional organizations and municipal amalgamation reforms were initiated. What happened and why? The first part of this chapter provides an outline of the institutional development of the regional administration in the Nordic area between 1999 and 2010. The second section of the chapter places this development in relationship to a number of larger trends in society.

Scandinavian and Finnish Models of Local and Regional Government

We can distinguish between two main models of organizing relationships between the local and the regional levels of government in the Nordic area: the Scandinavian model and the Finnish model.

The *Scandinavian model* has traditionally been based on two levels of self-government: local self-government (municipalities) and regional self-government, organized as county councils (*amtskommuner*, *fylkeskommuner*, *landsting*). The two self-governmental levels are neither subordinate nor superior to each other, but have different functional and territorial scopes. The regions do not enjoy any legislative powers that would influence local government, but have the right to levy taxes. The main public image of the Scandinavian regions is that of health-care regions, since hospital care until recently formed 60–80 per cent of the regional budgets. Furthermore, the Danish, Norwegian and Swedish regions assume some responsibilities in education, social services, zoning and public transport.

The *Finnish model* differs from the Scandinavian one in two respects. While the tasks organized on a regional basis are the same as in the other Nordic countries – health care, regional planning, vocational training and specialized tasks within social services – the organizations at the regional level do not enjoy any formal self-governmental status. The regional self-governmental level in Finland, although to some extent regulated by national legislation, is a creature of local government. Local elections decide the composition of the governing bodies on regional councils and local taxes finance the services organized at the regional level.

The regional level consists of a number of mandatory and voluntary joint municipal bodies. The joint municipal bodies are judicially independent and functionally specialized, but depend on their owners – the local authorities – for finances and democratic control. Membership of joint municipal bodies involving specialized health care (hospital districts) and regional planning (regional councils) is mandatory. Moreover, there are voluntary joint municipal authorities for vocational education that can also be regarded as part of the regional level. They have no right to impose taxation and state grants are usually given to the owners, the local governments, not to the regional bodies themselves.

Table 2.1   The democratically elected regional levels in the Nordic countries at the beginning of the 2000s

	The Scandinavian model			The Finnish model
	Denmark 14 county councils (*amtskommuner*)	Norway 18 county councils* (*fylkeskommuner*)	Sweden 24 county councils	Finland*** 19 regional councils, 20 hospital districts plus other joint municipal authorities
Democratically elected council (or equivalent)	Yes	Yes	Yes	No
Right to levy taxes	Yes	Yes**	Yes	No
Multifunctional organization	Yes	Yes	Yes	No

Note: *The capital city of Oslo is often counted as the 19th county council since it is responsible for county council as well as municipal functions

** The right of local and regional government to impose tax in Norway is restricted by parliament

*** The summary of Finland does not consider the Åland islands which enjoy autonomy based on international treaties

Reform Proposals and Institutional Change in the 2000s

During the 2000s, the structure of public administration attracted political attention in all the four Nordic countries. The types and extents of the initiatives varied, as did the degree to which the proposals were put into effect.

Denmark: A Sweeping Reform of Territorial Divisions, Task Distribution, Finances and Governance

In the autumn of 2002, Prime Minister Anders Fogh Rasmussen's liberal-conservative government appointed a parliamentary commission (*Strukturkommissionen*) to review the structures and functions of public administration in Denmark. This initiative was surprising since another commission, *Opgavekommissionen*, only four years earlier in 1998, had concluded that public sector responsibilities had by and large been placed at the right administrative level. Even more surprising was the fact that the proposal laid the basis for a political agreement on structural reform in the summer of 2004, and that the reform was carried out without any substantial opposition from the municipalities. The reform was enacted on 1 January 2007 (*Indenrigs- og Sundhetsministeriet* 2004, Mouritzen 2006, Christiansen and Klitgaard 2008).

The structural reform fundamentally revised the territorial structure of Danish local and regional government; it affected the system of public finances as well as the division of functions between the state, the regions and the municipalities. Moreover, the reform introduced novel modes of democratic governance at the regional level. The most spectacular element was the comprehensive amalgamation of the municipalities, with 271 municipalities being reduced to 98; the average population of the Danish municipality thus became approximately 50,000 inhabitants. The new municipalities were given a larger portfolio of tasks, which included an expansion of their responsibilities for employment and regional development.

For the regional level, the reform had dramatic consequences. The 13 county councils were terminated and replaced by five new regions. The regional divisions were carried out as an enforced reform by the state, unlike the municipal division reform, where the state put forward the aims for the size of the new municipalities and the municipalities could then find their own suitable partners.

The new regions are governed by a popularly elected body but do not have the general mandate that the former county councils enjoyed, nor do they have the right to impose taxes. Consequently, the regions cannot operate outside the areas of responsibility delegated by the state and are not able take upon themselves tasks at their own discretion. The regions are 90 per cent financed through funds allocated by the state and 10 per cent by funds allocated by the municipalities.

Of the earlier tasks of the county councils, responsibility for hospital care remains with the new regions, as well as certain responsibilities for overall regional planning. Upper-secondary schools were reorganized as independent, state-owned bodies, while the local authorities took over tasks from the former county councils in environmental protection and social services.

Finland: Local Government Reform

In Finland, attempts to reform regional and local government in the late 1990s and early 2000s can be divided into two phases: the first phase with a number of small reform initiatives at the beginning of the 2000s and a series of comprehensive reform proposals after 2005 (Sandberg 2004). The attempt to reorganize the Kainuu region was part of the smaller reform proposals from the beginning of the 2000s. Kainuu, one of Finland's smallest and poorest regions, was selected to be the object of an administrative experiment from 2005 to 2012.

The region of Kainuu has assumed responsibility for all the services and development tasks that had previously been organized by separate joint municipal authorities. Moreover, the municipalities in Kajanaland have undertaken to transfer approximately 60 per cent of their tasks to the region. The region is governed by a directly elected council (Airaksinen et al. 2008).

In March 2005, the Finnish centre/social democratic cabinet, inspired by the Danish reform, surprisingly introduced an extensive review of the structure of local government and the provision of welfare services. Finnish municipalities are comparatively small compared to the heavy responsibilities they bear. As noted above, local governments are accountable for final financial responsibility for health care and education. In 2005, the median size of a Finnish municipality was about 5,000 inhabitants. The government expressed concern as to the future capacity of the municipalities to cope with their responsibilities as most local governments would face demographic challenges, including an increase in the number of elderly inhabitants needing social and medical care and a decline in the number of tax payers. In keeping with Finnish reform traditions, the government laid out a reform scheme whose aim was to have larger units for the production of local government services, while allowing the local authorities to choose how to reach that goal (Sandberg 2010). The reform encourages mergers of municipalities, but municipalities can also join together in cooperative agreements to reach the 20,000 inhabitants set as a minimum for the provision of high-quality social and health-care services.

The reforms were scheduled to take place between 2007 and 2013 (RP 155/206). During the first wave of the reforms, the number of municipalities was reduced from 400 to 332 and over 200 municipalities have established new cooperation structures for social services and health care (SRR 9/2009).

In addition to the reform of local governments and their service responsibilities, an extensive reform of the state regional administration took place in 2010, finally abolishing the state provinces, whose origins could be traced to the 1700s. This reform will have some repercussions for the regional councils, even though no substantial changes were made either in their portfolio of responsibilities, or in the territorial divisions of the democratically appointed regional level.

Norway: The Decline and Return of the County Councils?

The development of the regional level since the late 1990s in Norway should be interpreted against the background of the deep cleavages between political parties in their view of local and regional self-government. It is hard to find two parties with identical sets of preferences concerning the need for municipal mergers, the existence of a regional level at all and and the ownership of public hospitals. Change of government can involve abrupt shifts in the views of the reforms deemed necessary. In 2001, the government headed by a social democratic prime minister, decided to transfer responsibility for hospitals from the county councils to five state-owned regional health-care companies. That decision left the county councils (*fylkeskommunene*) with only 20 per cent of their original budget and portfolio of tasks and, quite naturally, this initiated a political debate about the future of regional self-government.

Prime Minister Bondevik's right-wing government from 2001–05 chose to focus on the municipalities and initiated a bottom-up process, in which municipalities were encouraged to investigate the options of inter-municipal cooperation versus future amalgamation. The minister of local government affairs would have preferred extensive mergers of municipalities and the abolition of the county councils, an option far too radical in the eyes of most local and regional politicians.

The subsequent centre-left coalition (2005–09) declared its ambition to carry out a radical reform of regional government while leaving municipal borders intact. The proposed administrative reform in 2010 would have preserved a democratically elected regional level in Norway, but reduce the number of regions from 18 to seven to nine. The regions would have gained new responsibilities primarily from ministries in Oslo and from diverse bodies of the state provincial administration. The idea was that important decisions about regional development – for example investment in roads – now taken by anonymous civil servants would be given to politicians elected by the people of each region.

The passage of the proposed 2010 administrative reform through the political system was not, however, straightforward. The two prerequisites of the reform – that the state authorities give up some tasks and that the county councils voluntarily agree to establish larger regions – proved difficult to achieve. The outcome of the attempt at grand regional reform was relatively modest. Norway continues to have 18 directly elected county councils, which, since 2010, have gained some new responsibilities (Ot.prp.nr 10 (2008–09)). During its second term in power (2009–), the focus of the centre-left cabinet has been on the organization of health care and better coordination between primary and specialized health care. Overall, the many contradictory reforms taking place over a limited number of years show that the position of regional government in Norway remains ambiguous and controversial.

Sweden: Larger Regions – Will the Proposal be Realized?

Like in the other Nordic countries, the necessity of a regional self-governmental level has been a much-debated issue in Sweden. In 1996, in the wake of Swedish EU membership and the new tone in the debate about regions, the government decided to launch a number of regional experiments to gain evidence for the renewal of regional government. Skåne and Västra Götaland represented the most radical regional undertaking (Bäck 2004, Nilsson 2007). As well as the experiment in these regions involving taking over the responsibility of the state's county administration for regional development, counties were also permanently merged at the beginning of 1999.

Other regions chose a more moderate model, with regional development issues jointly organized by the county council and all the municipalities within a region (Landstingsförbundet 2003). This model resembles the Finnish regional councils and brings local and regional interests more closely together. New legislation passed in 2002 made the model of regional cooperative bodies available for any region. The model is a complement to, not a substitute for, county councils.

In 2003, the social democratic government appointed a commission on government responsibilities (*Ansvarskommittén*) to produce suggestions concerning, among other things, the future organization of the regional level. (SOU 2003: 123, Dir 2004: 93). In its final report in February 2007, the commission suggested that fewer and larger regional councils modelled on the regional experiments in Skåne and Västra Götaland should be given responsibility for health care, infrastructure and regional planning functions with a territorial scope larger than the municipality and smaller than the state. Furthermore, it was suggested that potentially controversial issues would best be resolved by political assemblies. Unlike many other commissions dealing with the regional issue, the *Ansvarskommittén* was unanimous in its suggestion and in general the response from local and regional authorities was encouraging. Furthermore, the Swedish Association of Local Authorities and Regions strongly advocated the new model, which might seem surprising against the background of the frequent and intense conflicts between advocates of local self-government and advocates of regional self-government as late as at the beginning of the 1990s (Feltenius 2008).

The right-wing government, however, never made the proposal part of its agenda. The response to the commission's report has been merely procedural: in 2007, the government appointed a coordinator to investigate the interest in forming larger regions (Björklund 2008). In 2009, it laid out procedures for county councils willing to form new regional councils (*Statsrådsberedningen* 2009). So far, initiatives have been rare. Bottom-up activities by the county councils and local governments are seen as a prerequisite for renewing regional government, since according to established practices over recent decades, Swedish governments are reluctant to force territorial reform. The regional issue might, however, be politicized in the 2010 elections.

Summary

In terms of functions, similar tasks are organized at a level larger than the municipality and smaller than the state in all the Nordic countries. These functions include health care, secondary education, regional planning and development policies. With regard to the organization of regional functions and the governance and financing of the regional entities, differences between the Nordic countries are considerable and growing.

The recent reforms have challenged the traditional division of structuring local and regional government into a Scandinavian and a Finnish model. In fact, the three

Table 2.2   The regional level in the Nordic countries 2010

	The Scandinavian model			The Finnish model
	Denmark 5 regions (regioner)	*Norway 18 county councils (fylkeskommuner)*	*Sweden 20 county councils/ regions*	*Finland 19 regional councils + other joint municipal authorities*
Democratically elected council (or equivalent)	Yes	Yes	Yes	No*
Right to levy taxes	No	Yes	Yes	No
Multifunctional organization	Yes, with fewer tasks	Yes, with fewer tasks	Yes	No*

Note: * Kainuu experiment

Scandinavian countries are increasingly diverging from one another, especially in the functioning of regional government. Only Sweden – the one country in which a major reform has not taken place – can be said to continue to represent the traditional Scandinavian model. The Finnish model, with an indirectly constructed regional level, remains largely intact, even though the administrative experiment in Kainuu has introduced elements of the Scandinavian model – directly elected bodies and multifunctional organizations – into the Finnish setting.

One illustration of the divergence in the last decade is in the organization, governance and financing of public hospitals and. In Denmark, hospitals are the responsibility of the new regions and strategic decisions are taken by directly elected councils. However, the political leadership has limited opportunities to affect the income side of the budget, since regions lack taxation powers and formal autonomy. In Finland, hospitals are run by joint municipal authorities, indirectly governed and financed by local authorities. In Norway, state-owned health companies with no direct links to the local and regional electorate manage the hospitals. Professional rather than political governance is the rule. In Sweden, hospitals are part of the portfolio of county councils, governed by directly elected politicians and financed by regional taxes.

Summing up the findings from the research project "The Nordic Countries in the Europe of Regions", Sandberg and Ståhlberg (2000) and Baldersheim et al. (2001) concluded that, despite mixed signals, the position of the regional levels in the Nordic countries seemed to be growing stronger. One of the reasons for this was the importance of the European Union in opening up a new playing field for the

Nordic regions. The traditional concept of county councils and regional bodies as mainly producers of welfare services, such as health care and education, was partly replaced by a discourse emphasizing regions as stewards of economic growth. Furthermore, traditional tensions between advocates of local self-government and advocates of regional self-government seemed to have diminished, paving the way for a new concept of local and regional democracy.

If the new institutional settings created by the reforms of the 2000s are viewed against the three trends observed in the late 1990s, an interesting and contradictory mosaic appears.

The Position of the Democratically Elected Regional Level in the Nordic Countries

The position of the regional level in the Nordic countries remains ambiguous. In Sweden (2007) and Norway (2005), recent initiatives have aimed to create a stronger regional level with broader competencies and larger units. The theoretical arguments in favour of regionalization have met with little political enthusiasm. The Norwegian reform, although preserving directly elected county councils, contracted to a minimum of the intended reform. The bottom-up and gradual path to a new regional level in Sweden has not yet achieved any striking success and large-scale reforms seem unlikely.

The Danish reform transformed the idea of regional self-government. The new Danish regions, although governed by directly elected councils, are creatures of the state, not self-governing institutions.

The regional reforms of the 1990s were partly motivated by the need to find alternative solutions to capacity problems in the public sector as the option of amalgamations and the nationalization of public services were blocked. In the reforms of the early 2000s, both options emerged. Large-scale amalgamations of local authorities have taken place in Denmark and Finland. Responsibilities for hospitals in Norway and secondary education in Denmark have been transferred from self-governing bodies to the state.

The Importance of the EU for the Nordic Regions

Although EU membership and European regional policy were important reasons for regional reforms in the 1990s (Baldersheim et al. 2001, Jerneck and Gidlund 2001), with the establishment of regional councils in Finland in 1994 and the regional experiments in Sweden from 1996 onwards, the EU as a driving force for regional action seems to have faded.

EU regional policies are part of the daily activities of any public authority in the member states in the 2000s, but the restructuring of regional government during the last few years has usually been motivated by domestic rather than international reasons. Since the Danish public sector reform, Denmark is viewed as one single region within the EU structural fund programmes. In the other countries, the direct connection between the regional authorities and structural fund programmes has diminished. Fewer Nordic regions are eligible for EU funds since the eastwards extension of the EU (http://ec.europa.eu/regional_policy).

Welfare Production and Regional Development Policies

When the discourse of the Europe of Regions entered the Nordic political scene in the mid-1990s, one popular argument was that regions should not be seen as mere welfare producers – as had been the case in Scandinavia – but as arenas and agents of growth and development. Competition between regions was, in contrast to traditional Nordic ideas of equalization, presented as an asset.

The argument about regional authorities as development agents remains vigorously debated in all countries. It is seen as important for regional authorities to possess a combination of competencies, enabling regional politicians and administrators to act and react to the specific assets and problems in each region. Even though the Danish reform stripped regions of many of their earlier functions, it also constructed an institution called "growth forums" as a meeting place for regions, local authorities and private businesses to promote the economy of the regions. Empirical evidence presented in subsequent chapters of the book shows that regions are intensely involved in regional, national and international development projects.

Despite the consensus on the importance of regional development policies, welfare production, especially health care, has been the prime motivator behind the reforms of local and regional government in the last decade. Welfare services constitute the vast share of the national budget and among policy-makers it is regarded as more important to create structures optimal for health care than examining how competent the new regional structures will be in terms of regional development. Furthermore, the legitimacy of the Nordic public sector is vested in the welfare services. Reforms that do not include functions which the people deem important – which was the case with the latest proposed regional reform in Norway – are likely to fail (Fimreite 2008: lecture). Since regional government is responsible for functions more distant from the general public than the functions of local government, proponents of stronger regions are unlikely to be able to count on broad popular support for their endeavours.

Ever since the 1990s, some of the political elites, especially leading figures in the national associations of local and regional government, have advocated stronger regional levels in the Nordic countries. Until now, this unification of local and national self-governmental interests has had little success in terms of actual decisions. In national politics, the future of the regional level is a recurring problem, resulting in repeated initiatives to examine public responsibilities and new regional governmental structures – Sweden has had 11 or 12 such examinations since the 1960s, Finland and Norway nearly as many. However, the windows of opportunity for acting politically upon the recommendations of various commissions open rarely and close rapidly (Krasner 1988).

Chapter 3

Knowledge Brokerage and Institutional Retooling: Policy Preferences for Regional Development in a Competitive World

Harald Baldersheim

Introduction – The Development of Regional Policy

Policy options for regional development have multiplied in recent decades. Several of these options are politically controversial. Choices regarding the appropriate institutional frameworks for implementing regional policies can also be controversial, as highlighted in Chapter 2, especially the distribution of functions and powers between national, regional and local decision-making bodies. What are the policy and institutional choices most likely to be adopted and/or implemented in the context of a more competitive world in which regions have found themselves since the 1980s? Our approach to answering this question is based on surveys carried out in 1998 and 2008 of regional and urban politicians from the four Nordic countries of Denmark, Finland, Norway and Sweden. What are the views of regional politicians today regarding appropriate policies for regional development? And how have these views changed in recent decades within the context of Europeanization and internationalization?

As a separate policy field that of regional development emerged out of measures of reconstruction in the wake of WWII. The policy field was supported by a veritable "regional science" drawing especially on regional economics and urban geography but also on other social sciences.[1] However, regional development as a political concern has been a on the mind of national policy-makers as long as the nation-state has been with us. In the well-known scheme of Stein Rokkan et al. (1987), the stages of nation-building have been conceptualized as those of territorial consolidation, cultural standardization, political mass mobilization

---

1   Walter Isard is considered by many to be the founder of the field as an academic dicipline. Cf. Isard, Walter. 1956. *Location and Space-Economy: A General Theory Relating to Industrial Location, Market Areas, Land Use, Trade and Urban Structure.* Cambridge, Massachusetts: The MIT Press and Isard, Walter. 1975. *Introduction to Regional Science.* New York: Prentice Hall. *The Journal of Regional Science* was founded in 1958.

and redistribution through welfare state mechanisms. In the first of these stages, "the regional problem" was that of physical control over sometimes rebellious regional counter-elites. The second challenge was that of overcoming the cultural diversity of disparate regions to create a common denominator of national identity and language through education and the propagation of manners and mores. Further nation-building included a gradual extension of political rights that granted admission of peripheries into national political arenas and also leverage for demands for special consideration by national elites. In the Nordic countries, in the post-war period, the political leverage of peripheries has driven territorial distributional and redistribution policies that have resulted in levels of welfare largely on a par with those of central regions.

Nevertheless, "the regional problem" has remained on the agenda of most European states as one of "underdeveloped" peripheries. In the terminology of Rokkan and Urwin (1983), the problem of the periphery is threefold: peripheries tend to be geographically distant, culturally different and economically backward. Of course, peripheries may vary in the extent to which they possess these characteristics; whether regional disparities are considered to be a problem of national concern may also vary from one country to another.

In the post-war period, the demands on the welfare state came to include not only various social benefits but also rights to employment and a concomitant obligation on the welfare state to create employment opportunities. In the industrial age, such obligations gave rise to policies of industrialization of peripheral or declining regions. Since market forces often worked against peripheries as industrial locations, industries located in peripheries were often state-owned or heavily subsidized. Regional policy in this vein was an expression of a belief in the power of socio-economic planning. In most countries, the state had a central role in elaborating and implementing regional policies. With the decline of the industrial order in Western Europe and the rise of post-industrial society, the ground was cut away from the planned economy – types of regional policies. How could jobs be generated in disadvantaged locations when there was little or no industry to spread around?

The answer emerging in the 1970s and 1980s was that of *endogenous development*, meaning that regions had to mobilize their own resources, above all human capital. Men of ideas – entrepreneurs – became the heroes of the day (Vazquez-Barquero 2002). This also opened up a natural policy space for local and regional governments: with roots in their regions and ties with potential entrepreneurs they could act effectively as coordinators of growth policies. During the 1980s, decentralization of development policies took place in all of the Nordic countries with more powers placed in the hands of elected regional bodies (Baldersheim 1990).

However, in a Nordic perspective decentralization in this regard was an uneven process and also an inherently unstable one (Baldersheim et al. 2001; Mydske et al. 2006; cf. Chapter 2 in this book for an updated overview). In Norway, regions lost important development functions in the 1990s. In Finland, the state never let elected bodies venture very far into regional development administration. In Sweden, a pattern of asymmetrical power distribution has emerged (Sandberg 2007). In short the institutional pattern – the distribution of powers and functions between local, regional and national bodies – is controversial as well as unstable.

Furthermore, in policy theory the focus on human capital has shifted from that of the endogenous mobilization of entrepreneurs to an interest in knowledge workers, i.e. how to develop regions and cities to become attractive locations for the footloose "creative class" of knowledge workers (Florida 2002, 2005). Initiatives to harness the growth potential inherent in institutions of higher learning and research have become known as "the Triple Helix Model" (Etzkowitz 2008). In practice, the latter has meant seeking to organize meeting places between business and academia, often in the form of joint consortia at premises located on the outskirts of university campuses. Today, most universities have a science park. Another sign of the acceptance of the knowledge-focused model of development is the spread of universities from being primarily located in central areas to locations in many peripheral regions. Norway, for example, had four universities in 1990 and eight by 2010.

The Policy Preferences of Regional and Urban Politicians: Knowledge Brokerage and Institutional Retooling

In our survey, policy preferences of regional and urban politicians were identified through their responses to the following question: "Internationalization is leading to increasing competition between regions/cities in Europe. In your opinion, what should your region/city do to maintain its position in this situation? Please indicate your preferences regarding the following policy options". A list of 24 policy options was presented to the politicians for their responses. The list is found in Table 3.1, including average scores for the respective options. The higher the scores, the more widespread the support for the respective options.

Table 3.1 Policy preferences of regional and urban politicians. Mean scores 1998 and 2008

	Policy type*	Scores 1998	Scores 2008	Change
More efforts regarding higher education	1	4.64	**4.41**	-.23
Improve communications and electronic infrastructure	1	4.58	**4.38**	-.20
Establish strategic alliances between universities and business/industry	1	4.42	**4.27**	-.15
Become a better service provider	1	4.27	**4.16**	-.11
Strategic alliances with other regions/cities	1	4.40	**4.13**	-.27
More emphasis on economic development issues	1	4.22	**4.08**	-.14
Develop technology centres	1	4.04	**3.85**	-.19
Alliances with regions/cities in other countries	2	3.82	**3.58**	-.24
Improve international expertise in own organization	2	3.84	**3.61**	-.23
Market region/city better	2	3.87	**3.78**	-.9
Establish separate international committee	2	2.92	**2.98**	+.6
Augment travel budgets	2	2.80	**2.88**	+.8
Take over functions from the state	4	3.19	**3.42**	+.23
Transfer developmental functions from state to regions/cities	4	4.00	**3.85**	-.15
Merge municipalities/counties (enlargement)	5	2.62	**3.35**	+.73
Transfer functions from municipalities to regions/from regions to municipalities	6	2.62	**2.97**	+.35
Improve interaction between region/municipalities	-6	4.33	**4.14**	-.19
Concentrate region/city on developmental tasks	7	3.43	**3.36**	-.7
New options 2008:				
More efforts to attract highly educated workers	1		4.26	
Establish or strengthen regional Brussels office	2		3.44	
Develop recreational facilities, attractions in urban centres	3		3.75	
Stimulate new companies in the fields of culture and knowledge creation	3		3.40	
Establish attractive cultural facilities (theatres, cultural centres, etc.)	3		3.48	
Improve management and organization in own institution	5		3.30	
N		1,123–1,234	545–828	

Note: Scale: 1=not important at all; 5=very important. Clusters of policies 1–7*. *Clusters based on factor analysis; cf. explanations p. 27.

a. In 2008, the most popular policies are related to *information age* types of development strategies: enhancement of educational levels and expertise among the working population, strategic alliances between regions and universities and improving structures of electronic communication (e.g. broadband connections). The Triple Helix model of development has definitely had a breakthrough among Nordic regional policy-makers. Examples of less popular strategies include changing the distribution of functions between regions and municipalities or higher travel budgets for politicians.

b. *Comparing the 2008 responses with those of 1998* yields an overall picture of remarkable *stability* with regard to the preferred policy options. The three most popular policy options are the same on both occasions: more efforts in the field of higher education in the respective regions, improve communications and electronic infrastructure and establish strategic alliances between universities and business/industry. The changes in average scores in no case reach one full point (on a scale from one to five). The largest change is a very interesting one, though: there is growing support for the idea that *municipalities and regions should be merged to form larger units*. A belief in larger size as a response to competitive internationalization is spreading among regional and urban policy-makers. Furthermore, in 2008 more politicians than before believe that it is necessary to change the distribution of functions between cities and regions. This is an issue ripe with controversy of course, since regional politicians think *they* should take on more functions while their urban counterparts tend to hold the opposite view. However, in the larger picture functional redistribution (cities/regions and regions/state) is not thought to be of the greatest importance for the competitive position of regions and cities.

c. In 2008, a series of additional policy options was introduced. These mostly reflected options associated with ideas about the developmental role of "the creative class". Especially the suggestion that regions or cities ought to develop measures to attract highly educated persons from outside was favoured by the politicians. Follow-up questions intended to indicate specific projects in this regard, e g. building new theatres or concert halls, did not meet with the same high level of support (although with overall approval). This may raise doubt as to whether the politicians will in fact be able to carry through the necessary measures to realize their favourite policy options.

Through factor analysis the 24 policy options were reduced to seven factors: 1) Triple Helix strategies, 2) internationalization, 3) cultural strategies (development of attractive cultural events/facilities), 4) regionalization of state functions, 5) enlargement of regions/municipalities, 6) functional redistribution between cities and regions, and 7) concentration of regions/cities on developmental tasks (rather than service provision). The emergence of these seven factors implies that politicians form seven groupings of policy advocates. One group champions knowledge-related strategies, another favours internationalization and a third one spearheads culturally driven development, etc. Although the seven groups are statistically distinct there are two overarching conceptual dimensions: *knowledge brokerage*, which units the three first groups and *institutional re-tooling*, which links the last four ones.

Knowledge brokerage is concerned with refocusing academic and research institutions in a developmental perspective, establishing links between such institutions and the business world and public administration and building local environments attractive to knowledge workers, especially by way of interesting cultural events. Knowledge brokerage is different from the more well-known concept of "knowledge management" as the former is concerned with building networks across different social spheres, with research and development institutions at the core of the networks, while the latter is concerned with improving the sharing and processing of knowledge inside one particular organization (Nonaka and Teece 2001). Knowledge brokerage is a prime domain of *politicians* while knowledge management is of an administrative nature. Brokerage between social and interest groups is, of course, what politicians are especially good at and there is thus a natural function for politicians in such a paradigm of regional development.

Knowledge brokerage is also distinct from – although related to – "regional learning". Regional learning is the hoped-for outcome of sharing skills and expertise among a cluster of firms in a particular region, often assisted by public organizations (Boekema 2000). Knowledge brokerage is the *process* through which regional learning may come about. Political involvement is often necessary to kick-start such processes of sharing, which are based on mutual trust rather than formal contracts, at least initially. Sharing knowledge with competitors is a risky business subject to classical collective action problems (the free-rider syndrome) (Olson 1965/1971). The political skills and public trust of politicians may be needed to overcome risks of free-riding.

Institutional re-tooling in the field of regional development administration has been taking place almost for as long as the field has been a recognized public concern (Mydske 1978). Powers and functions have shifted back and forth between regional and state bodies. Two sets of innovations occurred in the 1990s: the proliferation of public-private partnerships, largely driven by the stipulations of EU structural programmes, and the creation of semi-independent bodies which kept politicians at arm's length from the implementation of concrete programmes of support (e.g. Innovation Norway). The four items indicated above as expressions of institutional re-tooling today (regionalization of state functions, geographic enlargement, functional redistribution between cities and regions and concentration on development/divestment of service functions) are all on the political agenda of the four countries, and they are all sources of controversy.

Knowledge brokerage measures, in contrast, are less controversial, as witnessed by higher levels of support for these items reported in Table 3.1. However, as a new paradigm of regional development there is also more uncertainty with regard to how the paradigm should be concretized. There is as yet no definite summary study of action models or results, only scattered outlines of initiatives of this nature around Europe. Much research remains to be done to fill in the picture of knowledge brokerage at the regional levels in the Nordic countries. However, as contributions in this regard, specific initatives are analysed in subsequent chapters of this volume.

Box 3.1

Knowledge brokerage: The Norwegian region of Agder as an example

With the ardent support of the two south coast county councils of Aust- and Vest-Agder, the District College of Agder became the University of Agder in 2008. The support of the county councils was augmented by a research foundation set up by a group of municipalities to finance and enhance research efforts in the district college to speed up the drive towards university status. Furthermore, the City of Kristiansand, where the university is located, created its own foundation in 2003, financed through the sale of shares in power plants, with the overall aim of stimulating innovations in the field of culture and research, which has also become an important source of finance for research projects in the new university. The foundation, named Cultiva, also supports innovative cultural projects aimed at making the city an attractive location for new business ventures. Policy in this field is developed through a series of networks as well as formal bodies which provide meeting grounds for politicians from the two county councils, the central municipalities of the region and business and industry. Such networks include e.g. Knutepunkt Sørlandet and Spydspissen, while Agderrådet forms an overarching political body providing advice and recommendations regarding development initiatives. Agderrådet was formed as a joint advisory board for the two county councils for matters of mutual interest and also as a prelude to a merger of the two counties into a larger region. The merger is still under consideration, however.

In the next section, the distribution of support for and opposition to the respective policy types will be analysed.

Seven Policy Types: Support and Opposition

As noted above, some of these policy options may be highly controversial, while others meet with general approval. The level of controversy as well as the patterns of conflict – the cleavage systems – associated with the various policies may influence their chances of adoption or implementation. Support and opposition to the seven types of policy options are analysed in Table 3.2. For the analysis of cleavage patterns, three sets of independent variables are used.

Table 3.2   Policy options: who is in favour and who is against? Regression analysis. Beta coefficients. N=887

	Regional development policies (factor scores)						
	Triple Helix	Inter-nationalization	Culture	Regional-ize state functions	Enlarge-ment	Redistr-bution city/ region	Concentrate on develop-ment
Norway dummy	.218**	-.019	.061	.090**	-.043	-.021	-.259***
Finland dummy	.171***	.059	-.199***	-.119**	.009	-.021	.214***
Sweden dummy	.188***	.118**	.044	-.017	-.085	-.140**	-.087*
Region – city (1–2)	.059*	-.087**	.156***	-.342***	-.130***	.264***	-.110***
Centrality of region (low–high=0,1)	-.001	.014	-.043	-.070*	-.047	.123***	-.047
Party left – right (1,2,3)	.079**	-.067	-.107***	-.111***	.048	.022	-.061*
Age	.094**	.123***	.065*	-.093**	.033	.039	.017
Gender (1=f, 2=m)	-.144***	-.091**	-.050	.103***	.091**	.067**	-.041
Adjust.r²	.066	.049	.100	.147	.029	.103	.165

Note: ***.001/**.01/*.05

First, three potential drivers of conflict are analysed: positional interest (region/city), centrality[2] of regions (and, by implication, of cities located in that region) and ideology (left-right party continuum). Furthermore, national context is also expected to influence the chances of policy adoption and so the country of the respondents has been included. Finally, the age and gender of the respondents are included as control variables.

The relationship of cities and regions may be that of occupying complementary positions or one of competition and rivalry in the distribution of public functions and powers. Their views on policy options and institutional choice often follow from their respective positions in institutional space. Hence, positional interest is one of our explanatory variables. Conflicts between cities and regions are expected especially in institutional retooling, i.e. the distribution of functions and powers.

---

2   Our notion of centrality builds on central place theory (Christaller 1933). Central regions are defined as regions with cities of at least 100,000 inhabitants.

Table 3.3 Policy options and cleavages: commentaries and summaries

POLICY TYPES	CLEAVAGES	Primary cleavage between
	Groups supporting/opposing policy	
Knowledge brokerage		
-Triple Helix	The most important line of division is between **the Danes** on the one hand and the **Norwegians, Finns and Swedes** on the other. The Danes support these strategies less than do politicians from the three other countries. **Cities** are somewhat more supportive than **regions,** and parties on **the right** more than those on **the left.**	Countries Cities/ regions Left/ right
-Internationalization	Internationalization strategies are approved of somewhat more by **the Swedes** than the rest, and by the **regions** more than by the **cities**.	Countries Cities/ regions
-Culture	**The Finns** stand out as being more negative to cultural strategies than the others, while **cities** are more in favour than **regions**, which may be explained by the former being the natural locations of new cultural institutions in their respective regions.	Countries Cities/ regions
Institutional retooling		
-Regionalize state functions	With regard to the regionalization of state functions, **the regions** support such moves strongly while **the cities** are against; this is the most conspicuous line of division in the whole material on policy options. There is also an ideological dimension to this conflict as parties on **the left** support regionalization initiatives more strongly than those on **the right**.	Cities/ regions Left/ right
-Enlargement	The main line of division regarding enlargement is the one between **cities** and **regions**, with the latter being in favour and the former being against. This pattern of course also tallies with the one noted above: the cities being against the transfer of state functions to regions. Keeping regions small may be seen as a guarantee against strong regions	Cities/ regions
-Redistribute functions city/region	Redistribution of functions is supported strongly by **cities** as long as it favours them. **Swedish** politicians are more sceptical than those of other countries in this regard.	Cities/ regions
-Concentrate on development	Concentrating regions on development functions and divesting them of service provision is an idea that is strongly resented in **Norway**, but not so much in the other countries. Evidently, the Norwegians would like to see the regions being restored as important service producers. The Finns, in contrast, think such concentration is a good idea – perhaps a reflection of the lack of such functions in Finnish regions in the first place? **Regions** on the whole find the idea of concentration attractive.	Countries Cities/ regions

The centrality of regions and cities defines their positions in geographic space. A central location may presumably lead to other policy choices than a peripheral location – as the challenges of the periphery are different from those of central places.

Ideology may also play a role in the choices of policies. Left-wing parties mostly favour a more active and interventionist public sector than do parties on the right. Hence we expect left-wing politicians more than those on the right to applaud the "new" policy options associated with the triple helix and cultural strategies. Left-wing politicians are also expected to favour stronger regions and wish to transfer more functions and powers to them.

As outlined in Chapter 1 (Figure 1.2), for our purposes we concentrate on two features of the national contexts: the relationship to the EU (membership/ non-membership) and the overall position of regions. EU membership is expected to intensify exposure to international competition but also to open up policy opportunities, both of which are expected to augment regional activism. The position of regions is defined through the autonomy (range of functions) of regions; Swedish regions have been on the ascendancy in this regard, while Norwegian ones have become somewhat reduced and the Danish regions are hardly worthy of the name any more. Finnish regions remain in their limbo as advisory boards to strong national planning agencies (cf. Chapter 2). A greater range of functions means a greater range of responsibilities, which again presumably drives a search for new policy options and demands for more powers from the state. When the two features of the national contexts are combined, four types of context emerge: the weak outsider regions (Norway), the strong insider regions (Sweden) and weak insider regions (Finland and Denmark). The fourth position, strong outsider regions, is factually empty. Against this background, Norwegian and Swedish regions are expected to be the contrasts with regard to policy choices, while Denmark and Finland will occupy the middle ground. These hypotheses are tested through regression analysis reported in Table 3.2.

First of all, it is apparent that politicians are divided in their policy preferences by their country of origin. Information age policies (Triple Helix), for example, are less likely to be adopted by Danes than by their counterparts in the other countries. Furthermore, divisions between cities and regions are recurring phenomena in all of these policy fields. Ideological cleavages are less frequent: a division between politicians on the left- and on the right-wing of the continuum was found in only two cases: information age types of policies and regionalization of state functions. The right wing is largely against stronger regions and therefore also against transferring more functions in the field of development policies.

The overall conclusions are that while national contexts matter for the likelihood of the adoption of specific policies, the implementation is likely to be affected by cleavages according to city/region divides and ideological divides inside all countries. The most important cleavage is that between cities and regions. When this divide coincides with the ideological one, the pursuit of regional development policies will face an uphill struggle.

Conclusions

The question asked at the outset was: what are the policy options most likely to be adopted and/or implemented in the context of a more competitive world in which regions have found themselves since the 1980s? The question has been addressed on the basis of surveys carried out in 1998 and 2008 of regional and urban politicians. We found, first of all, that policy preferences have remained remarkably stable over the decade. Information age types of policies are those most favoured by politicians. They clearly want their regions and cities to adapt to a knowledge-driven world.

We find that policy options can be linked to form clusters that we have termed knowledge brokerage and institutional retooling. Knowledge brokerage represents the new paradigm for regional development policies. The paradigm presents natural roles for politicians in their capacity as brokers between different socio-economic spheres, which is the essence of knowledge brokerage. However, from an analytical point of view, how knowledge brokerage actually works is only imperfectly understood. Chapters 8–11 in this volume take us some way towards a further understanding but much analysis remains to be done.

Chapter 4

Learning Ecologies:
Capacity-Building in Nordic Regions and
Cities through Cross-Institutional and
Cross-Border Cooperation

Harald Baldersheim and Morten Øgård

What is the role of politicians in cross-border networks? And why do they choose to spend their time in activities that may be of little immediate electoral benefit, and that often take place far from their home regions or home towns? It is well documented that cities and regions since the 1980s have established extensive cooperative networks; they also have a presence on the European stage, especially in Brussels, to influence decisions that affect them or simply to have listening posts in important places (Klausen 1996, Goldsmith and Klausen 1997, Baldersheim et al. 2001, Anderson et al. 2003). Less attention has been paid to the participation and roles of politicians in these networks. To what extent do elected politicians take part? What are their views on the benefits, if any, of participation?

In this chapter we address these issues with data from surveys of elected members of the governing boards of cities and regions in the four Nordic countries of Denmark, Finland, Norway and Sweden (cf. Chapter 1 for an outline of the procedures of data collection and overall project design).

Cross-border Networks and the Expertise of Politicians

Why should politicians be expected to take on roles in cross-border networks, and perhaps even play important parts in the workings of those networks? The answer hinges on the expertise of the politician that may be increasingly called for as globalization challenges existing institutions and policies. Globalization creates uncertainty and sometimes even upheavals through freer flows of capital across borders, higher mobility among core workers – the creative class – and faster transmission of information and ideas thanks to digital information technologies. As suggested by Robert C. Tucker (1981: 15) in a classic text on political leadership, the expertise of the politician is related to struggles with problems of collective action. The more globalization affects regions, the more they can be expected to experience new, unprecedented problems of collective action, and the more the expertise of the politician will be in demand. Problems of collective action entail problems of direction as well as problems of coordination. The question of direction may trigger a search for policy responses. The hope of finding new policy ideas is one source of motivation for participation in networks. The more regions feel the pressures of globalization the more politicians can be expected to take part in networks as arenas for policy renewal. In Chapter 3 we analysed what regional leaders today think are appropriate policy responses to the challenges that their regions face. Often, new policies require both mobilization of support and also recombination of resources and reconstruction of institutions if they are to be implemented properly. Networks may enable regions to pool their resources in new ways and engage in joint problem-solving across institutional borders. Regions around the North Sea, for example, have under the auspices of the North Sea Commission developed a network of cycle paths to encourage eco-friendly tourism across borders.

Joint action through networks, however, without the guiding hand of government authority, depends upon mutual trust to control "the free rider syndrome", i.e. to prevent defection from a common obligation when there is no sanction against defection (Olson 1965/71). Building trust and support is the speciality of the politician. Regional politicians, elected to important political offices in their respective regions and cities go to network meetings with a store of individual political capital, which is the token of their standing on their home ground and therefore an indication of their capacity to commit and bind their home regions to joint projects. Of course, their standing on the home turf is only a foundation for building mutual trust among network participants, but it is an important beginning. In sum, problems of collective action open up space for political leadership.

European integration may also create dependency relations between regions and the institutions of the European Union. Regions are affected by a long series of EU directives and may naturally seek to influence such decisions. Relations between the regions and the European Commission have been characterized variously as clientellism and a conspiracy against the nation-states (Scully and Jones 2010: 2). Be that as it may, we assume for the purposes of the analysis here that the more regions are dependent upon the EU, the more they can be expected to emphasize the importance of some kind of presence in Brussels.

So far we have outlined network participation as a problem-driven activity. Participation may, of course, also reflect altruistic motives as well as serving symbolic purposes. Regions and cities may respond to calls for *solidarity*, trying to help more disadvantaged regions; this has traditionally involved contacts with third-world regions but after the collapse of the Communist bloc, many Nordic regions established bonds with regions or cities in post-Communist countries, especially in Russia and the Baltics (Baldersheim and Ståhlberg 1999). Furthermore, regional representations in Brussels, for example, may have been established for reasons of prestige rather than as problem-solving or policy-generating activities. An ambitious region may be quite simply expected to have its own office in Brussels, or to take part in joint Interreg projects with other regions.

Networks as Learning Ecologies

How networks actually function as adaptive mechanisms for cities and regions can be conceptualized by applying theories of *organizational learning* (e.g. Argyris and Schön 1996, March and Olsen 1976, Levitt and March 1988). Organizational learning takes place in response to performance gaps which institutions experience in the pursuit of goals (Cyert and March 1963). A performance gap is the discrepancy between aspirations and actual performance. Organizations can close such gaps either by trying harder to achieve goals or by lowering aspirations. In practice, at the organizational level, learning means changing routines in the light of information about (a lack of) goal achievement. However, participating in external networks may also result in learning that leads to *higher* aspirations in the light of information about what has been achieved in other, similar organizations (reflexive learning). Thus network participation may lead to organizational stress, not necessarily to improved performance, at least not in the short run.

The sum of networks creates *ecologies of learning* that serve the adaptive needs of regions and cities at times when flexible, creative and experimental responses are needed. By joining (and leaving) networks, a region or city is constructing or changing its learning ecology and thus its adaptive capacity. A learning ecology is the set of networks to which a particular city or region belongs.

The emergence of and inclusion in learning ecologies may not be of unmitigated advantage to regions and cities, however. Learning ecologies may also entail unfortunate lock-in effects that prevent regions and cities from discovering or trying out new options. Learning ecologies may have much the same effect as group thinking on corporate planning in blocking out fresh perspectives and new ideas (Janis 1972). A region or city may become too well adapted to its learning habitat so that environmental changes go unnoticed and opportunities are missed, just as species become extinct when their habitats change too quickly.

The research question of particular importance here is whether network involvement forms transient, diversified or segmented learning ecologies. These patterns influence the processes of learning and adaptation. Transient ecologies mean that involvement is open and often short-term – each politician is involved in a number of different networks and network involvement changes over time. Diversified ecologies mean that regions and cities are involved in many different networks but there is stability of membership. Segmented ecologies mean there is a highly stable pattern of specialization in terms of network involvement and little communication and learning across specialities. Each segment operates in a way that is insulated from the others.

Understanding Variations in Networking Activities

Some regions are more eager to join networks than others. Why? Our point of departure is that regions join networks in search of new policies to help cope with uncertainties generated by processes of globalization and dependencies entailed by European integration. Consequently, the search for new policies is expected to trigger network participation, and the more intense the search is the more eager networkers regions are expected to be. Policy search drives networks! This is our primary hypothesis. However, a number of intervening factors may modify such a direct link between problems, policy search and network activities.

Globalization often hastens the geographic concentration of investments, job opportunities and settlement patterns. Thus, in the new economy peripheral regions[1] are often more disadvantaged than central regions and can be expected to be more active in building or joining networks. What may be seen as new opportunities in centrally located regions may be felt as "wicked problems" (Kopenjan and Klijin 2004) in peripheral regions that are less attractive sites for the companies of the new economy or the core workers of those companies", the creative class". Recent theories of networks emphasize the origin of networks in attempts by public authorities to deal with "wicked" problems that cut across established jurisdictions and institutional boundaries (Ansell 2001, Mandell 2001, Agranoff and McGuire 2003, Kopenjan and Klijin 2004, Sullivan and Skelcher 2002, Hulst and van Montfort 2007). Many of the developmental problems of peripheral regions belong to the category of "wicked problems".[2] Consequently, central regions and cities can be expected to be less active networkers than the peripheral ones.

Dependency relations are also expected to drive networking across borders. Regions in countries that are members of the European Union are more dependent upon EU regulations and also have more chances of obtaining funds from the various sources that finance development projects. These regions, therefore, will have more active relations with the institutions of the European Union, e.g. the various DGs. In concrete terms this means that a contrast is expected in terms of network activities between Norwegian regions and the rest.

A corollary of the policy learning thesis is that institutional features of cities and regions will influence choices of network involvement. The wider the range of functions for which local authorities are responsible, the wider the range of networks in which local authorities will engage. Similarly, as suggested by Marks et al. (1994), the more autonomy local authorities enjoy, the more inclined they will be to join networks to fulfil obligations entailed by autonomy. Consequently, reforms of regional structures in Denmark, Norway and Sweden may have

---

1   Rokkan and Urwin (1983) list the classical features of the periphery as distance, difference, dependency: geographically far from the capital city, culturally different from the nation's core regions and economically backward.

2   Cf. e.g. Dunn (2008: 79) for an analysis of "ill-structured" or "wicked" problems.

repercussions for network involvement. In Denmark as well as Norway, regions have lost functions and in the Danish case, regions have also been downgraded in autonomy while Swedish regions have been upgraded as development agents as well as service providers in some cases (especially the two south-west coastal regions; cf. Chapter 2 for further details).

As pointed out above, networks may also grow out of feelings of cross-border solidarity with worse-off regions. This motive may rouse the networking impulse of politicians according to their ideological position on a left-right continuum; those on the left have traditionally responded more to the underdog and may be expected to do so, too, with regard to regions and cities in distress.

Finally, the basic requirement of *trust* among participants in networks may shape the overall patterns of networks. Regions may cooperate more with neighbours than with more distant regions; cross-border cooperation will take place more frequently across borders of adjacent countries than with regions in distant countries; cultural proximity or distance will work in similar ways.

Before attempting an analysis of the hypotheses outlined above, a series of more descriptive issues will have to be addressed. First, to what extent do politicians from Nordic cities and regions actually engage in cross-border activities? What are the focal points of those activities, with whom do they engage? How do they assess the benefits from those contacts? Are they satisfied with the outcomes of cross-border activities in which their regions and cities engage? Do they actually learn something from network participation?

Involvement in Cross-border Networks – Towards Learning Ecologies?

Patterns of Network Involvement

This part of the chapter outlines the extent to which Nordic politicians are involved in both national and international (cross-border) networks and the types of networks and contacts. The aim is to identify the learning ecologies of the respective regions and cities. The analysis proceeds in two steps. First, we outline the extent and range of the network involvement of politicians. An important issue in this respect is how international involvement has changed over the last decade. Second, the patterns or profiles of network involvement are analysed. These profiles represent the *learning ecologies* of politicians. Furthermore, by aggregating the learning ecologies of politicians according to their regions and cities, we may also be able to identify the learning ecologies of regions and cities as institutions. The basic issue we address is whether learning ecologies are transient, diversified or segmented.

Table 4.1 presents the politicians' involvement in joint activities with other regions in their own country as well as with regions abroad. Other international contacts and activities are also listed, such as study visits to foreign municipalities or contacts with EU agencies. First of all it should be noted that in column two the various activities have been grouped in three categories: Cross-border

Table 4.1   Cross-border and cross-institutional involvement among Nordic regional and urban politicians 1998 and 2008. Mean scores (2008) and percentage "yes"

	Cluster type**	Mean scores overall 2008	Pct "yes" 2008	Pct "yes" 1998
Study visit to region/municipality in other countries	1	1.59	57	60
Participation at international conferences	1	1.44	42	38
Visits to twin region/city	1	1.36	35	
Membership of committees with regions/ municipalities in other countries	1	1.39	32	39
Involved in preparing projects with regions/ municipalities in other countries	1	1.32	29	42
Participation in projects with regions/municipalities in other countries	1	1.30	25	
Participation in regional collaboration across Nordic borders	1	1.27	24	
Participation in other European regional collaboration	1	1.22	21	
Participation in collaboration with other Baltic or North Sea regions	1	1.20	18	
Participation at meetings of European regional associations	1	1.15	14	
Contacts with regional Brussels office	1/2	1.45	38	
Contacts with other EU institutions	2	1.19	16	
Contacts with DG Regional Policy (EU)	2	1.08	8	
Contacts with other DGs (EU)	2	1.10	8	
Membership of committees with other regions/ municipalities in home country	3	1.79	55	59
Participation in projects with regions/municipalities in home country	3	1.59	45	
N		744– 857	744– 856	1,229– 1,240

Note: Scale: 1 = rarely/never; 5 = almost daily*. Cluster types of networks/contacts
*Q.: How often have you been involved in the following activities during the last year?
1: Rarely/never, 2: a couple of times, 3: almost monthly, 4: almost weekly, 5: almost daily
**Based on factor analysis; the numbers indicate items that form a common factor

collaboration and contacts with regions and municipalities in other countries, contacts with EU institutions, and collaboration with regions at home (the reason for this grouping is presented in the next section). Inside these clusters the various activities are ranked according to the proportion of politicians who claimed to have been involved in the respective activities at least once over the last year. The proportions are reported in column four while the mean scores or frequencies of involvement are given in column three.

Quite a large proportion of politicians claim to have had some networking experience during the year preceding the survey. If we concentrate first on category one, contacts with regions and municipalities in other countries, more than half of the respondents have been on study tours and nearly half have participated in international conferences or gatherings of regions. Membership in standing groups ("committees") that work across national borders is also fairly common, this is something that around one third claim to be involved in. Almost the same proportion has experience from project development with foreign partners. However, these activities are not very frequent occurrences; mostly they take place once or twice a year. The seemingly low frequency may not be so surprising but suggests instead that such meetings and contacts are not routine events in the life of the politicians and may also highlight the workshop like character of these meetings.

What about the direction of contacts? Are contacts among Nordic neighbours more frequent than contacts with other European partners, as suggested above? This is in fact not the case. Almost the same proportion of politicians claims to have been involved in collaboration across Nordic and other European borders. A quarter has collaborated with colleagues from other Nordic countries while a fifth has worked with regions in other European countries. When asked whether their networks also included ties across the Baltic Sea or across the North Sea almost 20 per cent said they did.

Contacts with the institutions of the European Union are much less frequent. Contacts especially with the DG for regional policy were expected to be quite high but are in fact something few politicians engage in. The explanation may be that this is a type of bureaucratic contact that their permanent Brussels offices handle. And interestingly, the politicians are frequently in touch with their respective offices there (almost 40 per cent of them during one year).

The primacy of collaboration with neighbours is borne out when we look at the ties between regions in the same country. Around half of all the politicians are involved in standing work groups with neighbouring regions or in more short-term projects. Clearly, there is intense activity across jurisdictions inside the respective Nordic countries.

How has networking developed over time? Is the cross-border collaborative urge subsiding when the EU is moving more of its attention and funding priorities towards the new member countries? This question can only be answered partly since the full range of items was not used in the survey in 1998. However, where a comparison between 2008 and 1998 is possible the results indicate that the level of contacts and collaboration is remarkably stable. Much the same proportion of respondents reports in both years that they go on study visits or to international conferences or take part in cooperation with regions in other countries. The numbers involved in domestic cooperative ventures are also much the same. There is a substantial change in one respect, however. More politicians were involved in the preparatory stages of project development regarding cross-border cooperation in 1998 than in 2008 (42 vs. 29 per cent). We cannot give precise reasons for this change but would suggest that the explanation may be found in the maturation of international involvement in cities and regions. As international cooperation matures and becomes more routinized, the participation of politicians focuses on strategic issues regarding international involvement, while details such as actual project development and concretization are assumed by administrative staff. The case studies reported in section two of this report indicate that a number of regions have specialized staff dedicated to international issues. However, the overall picture is that networking and international contacts are still a priority of Nordic regions and cities.

We have so far ascertained that there are in fact extensive cross-border contacts and network activities taking place involving regional and urban politicians. But are there more overall patterns of network involvement? Is it transient and fleeting or diversified and specialized, possibly even segmented? These questions have been followed up by factor analysis seeking to identify groupings of politicians according to their involvement patterns. If involvement is transient, no clear pattern is expected to emerge, i.e. no factors will be found. If involvement is diversified and specialized, a smaller number of clusters should emerge. The issue of segmentation cannot be addressed only through factor analysis, however, but will be broached at a later stage of the analysis (cf. below).

Three factors were identified through factor analysis. The composition of the factors is indicated in column two of Table 4.1. The three groupings are: 1) foreign cross-border cooperation (including Nordic, Baltic/North Sea and other European regional/municipal cooperation) plus study tours and international conferences; 2) contacts with EU institutions; and, 3) cooperation between "home" regions/ cities. In other words, politicians seem to prioritize their cross-border activities in a way that results in clusters of networks. This result suggests that politicians form specialized groupings in cross-border involvement – they are grouped into three types of learning ecologies. One set of politicians collaborate with adjacent regions in their own country. As noted above this is the most frequent type of collaboration. A second set is involved in "international relations", i.e. they take part in networks and contacts that extend beyond national borders. And a third set of politicians have contacts primarily with agencies of the European Union. The specialized, possibly the segmented, nature of networking raises the question of whether and how learning is organized *across* these groupings. Is there any organized summary of information flows from the various sources covered by the politicians? This issue is addressed in Chapter 9.

Table 4.2   The usefulness of involvement in international networks according to the assessment of regional and urban politicians, and totals for 2008 and 1998. Mean scores. Scale: 1= not useful at all, 5= very useful

	Finland	Sweden	Norway	Denmark	Total 2008 1998
Usefulness of:					
Contacts with twinned regions/cities	3.68	3.55	3.42	3.04	**3.24** 2.49
Regional/municipal collaboration in Nordic countries	3.53	3.74	3.02	3.33	**3.24** 2.57
Regional/municipal collaboration in the Baltic area	3.52	3.76	2.61	2.99	**3.13** 2.46
Regional/municipal collaboration in other European countries	3.44	3.61	2.89	3.16	**3.24** 2.38
Membership of European regional/municipal associations	3.47	3.64	2.89	2.92	**3.14** 2.27
Overall satisfaction with international involvement of own region/municipality	3.27	3.33	3.45	3.33	**3.34*** 2.80**
N	164–179	255–281	159–191	177–205	765–856

Note: *Scale: 1=very dissatisfied, 3=neutral, 5=highly satisfied
**Scale: 1=too little, 3=about right, 5=too much international involvement

Learning from Network Involvement

Do politicians actually learn anything through the networks in which they are involved? The second part of the analysis presents the respondents' assessment of *the benefits* of networking and what sort of benefits they derive from networks. The analysis of this issue is limited to international network involvement such as contacts with twin cities, cooperative projects with regions in other countries or membership of international regional or municipal associations. Cf. the list in Table 4.2.

Mean scores of three or above indicate a positive assessment of the region's or city's collaborative arrangements across national borders. Overall, in 2008 politicians find that the relationships listed in Table 4.2 yield useful results for their regions/cities; there are no partnerships that stand out as clearly more or less useful than others. Evidently, regions and cities take care in selecting the partners with which they become involved so that they obtain the results that they expect.

Of, course, when data are analysed in greater detail groups of politicians do emerge who think that international involvement is a waste of time, but these are few in number and do not dominate the responses given on this issue. When the data are analysed by country, variations become apparent, however. Norwegians seem slightly more reserved as to usefulness of international collaboration than the other countries when it comes to collaboration across the Baltic Sea and through European regional and municipal associations such as the Association of European Regions. The Danes are close to the Norwegians in these respects, however.

Appreciations of international involvements have become more positive over the years. Politicians are more satisfied in 2008 than in 1998. In 1998 assessments overall verged on the negative side, while in 2008 Nordic regions and cities feel they derive positive benefits from their contacts across borders. This development may indicate an enhanced capability to learn from international contacts. Precisely how learning processes are organized in individual regions is illustrated by case studies Chapter 9.

There are, however, variations in perceptions of the usefulness of these relations. What do these variations depend upon? This matter will be broached in the section below.

Drivers of Network Involvement and Learning

In this part of the chapter the hypotheses outlined above are tested through regression analysis. Our main hypothesis pinpoints novel policy ideas as drivers of networks. Testing the hypothesis draws on the data on policy preferences presented in Chapter 3. Chapter 3 outlined how factor analysis reduced 24 policy options to seven factors or policy groupings: 1) information age strategies or triple helix, 2) internationalization, 3) cultural strategies (attractive cultural facilities and events), 4) regionalization of state functions, 5) enlargement of regions/municipalities, 6) functional redistribution between cities and regions, and 7) concentrate region/city on developmental tasks (rather than service provision). The seven policy types are used as independent variables for the regression analysis presented in Table 4.3 (in practice, the factor scores of the seven factors were used for this purpose). We regard policy types numbers 1, 2 and 3 as indicative of new types of policies that are expected to drive network involvement in particular while the remaining types are "old" policy options, at least as policy ideas (the last four represent ideas about systemic change that have been around in the Nordic polities for a rather long time).

To test hypothesis no. 2 ("wicked problems"), the analysis distinguishes between politicians from central and peripheral areas. We have defined central areas as regions with a city of at least 100,000 inhabitants.

Hypothesis no. 3 highlights dependency relations. Regions and cities highly dependent on EU regulations and grants will be involved more overall in networks

Table 4.3   Determinants of network participation and satisfaction with outcomes. Regression analysis. Beta coefficients. N=887

	Network participation (cf. Table 4.1)				Satisfaction with outcomes (cf. Table 4.2)	
	Overall network participation	Foreign networks	EU contacts	Domestic cooperation	Model 1	Model 2
Policy orientation:						
Policy 1 Triple Helix advocates	-.018	-.022	.037	-.013	.125**	.126**
Policy 2 Internationalists	.233***	.198***	.070	.169***	.433***	.399***
Policy 3 Culturalists	.036	.067	-.003	.072	.190***	.180***
Policy 4 Radical regionalists (Take over state functions)	.233***	.176**	-.033	.256***	.145**	.123**
Policy 5 Enlargers	-.025	-.054	-.025	.041	-.017	-.004
Policy 6 Re-aligners (Redistribute functions regions-cities)	.001	.030	-.035	-.023	.022	.017
Policy 7 Developmentalists	.035	.018	.054	.035	-.002	-.007
Centrality of region/city	.096*	.088	.057	.095**	-.005	-.020
Norway (dummy)	.071	.106**	-.085	.103**	-.172	-.184***
Region or city	.015	-.002	-.048	-.003	-.187***	-.187***
Left-right party	.081	.088	.073	.061	-.103**	-.122**
Age of resp.	-.060	-.018	-.107**	.020	-.011	-.002
Gender	.062	.029	-.004	.064	-.098**	-.102
Foreign networks involvement						.198***
EU contacts						.047
Domestic networks involvement						-.050
Adj. r²	.094	.069	.016	.075	.335	.366

and especially those focusing on EU institutions. Here, a contrast between Norway and the other three countries is expected.

We also suggested that involvement in international networks may spring from altruistic motives – a wish to aid worse-off regions; such motives may be related to the political ideologies of left-wing politicians in particular. The politicians have therefore been classified on a left-right continuum according to their political parties.

The same set of independent variables is used to investigate variations as to the learning impacts or perceptions of benefits of cross-border network involvement. Results of the regression analysis are reported in Table 4.3.

Several of the hypotheses are supported by the pattern of relationships demonstrated in Table 4.3. First, policies drive network participation, especially policies regarding internationalization and preferences for the take-over of state functions. The latter are a preference of hardline regionalists. The hardliners are driven to participate in foreign as well as domestic relations more than "soft" regionalists are. However, such "modern" policy options as knowledge-related and cultural strategies are not specifically associated with network participation. Apparently, these are not options that seem to demand direct cross-border cooperation from their advocates.

Second, "wicked" problems, presumably possessed in abundance more often by the periphery than by central districts, are related to networking in the way we suggested. There are statistically significant variations in terms of network activity between politicians from central and peripheral locations. The effect of peripheral location is seen in terms of overall network activity and in terms of domestic cooperation.

Third, dependency relations, operationalized as a split between members and non-members of the EU (Norway), were expected to drive contacts especially with the EU but with spill over effects also to other networking relations. Networking is indeed related to membership status but in the opposite direction of our expectations. Norwegians are more active than the other Nordics in foreign networks as well as domestic networks while there is little difference in contacts with EU institutions (although the negative sign of the coefficient suggests slightly less activity in this regard in Norwegian cities and regions). What we observe here may be an interesting side-effect of Norway's outsider status: Norwegian cities and regions have to be *more active* network participants than their counterparts in member countries to compensate for the disadvantages of the outsider situation (it should be noted that all Norwegian regions and most of the larger cities are represented by information offices in Brussels).

Can we, finally, find any sign of solidarity with underdog regions as a motive in cross-border contacts? Are left-wing politicians more active than those from right-wing parties? The answer is that there is no party-related division to be found among the politicians, at least not as far as the propensity to participate in networks is concerned.

We also wanted to test how well these variables can account for variations in *learning outcomes from international contacts,* which were analysed in detail in Table 4.2. This is the purpose of the two right-hand columns of Table 4.3. Model 1 includes the explanatory variables that were used in the preceding analysis of networking activity. Model 2 also includes indicators of network participation (the same set of variables that were used as dependent variables in the analysis above).

We find, first of all, that some policy preferences do contribute to a positive appreciation of networks, i.e. policy types 1–4 are of importance in this regard (policies associated with knowledge brokerage, as presented in Chapter 3), which means that politicians who want to pursue knowledge-related and cultural strategies find that international contacts are of great value. Second, regional politicians find international collaboration to be of more value than their urban colleagues while there is no difference between peripheries and centres in this respect. Norwegian politicians are somewhat less appreciative of international contacts than their colleagues from the EU countries. Furthermore, right-wing politicians value the lessons from international networks less than those of a left-oriented leaning.

Finally, looking at the rightmost column (Model 2), there are also direct learning impacts from involvement in foreign networks but no impacts from contacts with EU institutions or domestic cooperation. This last point is not that surprising since the issue was to what extent respondents found international contacts useful.

What about the overall issue of the chapter? Are learning ecologies transient, diversified, specialized or segmented? Learning ecologies cannot be said to be transient since network involvement forms stable clusters and the level of political participation has remained fairly stable over time. Overall, we conclude that these clusters form specialized patterns bordering on segmentation. There may be signs of segmentation inherent in these patterns because of the close relationships between policy preferences, network involvement and network appreciation. As shown above network participation is specialized into three separate clusters. Participation is driven (to some extent) by policy preferences. Participation also drives the appreciation of outcomes although appreciation is driven even more strongly by policy preferences. So we may speak of a segmentation circle: from policy preferences via network participation to learning/appreciation of useful benefits of networks. If these relationships work as a self-reinforcing circle, we may talk of strong segmentation. However, the relationships indicated in Table 4.3 point only to moderately strong processes of segmentation. At present, the patterns indicate learning ecologies between specialization and segmentation. The dangers of lock-in effects are not that imminent.

Conclusions

We have found that regional and urban politicians are quite extensively involved in networks both in their home countries and across national borders. In 2008 they have fairly positive views of the benefits of the involvement of their respective institutions in various international channels, but there are also exceptions. Perceptions of benefits have become more positive since 1998. We interpret this as a sign of better learning capacities in cities and regions. They have developed structures enabling them to actually make use of information gained through international contacts in their own operations. The case studies presented in Chapters 7–9 demonstrate how this works in selected regions.

Network involvement is largely driven by policy preferences. Politicians take part in networks because they have policy views and seek confirmation and additional information regarding those views. Patterns of network involvement are specialized with signs of segmentation. Segmentation is quite moderate, however, so cross-border networks as learning ecologies still represent flexible channels of adaptation to changing environments.

Chapter 5

Regions in the European Architecture of Governance: Towards Integrative Regionalism. The Attitudes of Regional Policy-Makers

Harald Baldersheim

Beyond Lobbying in Brussels

What is the proper role of the regions in collaboration beyond national borders? Is there a role for regions in the wider European architecture of governance? What should that role resemble? How much autonomy should regions be allowed to exercise in pursuing their interests beyond the nation-state? This last question also raises controversial issues regarding the relationship between regions and the nation-state itself.

The dominant view of European regionalism has largely been framed by a vanguard of assertive identity regions since the collapse of the Warsaw Pact (Harvie 1994). Another view has highlighted competitive regionalism in the search for investments and entrepreneurs to stimulate job-creation schemes (Keating 1997) following the creed of "endogenous development" (Vazquyez-Barquero 2002). Competitive regionalism has also been taken to entail, at a further stage of development, a Europe composed of competing super-regions covering large tracts of land and cutting across several countries, such as an Atlantic Coast region, an Alpine region, a Baltic region or a Danube Basin region (Delmaide 1994). These super-regions have the potential, according to Delmaide, not only to dwarf the nation-states of Europe but also to put a stop to the overall European integration project because of their very competitiveness. The Nordic cooperation project could also be threatened by the rise of super-regions as the new forces of gravitation would cut across traditional Nordic bonds of cooperation and divide the Nordic countries into an Atlantic and a Baltic league.

In this book we have sought particularly to map the extent to which regional policy-makers advocate comprehensive roles for regions in European processes of decision-making, as opposed to those who think that regions should be limited to national roles or, at most, a role in established Nordic structures of collaboration. Policy-makers who advocate more influential roles for regions in European affairs are designated champions of *integrative regionalism.* The term integrative regionalism has been coined to capture a role for regions *beyond* the one often outlined in accounts of multi-level governance. The role of regions in multi-level governance has largely been portrayed as that of *lobbying* in Brussels (Marks et al. 1996, Lein-Mathisen 2005). This is a role that regions increasingly took on during the 1990s as they established offices or other listening posts to gather information, monitor decision-making in EU institutions and collect as much money as possible from the structural and other EU funds. In this account multi-level governance, as far as regions are concerned, is about the construction and management of clientellistic relations to the EU Commission. Integrative regionalism, in contrast, is a movement to make regions institutionalized partners in decision-making at levels beyond the nation-state and especially in EU affairs.

This is a development both welcomed and stimulated to some extent by EU agencies. The Commission of the EU stated as early as 2001,

---

The Commission will:

- Establish from 2002 onwards a more systematic dialogue with European and national associations of regional and local government at an early stage of policy shaping.

- Launch, from 2002 onwards, pilot "target-based contracts" within one or more areas, as a more flexible means of ensuring implementation of EU policies.

The Committee of the Regions should:

- Play a more proactive role in examining policy, for example through the preparation of exploratory reports in advance of Commission proposals.

- Organise the exchange of best practice on how local and regional authorities are involved in the preparatory phase of European decision-making at national level.

- Review the local and regional impact of certain directives, and to report to the Commission by the end of 2002 on the possibilities for more flexible means of application. The Commission will then consider a more systematic approach to allow such flexibility for some parts of Community law.

The Member States should:

- examine how to improve the involvement of local and regional actors in EU policy-making.

- promote the use of contractual arrangements with their regions and localities.

Source: Commission of the European Communities (2001).
*Europe*an Governance – A White Paper, Brussels, 25.7.2001, COM(2001) 428 final.

The way in which regions could be involved in European decision-making was further outlined in 2009 by the Committee of the Regions:

The Committee of the Regions
– considers multilevel governance to mean coordinated action by the European Union, the Member States and local and regional authorities, based on partnership and aimed at drawing up and implementing EU policies. It leads to responsibility being shared between the different tiers of government concerned and is underpinned by all sources of democratic legitimacy and the representative nature of the different players involved;
– recommends that each major Community strategic reform should be accompanied by a territorial action plan agreed between the European Commission and the Committee of the Regions, setting out the political mechanisms to facilitate the ownership ...

Source: Committee of the Regions (2009).
White Paper on Multi-Level Governance, Brussels, CdR 89/2009 fin FR/EXT/RS/GW/ym/ms.

Against this background, it would not take a long stretch of the imagination to extend the role of regions into "high politics" as actors in international relations. This is precisely what a conference sponsored by the Committee of the Regions was invited to contemplate in January 2010. The conference preamble outlined three "waves" of "substate diplomacy": The first was one of competitive regionalism concerned with attracting foreign investments; the second was spearheaded by regions that established their own parallel diplomatic services coordinating international contacts across the various departments of the regional administration, while:

> The current third wave is characterized by steps towards a "verticalization" of the organizational structure of the administration or department of external/foreign affairs, a strategic re-orientation of the geopolitical and functional priorities, and attempts to integrate the external instruments of a sub-state foreign policy into a well performing whole.
>
> International Workshop: Towards a "Third Wave" in Sub-State Diplomacy?
> Committee of the Regions, Tuesday, 19 January 2010

To what extent are Nordic regions influenced by this movement? Does such a movement threaten traditional inter-regional cooperation across Nordic borders?

The Structures of Integrative Governance

The structures of integrative regional governance include, of course, the Committee of Regions mentioned above. They also include a series of long-standing *direct cross-border* cooperative arrangements, a number of *platforms* for such initiatives as well as *funding arrangements* and a variety of *lobbying* organizations.

Direct Cooperation

In the Nordic area, the emergence of cross-border cooperation and accompanying governance structures predates EU initiatives in this field (Baldersheim and Ståhlberg 1999). Cross-border cooperation among regions in the Nordic area has a long tradition and is widespread, as illustrated by Map 5.1, indicating the cooperative ventures supported by the Nordic Council of Ministers. Some of these ventures date back to the 1950s. These networks have their own governing structures and are thus examples of the new patterns of governance to be explored here.

An advanced example of this kind of cooperation is found in The Border Commission of Østfold-Bohuslän/Dalsland. According to the Commission's own assessment,

> Of the collaborative arrangements found along the Swedish-Norwegian border, that of the region of Østfold-Bohuslän/Dalsland is the most highly developed in density and the frequency of contacts. The collaboration Østfold-Bohuslän/Dalsland started in 1980 to promote the development of the region and establish a forum for issues related to both countries (translation/HB).[1]

Funding Arrangements

Map 5.2 outlines the cooperation supported through the EU's Interreg programmes. These arrangements largely overlap with those found on Map 5.1, which demonstrates how long-standing cooperative initiatives manage to attract funds and projects from a variety of sources. These sources may also include other EU funds.

Since 2007, the Interreg programme has been followed by programmes for *territorial cooperation*, including traditional cross-border and EU-wide ventures.

Map 5.3 details the regions eligible for support from objective 1 and 2 funds in the period ending in 2006. The map specifies regions eligible during the period 2000–06. Eligible areas were located largely in Sweden and Finland and less so in Denmark (Norwegian regions, of course, fall outside). Maps 5.1 and 5.2 can be read as blueprints of the engine driving much of the cross-border networking and regional interest in multi-level governance – the availability of funding for

---

1   (http://www.norden.org/da/samarbejdsomrader/graensehindringer/links).

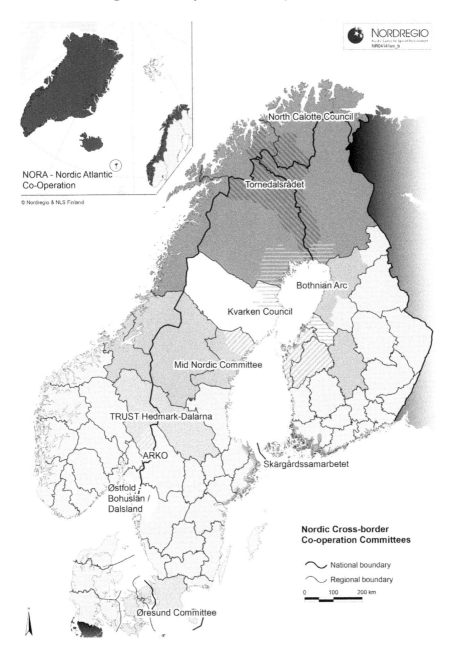

NORDREGIO
NR04141en_b

NORA - Nordic Atlantic
Co-Operation

© Nordregio & NLS Finland

North Calotte Council

Tornedalsrådet

Bothnian Arc

Kvarken Council

Mid Nordic Committee

TRUST Hedmark-Dalarna

ARKO

Skärgårdssamarbetet

Østfold
Bohuslän /
Dalsland

**Nordic Cross-border
Co-operation Committees**

⌇⌇⌇ National boundary
⌇⌇⌇ Regional boundary
0   100   200 km

Øresund Committee

Map 5.1   Nordic Cross-Border Cooperation Committes

NORDIC INTERREG III A/B PROGRAMME AREAS

— INTERREG III A
1 Sweden-Norway
2 Kvarken MittSkandia
3 Nord
4 Karelia
5 South East Finland
6 South Finland Coastal Zone/Phare CBC Estonia
7 Sweden/Finland Islands
8 Öresund
9 Storstrøm - Ostholstein/Lübeck
10 Fyn - K.E.R.N.
11 Sønderjylland - Slesvig

••• INTERREG III B
12 Baltic Sea Region
13 North Sea Region
14 Northern Periphery

European Union
∧ National boundary

Map 5.2   Nordic Interreg III A/B Programme Areas

development projects and the concomitant wish not only to access funds, but also to influence the regulations governing their distribution and use. The new programme period starting in 2007 will last until 2013 and emphasizes human resources and knowledge-driven development. For domestic reasons, however, Danish regions may not be able to access these funds directly. The Danish local government reforms (cf. Chapter 2) have entailed a marked centralization of decision-making in the use of regional development funds in Denmark and

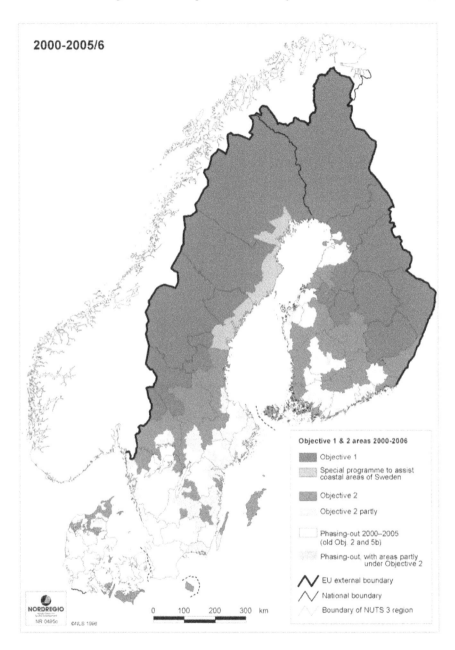

Map 5.3   Nordic Regions Eligible for Support from Objective 1 and 2 Funds 2002–06

a correspondingly diminished role for the regions.[2] The policy space open to regional politicians in Denmark is shrinking.

Platforms

While the funding arrangements mentioned above have a certain top-down character, regions have established a series of broad cooperative platforms that serve as forums for deliberation, policy initiation and workshops for project development. These platforms are established and run by regions of a larger area that are assumed to share certain joint geopolitically defined interests. The most well-known of these platforms are the North Sea Commission, the Baltic Sea Substate Council and the Barents Sea Council. The Nordic Council and the Nordic Council of Ministers can also be seen as platforms for the promotion of regional cooperation in the Nordic area. Map 5.1 details the actual fruits of these efforts. A new document[3] has been drawn up for the period 2009–13 and is intended to stimulate Nordic cross-border cooperation in regional policy, focusing on three "action areas":

- Exchanging experience and knowledge building;
- Globalization and cross-border cooperation;
- Third-generation regional policy.

The authors of the documents clearly envisage processes of integrative governance with regions actively involved in promoting third-generation regional policy at all levels of decision-making, including EU policies. The documents also states that,

> Contributing to the development of a third-generation regional policy requires active and powerful players with responsibility for regional growth and development issues. In early 2008, the Committee of Senior Officials for Regional Policy appointed a cross-Nordic group to prepare, at national level, Nordic input to the ongoing debate about the future development of the EU's territorial cohesion policy.

---

2   After the Danish local government reforms of 2007, a complex structure has been set up to manage regional development funds that used to be the responsibility of *amtsrådene*. Each of the five new regions has to establish a "growth forum", the members of which are appointed by the regional council, municipal councils of the area, associations of business and industry, research institutions and associations of employers and employees. The growth forums are to draw up a development plan for their respective regions. Overall responsibility including daily supervision rests with a central government agency (Erhvervs- og byggestyrelsen: http://www.ebst.dk/file/5467/Regionalfondsprogram_2007-2013.pdf). The influence of the regional council is reduced to the appointment of three members of the regional growth forum.

3   Nordic regional policy cooperation programme 2009–2012, pp. 55ff, Nordic Council of Ministers, 2009.

Lobbying Organizations

Of the lobbying structures, mention should be made first and foremost of the myriad of lobbying offices established in Brussels by regions. All Nordic regions are represented by an office, often established jointly by a group of regions (Dosenrode et al. 2005). There are also a series of European regional associations – some of them with a functional focus, others with a geographic delimitation. One of the most encompassing of these is the Assembly of European Regions (AER).

State/region relations in the Nordic countries have changed in the last decade. The EU has also changed through its eastward expansion and the stepwise revision of its institutional structure and procedures of decision-making. Fewer Nordic regions are eligible for support from the structural funds. Therefore, continued regional interest in international activities cannot be taken for granted, at least not an interest in European affairs. Integrative regionalism may be waning.

How Much Support is There for Integrative Governance Among Regional Policy-makers?

What are the features of cross-border governance favoured today by Nordic regional policy-makers? To what extent are regions champions of integrative regionalism? Have the attitudes of regional policy-makers changed since the heydays of EU accession? Do attitudes today reflect largely integrative or clientellistic positions? The rolling-back of regions that has occurred in two of the countries – Denmark and Norway – could indicate that the regionalizing influence of European integration, so pronounced in the 1990s, is now waning. This could have repercussions for the attitudes of regional policy-makers, producing indifference to rather than enthusiasm about the prospect of extended roles for regions in European governance.

In our previous project, three forms of regionalism were identified among regional and urban politicians: Euro-regionalism, regional activism and state-centred regionalism. *Euro-regionalism* was characterized by positive views among policy-makers regarding EU initiatives in regional policy and cross-border regional cooperation and a wish to play a part in European integration; this is a position largely in line with *integrative regionalism* as outlined above. *Regional activists* were highly concerned with strengthening the role of regions in national as well as in European decision-making and also agreed that it was high time for regions to develop their own foreign policies. *State-centred regionalism* was expressed through attitudes sceptical towards regional involvement in European integration while also favouring a strong nation-state as a defender of regional interests and seeing regional cooperation at the European level as an overcrowded arena (Ståhlberg 2001: 73 ff).

The Euro-regionalist position was the one most widely supported by policy-makers a decade ago, with around half of all respondents clearly in support of a

Euro-driven regional development. Regional activism came second, while state-centred regionalism had the fewest adherents. Overall, the pattern was the same in all four countries. Danish regions came on top in their support for Euro-regionalism. Interestingly, Euro-regionalism was somewhat weaker in Norway than in the other countries but not conspicuously so compared to Finland and Sweden.

In sum, in the Nordic countries 10 years ago a regionalist position meant being an advocate of an enhanced role for regions in European integration while seeking more autonomy from the state. However, there was also a group, although a much smaller one, that saw the state as a safeguard in a more competitive economic climate. To them, the role of the regions was to be developed with limited autonomy under the umbrella of a strong nation-state. While Euro-regionalism constituted the set of attitudes that most clearly reflected an integrationist position, that of state-centred regionalism is the one most in keeping with regional clientellism. However, there were clearly tensions among the representatives of the regions regarding the future of Nordic regions. Have those tensions continued or abated against the background of regional reforms in the Nordic countries and an expanding EU?

What are the Attitudes Like 10 Years On?

As mentioned above, the analysis of attitudes to various regionalist positions is based on a survey of politicians on boards of regional and city councils in the Nordic countries. In Table 5.1, responses to the question posed 10 years ago are reported alongside responses to the same question posed in 2008. One of the striking features of the table is the stability in patterns of responses. The three statements that received most widespread support from policy-makers are the same in 2008 as 10 years ago:

- EU promotion of regional collaboration is a positive force;
- Regions have much to gain from European regional collaboration;
- Cross-border collaboration among Nordic regions is an excellent platform for further collaboration in a European context.

Statements with *the least* support are also the same:

- Regions cannot have an independent role in processes of European integration;
- The costs of regional collaboration in Europe outweigh the benefits;
- It is time for each region to develop its own foreign policy;
- Nation-states, not regions, should run European structural policies.

Consequently, Nordic regionalism is largely in keeping with *the integrationist position* in the sense that *the majority* of regional policy-makers think that:

Table 5.1   **Attitudes to cross-border and European governance. Survey of regional and urban elected representatives in Denmark, Finland, Norway, Sweden. 1998, 2008. Mean scores**

	Cluster*	2008	1998
Regions have a lot to gain by collaborating in a European context	1	3.78	3.92
Cross-border collaboration among Nordic regions is a good foundation for their involvement in wider European collaboration	1	3.72	3.92
Nordic regions are the foundations of Nordic cooperation	1	3.30	3.55
Ultimately, only strong nation-states can defend the interests of their regions	2	3.09	3.21
There are too many organizations seeking to represent European regions	2	3.41	3.47
Regions cannot have extensive autonomy in the context of European collaboration	2	2.58	2.53
On the whole, regional collaboration in Europe is a waste of resources	2	2.64	2.78
The control of European structural policy is a matter for the nation-states, not the regions	2	2.97	2.99
The position of regions should be strengthened in European decision-making	-2**	3.47	3.70
It is a good thing that the EU stimulates regional collaboration	-2**	3.79	3.92
Nordic regional collaboration has been overtaken by European collaboration	3	3.02	3.12
The position of regions is too weak in the national system of decision-making	3	3.67	3.54
The elected officers of regions have too little knowledge of European collaboration	3	3.60	3.81
Baltic cooperation is more important than just Nordic cooperation	3	3.22	3.51
European integration has led to more competition between regions even inside countries	4	3.24	3.54
It is time for each region to formulate its own "foreign policy"	4	2.59	2.68
Valid N		824–650	1,223–1,199

Note: Scale: 1 (disagree completely) – 5 (agree completely). * Clusters of attitudes

Q.: "There are many different views of regional collaboration in the European context. Please indicate whether you agree or disagree with the following statements":

*Clusters are based on factor analysis

**The negative sign indicates that the proponents of state-centred regionalism reject this statement

- Nordic regions benefit from collaboration in a wider European context and support further EU initiatives in this field;
- Regions should have more say in European decision-making; evidently, the purely advisory position of the Committee of the Regions is not a satisfactory solution in the long run;
- Nevertheless, there should be limits to regional autonomy in a national context in the sense that regions cannot be allowed to have their own foreign policy;
- Regional collaboration across Nordic borders does not necessarily conflict with collaboration in a European context;
- There are also a number of fault lines permeating regional collaboration, e.g. between Nordic and further European regional collaboration and between Nordic and Baltic collaborative projects; at the same time, European integration has resulted in more competition between regions inside the respective countries.

Furthermore, the attitudes among regional policy-makers cluster in much the same way they did 10 years ago. Through factor analysis, we could identify four clusters of attitudes (the components of the respective clusters are indicated in column one of Table 5.1):

1. integrative, Euro-Nordic regionalism,
2. state-centred regionalism,
3. extra-Nordic regionalism, and
4. competitive regionalism.

These clusters correspond quite well to the three dimensions mentioned above: Euro-regionalism, state-centred regionalism and regional activism. The last two clusters identified in the 2008 material – competitive and extra-Nordic regionalism – can be seen as a split of the former regional activism cluster.

In short, Nordic regionalism is still characterized by strongly positive attitudes to collaboration in a European context and under an EU umbrella. The European project is not seen as a competitor to a Nordic project; rather, regional collaboration across Nordic borders is seen as an integral part of wider European collaboration. At the same time, Nordic regions are pressing for more autonomy in relation to their respective nation-states.

There are, however, three competing clusters. The most clear-cut one is *the state-centred view* that is also imbued with negative attitudes to European, or at least EU-driven collaboration. To the state-centric group, the state appears as the protector of regional interests. Another group of policy-makers prioritizes *extra-Nordic* collaboration, i.e. Nordic collaboration with an extra dimension, including collaboration across the Baltic Sea and the North Sea, while being sceptical of EU-oriented projects, agreeing that Nordic collaboration has been overtaken by the EU project; they are, however, regional activists in the sense that they think regions have too little sway in national decision-making in their respective countries. *Competitive* regionalists think above all that regions are being exposed to increasing competition and that they should have leeway to formulate their own foreign policies, presumably to meet the competitive climate in their own fashion.

In sum, Nordic regional policy-makers are divided in their views of the role of regions in cross-border governance. Four ways of thinking about regions in multi-level governance have been identified. Clearly, the pressure from globalization and European integration can also be sources of conflict.

Cleavages: Patterns of Support and Rejection

The remainder of the analysis will focus on the two main clusters. *Who* are a) the euro-Nordic and b) the state-centred regionalists and *where* are they found? These questions are addressed through regression analysis (Table 5.2). The analysis highlights six potential lines of division among respondents: the national context of the respondents, whether they are representatives of regions or cities, the position of regions and cities in market-geographic space (the centrality/peripherality of the location), political ideology (left-right) and the policy preferences and network involvement of respondents.

The main features of the framework of comparative analysis were introduced in Chapter 1. In terms of national contexts (EU membership and regional autonomy), Norwegian and Swedish regions are expected to be the contrasts with regard to championing integrative regionalism, while Denmark and Finland will occupy the middle ground.

The relationship of cities and regions may be that of occupying complementary positions or one of competition and rivalry in the distribution of public functions and powers. Their views on policy options and institutional choice often follow from their respective positions in institutional space. Hence, positional interest is one of our explanatory variables.

The centrality of regions and cities defines their positions in geographic space. A central location may presumably lead to other policy choices than a peripheral location – as the challenges of the periphery are different from those of central places (Rokkan and Urwin 1983).

Ideology may also influence views of governance. The pattern of support for European integration is different in the Nordic countries compared to the rest of Europe. In the Nordic countries, parties on the left tend to be more sceptical to European integration which is associated with neo-liberal "free trade" ideas, while parties on the right tend to sympathize with European integration. Hence, we expect respondents from right-wing parties to champion integrative regionalism more than those on the left; conversely, the left is expected to be more in support of state-centred attitudes.

The policy preferences of respondents and their involvement in policy networks have been introduced as additional variables. Policy preferences have been added to follow up the guiding idea of the analysis – policy as a driver of change (cf. Figure 1.1). While policy preferences probe the potential influence of ideas on attitudes to governance, network involvement may demonstrate the impact of experience on attitudes. Information-age policy preferences and extensive network involvement are expected to lead to favourable attitudes to integrative regionalism.

The data presented in Table 5.2 show that, with regard to *integrative regionalism*, three lines of division emerge: nationality, policy preferences, and network involvement.

The analysis proceeds in two steps. In the first step, only the basic features of the comparative framework are taken into account, i.e. national contexts and the geographical-institutional environment. Political-ideological orientation is added as a control variable. The results of the preliminary analysis are shown in the first column, in which the analysis focuses on support/rejection of the integrative position. The Finns seem to reject the position while there is no clear pattern in the other countries. There is also a division between regions and cities: cities reject integrative regionalism while regions embrace it. The party affiliation of the respondents is of no consequence. Will these divides remain when further explanatory variables are taken into account?

In columns two and three, the two additional sets of variables, policy preferences and network involvement, are brought to bear on the analysis. From column two of Table 5.2 it appears that Norwegian officials are decidedly less enthusiastic than respondents from the other countries about integrative governance. Two components of national contexts were expected to influence views on governance: outsider/insider status with regard to EU membership and regional autonomy measured as a range of functional responsibilities. Of these two components, the former seems to be the one that most decisively frames the views of policy-makers. Norway and Sweden were expected to be contrasts but, in reality, it is Norway against the rest. A contrasting pattern is brought out in the analysis of state-centred regionalism; here, it is Sweden against the rest, i.e. the Swedes reject the state-centred position while the others are on the whole indifferent or lean towards a certain acceptance (the Norwegians incline somewhat in the latter direction). However, when attitudes to the integrative and the state-centred positions are *taken together*, the Swedes and the Norwegians do indeed appear as opposing camps, as hypothesized.

Institutional position (region or city), location (centrality) and party do not matter significantly with regard to support for integrative regionalism when policy preferences and network involvement are also taken into account. Views of governance cut across the divides of region/city, centre/periphery and left/right. This is also true with regard to state-centred regionalism.

Table 5.2   Supporters and opponents of integrative and state-centred regionalism. Regression analysis. Beta coefficients

	Integrative regionalism	Integrative regionalism	State-centred regionalism
Norway dummy	-.081	-.204***	.090
Finland dummy	-.104*	-.090	-.016
Sweden dummy	.070	-.006	-.124*
Region or city (1,2)	-.117**	-.039	.005
Centrality of region, city	-.057	-.063	-.046
Party left – right	-.016	.002	-.009
Policy preferences*:			
• info age		.233***	-.079
• culture		.118**	-.034
• regionalize state functions		.235***	-.245***
Network involvement*:			
• with Nordic and European regions		.228***	-.212***
• with EU institutions		.113**	-.173***
• with national regions		.192***	-.119**
Adjusted r²	.031	.258	.194

Note: *Factor scores for the respective policy and network clusters are used as independent variables, cf. Tables 3.1 and 4.1.

Composition of integrative regionalism index and state-centred regionalism index: cf. Table 5.1 and p. 60.

Views on governance are, however, most conspicuously driven by policy preferences and involvement in policy networks. The three sets of policy preferences included in the analysis are all significant drivers of integrative regionalism. State-centred regionalism is *inversely* related to the same policy preferences. Respondents who support the three policy types tend to reject state-centred regionalism. The same pattern is found with regard to policy network involvement. And it is network involvement as such that matters. Experiences from collaboration with Nordic and European regions, EU institutions as well as with regions in the home country produce support for integrative regionalism and a rejection of state-centred regionalism.

Interestingly, the division between cities and regions found in the first round of analysis disappeared when policy preferences and network involvement were taken into account.

The results of the analysis support the basic notion that has guided the project. Policy preferences influence the formation of policy networks; both factors again shape attitudes to governance.

Conclusion: Policy Shapes Governance

Policy-makers in Nordic regions (including the main cities) are still, 10 years on, decidedly in favour of and prepared to take on extended roles in European structures of decision-making for their regions. Integrative regionalism is the dominant attitude. However, there are competing positions: those of state-centred regionalism, extra-Nordic regionalism and plain competitive regionalism. The role of regions in multi-level governance is clearly a divisive issue.

The lines of division can largely be explained through our comparative, analytical framework. National contexts matter. EU membership/non-membership is an important variable, meaning that the pull of European integration is felt through membership status and the concomitant access to decision-making bodies. Norwegian regions stand out as less integrationist than those of the other three countries. However, of the member countries, Swedish regions are clearly more enthusiastic than those of the other two countries. So regional status also matters – the more responsibilities regions have, the more they want to exercise influence in the European architecture of governance.

The second line of division – between cities and regions – emerged in a preliminary analysis but was much less pronounced when the policy preferences and network experiences of respondents were introduced into the analysis. Views on multi-level governance are most clearly influenced by policy ideas and a background in policy networks, including familiarity with EU institutions. Policy shapes governance!

Chapter 6

Transforming Governance in Cities and Regions in the Nordic Countries: Adapting to "the New Citizen"?

Harald Baldersheim and Morten Øgård

What is "Good Governance" in Regional and Urban Settings? A Longitudinal Approach[1]

"Citizen-orientation" has long been a watch-word in the pursuit of good governance in cities and regions. Such an orientation may take reforms in several directions, however. In what direction does it take reforms when cities and regions increasingly compete to become attractive locations for the so-called "creative class" of knowledge workers, upon which so much of the new economy is claimed to depend (Florida 2002, 2005)?

The present study is a continuation of an earlier one based on data collection in 1997/98 (Baldersheim et al. 2001, Øgård 2002, 2003). The previous study took as its point of departure the wave of reform then surging through many parts of the globe under the label of New Public Management, the core of which was a preoccupation with market-oriented models of management. Consumer choice and competition between providers of public services were features that were expected to enhance efficiency and sensitivity to consumer interests in government. The NPM programme could be seen as a part of a wider liberal agenda that in its more extreme ideological versions vowed to free society from the fetters of state and hierarchy. More restrained versions have sought to promote "lean" government rather than rolling back the state, celebrating the "entrepreneurial spirit" in the public sector (Osborne and Gaebler 1992, Borins 1998, Harris and Kinney 2003).

The heatedness of the NPM discourse on reforms may have blinded observers to the actual richness of local initiatives. Therefore, we added the watchwords of *roots* and *virtue* to that of *choice* in trying to describe reforms that were taking place in the Nordic countries at the time. A "quest for roots" describes initiatives attempting to build or strengthen a sense of community among the inhabitants of a municipality. Examples can be found in inner-city neighbourhoods suffering

---

1 This chapter is in parts an updated version of a text presented by Harald Baldersheim in Kersting and Vetter (2003) entitled "Local Government Reforms in the Nordic Countries. Bringing Politics Back in?"

from vandalism, decay and desolation as well as in small towns or rural areas wishing to celebrate their uniqueness or difference. Local patriotism and regional attachments may exist naturally or be consciously built by local authorities (Stewart and Stoker 1989). Initiatives of this nature range from neighbourhood councils to municipal chat pages and local festivals. Nordic cities with rather far-reaching neighbourhood governance include Oslo, Stockholm and Gothenburg (see e.g. Jönsson et al. 1995, Bäck 2005). Recent surveys of municipal home pages in the Nordic countries found that a good number had introduced citizen chat pages or debate forums (Baldersheim et al. 2008). A sociological term for this phenomenon is social capital formation (Putnam 1993, 1999). In philosophical terms these initiatives can be seen as parts of a communitarian movement seeking to address the social ills of an urban society by stimulating a sense of belonging and identity (Bellah et al. 1988, Reynolds and Norman 1988, Bell 1993). In some versions, communitarians represent a reaction to what they regard as egoistical, choice-driven individualism (Delany 1994). The movement seems to be gaining momentum, especially in the US, and has even established its own web site.[2]

The concern with "virtue" is particularly expressed through strategies that aim at enhancing the transparency and accountability of local governance. To maintain its legitimacy, it may not be enough for local government to offer a choice between service providers or delivering services with a smile. Citizens also expect moral rectitude at the town hall. They may not be satisfied with politicians who merely profess their honesty. Citizens increasingly want to see for themselves. At its core, the taxpayer's prime slogan, "value for money", is also about virtue and transparency. How is the taxpayer to know that he or she is getting value for money if there is a lack of transparency at the town hall? The concern with political virtue is gaining momentum worldwide. International watchdogs have emerged, e.g. Transparency International. Courses on bureaucratic ethics are increasingly in demand. Most donor countries offering development aid now insist on demonstrations of "good governance" as a precondition for their aid money. New as many of these offers may seem, they reflect classic republican ideals of good governance, according to which the highest value is to place the common good above individual self-interest. While in the history of ideas, a concern with virtue is often traced to Machiavelli's writings on the strong city state (Skinner 1981), neo-republicans share a belief in the power of the shining example of moral qualities (Østergård 1992). Whereas the communitarian programme may *in extremis* suggest a cultivation of a mythical, primordial, local solidarity, neo-republicans place their hope in the enlightened discourse of Public Man. Many of the present-day "innovations" in local governance are really about demonstrating practically that the common good is being served. Various ways of "giving a

---

2   "The Communitarian Network is a coalition of individuals and organizations who have come together to shore up the moral, social and political environment. We are a non-sectarian, non-partisan, international association. Visit our web site! http://www.gwu. edu/-ccps".

face" to local politics are demonstrations of such a quest, e.g. the spread in many countries (including Norway) of directly elected mayors (Larsen 2002, Bäck et al. 2006), or even the growing care taken in presenting municipalities on the Internet (West 2005, Baldersheim et al. 2008, Haug 2009). Perhaps the Internet represents an opportunity for the renewal of republican values of our time?

"The new citizen" as described in the theory of the creative class (Florida 2002, 2005, Clark 2004) have features in common with "the post-materialist citizen" (Inglehart 1971, 2008) as well as "the discursive citizen" (Habermas 1981, Eriksen and Weigard 2004). The postulates of these theories outline a citizen that is just as much concerned with "meaning" as with high levels of private and public consumption. If this is the type of citizen that regions and cities have in mind in their pursuit of good governance, we may expect that their efforts may indicate communitarian and neo-republican ideals as well as a consumer orientation.

Development Strategies: What, How Much, Where? Results from Two Surveys

To what extent do the reform initiatives of Nordic municipalities and regions reflect the ideals of good governance outlined above? And has there been a change of emphasis over time? Examples of initiatives illustrating the various ideals have been mentioned. However, these examples do not tell us much about the overall reform ideals of Nordic municipalities. To what extent are they as a group liberals, communitarians or republicans? This is the issue of this section. The section compares data on the actual reform initiatives pursued by municipalities in the Nordic countries with the patterns of governance that characterized the same cities and regions 10 years ago. The local authorities included are the main city (provincial capital) of each of the provinces of the Nordic area (apart from Iceland), and also the county councils of the respective provinces (note that Finland has no second-tier local government system similar to the county councils of the three other countries).

Based on a series of benchmarking studies,[3] a questionnaire was constructed seeking to map the various development strategies pursued by local government. Below, the survey material is used to assess the relative weight the respective ideals carry in local government in the Nordic countries.

The data was collected through a postal survey consisting of a checklist that the municipalities/county councils were requested to fill in.[4] The list was usually

---

3   The benchmarking studies largely followed the format established for the Bertelsman Prize 1993 (Bertelsmann Stiftung 1993).

4   The survey in 1997/98 was part of a larger project concerning "The Nordic Countries in the Europe of Regions" coordinated by Harald Baldersheim, University of Oslo, and Krister Ståhlberg, Åbo Academy. For details, see Baldersheim et al. 2001; especially Øgård 2001. The survey in 2007/08 was part of a larger project concerning "Internationalization

Table 6.1   Strategies and measures to enhance the responsiveness of local authorities, 1997/98–2007/08 (indices applied in surveys of Nordic cities and regions)

	To what extent have the following measures been introduced? Yes=1; No=0
Indices of user and choice orientation	*User orientation:*
	- citizens' charters
	- complaints procedures
	- user choice procedures
	- user surveys
	- service shops
	- training courses in dealing with the public
	Market orientation:
	- internal billing (between units in same authority)
	- competitive tendering
	- benchmarking of municipal services
	- establishment of quasi-independent service companies
	- transfers of functions to private providers or voluntary associations
Indices of community and participation strategies	- citizen discussion meetings
	- citizen panels
	- citizen question hour in local/ county council
	- citizen involvement in planning procedures
	- dialogue forum with voluntary associations
Indices of transparency and accountability strategies	- information department/officer established
	- newsletter published regularly
	- information column in local newspaper
	- TV/radio broadcasts from council meetings
	- Annual report sent to citizens
	- Council documents presented on the Internet
	- Communication with politicians via municipal home page
	- PCs and so forth available to citizens in public places

filled in by an official at the municipal/county head office (the town/county clerk's office) with a good knowledge of the municipality/county. In some cases, we were able to perform in-depth case studies of some of the municipalities that had responded to the surveys. As a rule, the correspondence between the questionnaire results and the case studies was convincing.

Based on the questionnaire data, summary indices have been constructed that reflect the respective ideals of good governance, as indicated in Table 6.1. The appendices have mostly been constructed on the basis of yes/no answers. A sum has been calculated that expresses the range of measures that have been introduced of a particular type in a specific municipality. The higher the sum, the larger the number of measures introduced. A sum of 100 would indicate that all authorities in the group have implemented all the reforms covered by a particular type of measure (for further details, see Øgård 2002).

To what extent are Nordic cities and regions oriented towards choice, community or transparency in their development strategies? Can we trace some changes in reform strategies during the 10 year period? The answers are provided in Tables 6.2 and 6.3.

Looking at the total scores (cities and regions together), the table first of all indicates that local government in all four countries still pursues a multi-faceted strategy. All of the three main types of development strategies outlined above find expression in the Nordic area. It would be correct to say that the strategies are becoming even more complex and multidimensional.

As can be seen from the data, strategies signalling a concern with market and user orientation predominated back in 1997/98. It is interesting to note that 10 years later, user orientation maintains its position, while market orientation experiences a minor drop compared with the scores from 1997. While Denmark demonstrates a drop in user orientation, both the Swedish and Norwegian authorities have increased their interest in such tools as user choice, user surveys, citizens' charters, complaint procedures and so forth.[5] Competitive tendering, benchmarking and the establishment of quasi-independent service companies (market orientation indicators) are less frequently applied now than they were 10 years ago by Swedish and Norwegian authorities. In contrast, Danish authorities show a somewhat greater interest in those kinds of management tools than they did before.

What about the two other strategies, the communitarian and the neo-republican? Here we touch upon the most significant patterns of change since 1997. As can be seen from Table 6.2, the community involvement indices and

---

of Regional Development Policies – Needs and Demands in the Nordic Countries" co-ordinated by NORDREGIO.

5   Here we have to bear in mind the structural reform in Denmark that completely changed both the regional structure and the functional responsibilities of the new regions. From being a service provider, they have become more of a regional developer and hospital controller.

Table 6.2   Nordic cities and regions: types of development initiatives by country, 1997/98–2007/08. Mean scores

		User orientation		Market orientation		Community involvement		Transparency/ Information	
		1997	2007	1997	2007	1997	2007	1997	2007
Finland	Mean	60		90		65		51	
	N	19		19		19		19	
Sweden	Mean	58	63	75	73	36	42	56	55
	N	45	26	45	26	45	26	45	26
Norway	Mean	41	49	61	57	24	41	28	47
	N	37	35	37	34	37	35	37	36
Denmark	Mean	76	63	61	68	41	51	45	58
	N	28	17	28	15	28	14	28	16
Total	Mean	57	57	70	65	38	43	45	52
	N	129	78	129	75	129	75	129	78

Note: Scale 0–100

transparency/information indices show interesting changes. This is especially true of the latter indices. This type of reform has gained interest in Norway and Denmark in particular. Swedish municipalities and regions have not changed with regard to transparency indicators. The community involvement strategies are being pursued more vigorously than before in all three countries.

As we have indicated, there are contrasts between local authorities when analysed according to country. Swedish and Danish authorities still definitely represent the most classical NPM-oriented reform approaches of the countries (highest score on user and market orientation). The Norwegian authorities and the Danish ones represent an interesting switch in the direction of community involvement strategies. The Danes in particular represent a change of focus in user orientation. For years this has been a hallmark of the Danish authorities. The explanation for this change of focus could be the introduction of the new regional authorities.

To check this, we will take a closer look at the scores for the cities only. As can be seen from Table 6.3, the drop in user orientation is clearly related to the new regional authorities. The data show that user orientation remains high on the agenda of the Danish cities. At the same time, Danish cities have become much more market oriented than they were 10 years ago. However, the same development has also taken place in transparency and citizen involvement.

With the exception of user orientation, the national patterns for cities are more or less similar to those of cities and regions together (cf. Table 6.2). The same strong and weak points emerge in the respective national groupings. Although the patterns are more or less similar, the scores for the indices are much higher for the cities than for the regions.

Table 6.3   Nordic cities only: types of development initiatives by country, 1997/98–2007/08. Mean scores

		User orientation		Market orientation		Community involvement		Transparency/ Information	
		1997	– 2007	1997	– 2007	1997	– 2007	1997	– 2007
Finland	Mean	60		90		65		51	
	N	19		19		19		19	
Sweden	Mean	55	71	81	73	40	49	62	66
	N	22	14	22	14	22	14	22	14
Norway	Mean	40	65	66	69	32	52	36	55
	N	22	17	19	16	19	17	19	18
Denmark	Mean	76	73	48	69	45	55	44	60
	N	14	12	14	11	14	11	14	11
Total	Mean	56	69	73	70	45	51	49	60
	N	74	43	74	41	74	42	74	43

Note: Scale 0–100

We will comment in more detail on some development patterns in the cities (cf. Table 6.3). Despite the stable situation in user orientation in Danish cities, among both Swedish and Norwegian cities we can register a strong interest in user-oriented reform tools. While the Danish cities demonstrate a stable and permanently high interest in user orientation, we also observe a conspicuous reorientation among them in market-like mechanisms. Both Swedish and Norwegian municipalities are also signalling an interest in market mechanisms, but far from on the scale of change found in Denmark. The Swedish municipalities show a decreasing tendency in the use of market-oriented mechanisms compared to the figures from 1997/98 (but all in all, still a high score in 2007/08). It is worth noticing an increasing interest in user orientation among the Norwegian cities. The same is true of the Swedish cities.

Cities in all three countries have showed greater interest in community involvement as a reform strategy during the 10-year period. A positive change rate between 10 per cent and 20 per cent – indicates that this reform strategy really has gained momentum in Norwegian and Danish municipalities. Here we could add that the Swedish cities have also introduced more community-oriented measures than before. Based on the divergence that has been underlined in the literature between an individualized user orientation and more collectivistically oriented communitarian thinking, it is surprising to note that the increasing communitarian inclination does not seem to have reduced the interest in user and market orientation. On the contrary, it seems that both user and market orientations stand out as still highly regarded reform strategies in Nordic cities.

There are interesting contrasts as well as parallels regarding national patterns. Back in 1997/98, Finnish cities definitely represented the most clearly NPM-inspired reformers while the Norwegian municipalities were the most moderate. At that time, Sweden was close behind Finland in market orientation while Denmark was ahead in user orientation. What we can see in 2007/08 is that both Swedish and Danish cities have stabilized their interest in market orientation and user orientation respectively, while signalling a substantial increase in their preference for user orientation (the Swedes) and market orientation (the Danes) respectively.

We may conclude that the cities in Denmark and Sweden are the most consistent NPM-oriented reformers. Norwegian municipalities also demonstrate the same trend as Danish and Swedish cities, but not with the same consistency. In the terminology of Rogers (1995), the Norwegians could be described as late innovators or laggards especially in user orientation, but also partly in market-oriented reform initiatives.

Governance Strategies – Specialized, Conflicting or Mutually Supportive?

The development patterns documented above suggest that the Nordic cities and regions pursue policies that are often regarded in the academic literature as contradictory or mutually inconsistent, e.g. those of liberal market orientation and neo-republican political accountability and citizen involvement. Consequently, cities and regions may experience increasing organizational tensions and some of the policies may soon be abandoned. However, it could also be the case that cities and regions experience these measures as mutually reinforcing and beneficial to their overall public mandate. It could also be that there are different sets of cities and regions that account for the different development trends. Is there a distinct group of market-oriented units, a second one that adheres to neo-republican strategies and a third one that pursues communitarian ideals? If cities and regions pursue specialized development strategies rather than composite ones, there should be little correlation between the various items. If strategies inter-correlate, the reinforcement hypothesis gains ground.

In Table 6.4, a correlation analysis is presented based on indices for the four types of development initiatives. Correlations are in general high, thus it is not easy to identify specialized development strategies. There is one interesting exception, however: namely, the correlation between market orientation and community involvement ($r=.205$). The correlation is positive but not significant; this could indicate that those that pursue a traditional market-oriented strategy are not necessarily the same authorities that pursue a community involvement strategy. This again could indicate that the communitarian orientation is a specialized development strategy, but the findings are not particularly strong. Furthermore, when examining the second type of NPM-measures – user orientation – a similar trend is not evident. On the contrary, the correlation between user orientation and community involvement is fairly high. A strong correlation is also evident between user orientation and market orientation; this is not surprising, however, since these strategies are conceptually close.

Table 6.4   Correlation matrix for the indices of user orientation, market orientation, community involvement, transparency/ information

	User Orientation	Market Orientation	Community Involvement
Market Orientation	.425**	–	–
Community Involvement	.350**	.205	–
Transparency/ Information	.481**	.455**	.389**

Note: ** Correlation is significant at the 0.01 level (2-tailed).

The strongest correlation is not between classical NPM-initiatives (market and user orientation), but between NPM-initiatives and transparency (.481** and 455**). The municipalities do not pursue single-track reform strategies. Instead, we observe strategic choices that are multi-facetted and more in line with what could be described as composite development strategies. Choices of development paths are observed through which different tools and ideologies reinforce one another in the quest for better governance capacities. These findings are in accordance with findings previously presented by both Gregersen (1999) and Øgård (2003). Øgård (2003) has shown that a development orientation with an emphasis on openness (providing information and insight into documents and political processes) correlates with both participatory strategies (participation in the political processes) and also with user-orientation (freedom of choice) and market orientation (competition and privatization). Based on Gregersen's (1999) major study of innovation in municipal social administration in Denmark and his own data, Øgård (2003) concluded that when a municipality was innovative in one area, the possibility was high that it also was innovative in other areas. In the municipal and regional context, innovative initiatives are mutually supportive, even when of seemingly different types or in different operational fields.

Does National Context Matter?

Although it is not the primary purpose of this chapter to search for explanations of patterns of variation,[6] it is, of course, relevant to point out the contrast between the

---

6   An explanatory study based on the data from 1997/98 has been carried out by Øgård (2002).

countries and to reflect on the development patterns seen over the 10-year period. Looking back at the mid-1990s, the national patterns could be explained by Finland and partly Sweden running into a period of economic stagnation and cutbacks in the public sector. Norway enjoyed a continuous boom and an expanding public sector (much thanks to the oil economy). Consequently, the pressure to seek new methods of governance and service provision was much stronger in the Finnish case. Sweden was in a mid-position in this respect, with a stagnating economy but not quite as badly off as Finland. The economic environment back in 1997/98 also makes it understandable that Finland more than the other countries should seek to enhance the efficiency of the public sector through market-oriented strategies, applying the pressure of competition to municipal providers. This was then a most un-Nordic way of dealing with efficiency problems, and it may have taken a crisis of the Finnish proportions to gain acceptance for such emergency measures.

The patterns are a great deal more complex and more challenging to explain today than back in 1997/98. The Nordic countries have gone through a decade of economic growth. The data illustrate a continuous interest in classical NPM reform strategies (market and user orientation), but we can also see an increasing interest in community involvement strategies (a communitarian orientation). This takes place in all four countries, but is especially pronounced in cities in Norway which also show more interest in user-oriented reform tools. Of course, the growth in communitarian thinking among the Nordic cities can be explained as a reaction to the market-oriented reform politics that dominated the 1990s. But user orientation is with us still and has been gaining ground. At the same time, most of the communitarian-oriented cities are still into benchmarking and competitive tendering.

If Norwegian reform patterns could be described as a peculiar combination of user orientation and communitarian thinking, the Danish case shows a reform pattern that combines market orientation and transparency/information (neo-republican) strategies. What is most striking in the Danish case is a pronounced and growing interest in market orientation. Of all countries, the Danes show the largest increase in market-oriented tools in combination with an increase in transparency and information measures. The structural reforms Denmark has recently experienced (cf. Chapter 2) may play a role in explaining this development pattern. The central aim of this reform was to create larger municipalities able to both economize and develop service quality. As has been reported so far through evaluation reports, most of the focus of the newly created municipalities has been on service provision (Blom-Hansen 2005, Blom-Hansen et al. 2006, Brøndum 2008). Less attention has been paid to issues related to participation and democracy more generally. At the same time, there has been much pressure from central government on cities and regions to realize the expected efficiency potential related to the amalgamation reforms. Perhaps this has resulted in an intensified interest in market-oriented reform strategies among the cities. They have to show results, and the easiest and most well-known route is by using a market oriented strategy. But what about the parallel high interest in transparency/information? This could also be related to the structural reform. Newly created and much larger units of local government entail a need for better information to the public, which may be what the Danish transparency measures are about.

What about the interest in neo-republican strategies in the Norwegian municipalities in the period covered? Norway has not experienced structural reform. One possible explanation could be related to a series of much-publicized cases of corruption in local government (Gedde-Dahl et al. 2008) and the growth of quasi-governmental service/development companies in and between the municipalities. The Swedish municipalities were early innovators in these new governance structures and market orientations; therefore, back in 1997/98, they had already developed a transparency/information policy now seen developing in Denmark and especially in Norway.

Conclusion

First of all, our data show that the reform patterns among Nordic local and regional authorities are much more complex than a mere series of NPM-inspired initiatives. It is also worth highlighting that complexity seems to have increased during the 10-year period covered by our data. This is especially true of the rise in communitarian and neo-republican orientations in the Nordic cities regarding reform strategies. The particularly interesting finding is that the heightened interest in communitarian and neo-republican measures does not seems to weaken the NPM-oriented reform patterns that we witnessed at the beginning of the period. Instead, we see a parallel development where the learning and adaptive capacity of cities and regions is developing by adding new dimensions to the already existing patterns. The result is a more complex governance structure that may enable cities and regions to deal more effectively with a more complex and dynamic environment. The transformation of governance we have identified can also be interpreted as adaptations to expectations among "the new citizens" of post-materialist or discursive leanings.

Chapter 7

Informatization of Political Roles and Communication Patterns: Regional Advantages through Information and Communication Technologies?

Are Vegard Haug

The Role of Information and Communication Technologies (ICTs) in the Emergence of the Networking Region: An Introduction

Globalization processes are continuously pressuring cities and regions to connect, learn, reject or adapt. This chapter examines the role of information and communication technology (ICTs) in this respect. One of the most important features of network technology, especially the Internet, is the potential to connect, thereby enabling individuals, groups and organizations to overcome numerous organizational, functional and territorial boundaries and barriers (Bekkers and Homburg 2005). The World Wide Web is claimed to play a key role, even reinforcing globalization (Castells 1996/2000, 2004). To what extent and in what way do ICTs bring advantages to city and regional politicians in the performance of their functions as councillors? Do such advantages also bring a competitive edge to regions as development agents and an enhancement of their qualities as democratic institutions?

Three aims have guided the analysis presented in this chapter. The *first aim* is simply to describe the use of and satisfaction with ICT among Nordic regional and city politicians: to what extent do regional and city councillors make use of modern ICTs and how sophisticated is their digital competence? The *second aim* takes the study one step further by analysing ICT in relation to classical aspects of the politician's roles. Being an elected politician encompasses several political roles: ombudsman, representative, controller and decision-maker (Offerdal 1992). Is each role equally affected by ICTs, or do local politicians utilize technology more selectively – even strategically? The *third aim* addresses directly a much vaunted positive relation between ICTs and conventional patterns of communication, i.e. local and national networks and wider Nordic and international contacts. What is – if any – the added value of digital technology for the emergent Nordic "networking" region?

Theoretically, the study is inspired by an ecological analogy. In their volume on *The Information Ecology of E-government*, Bekkers and Homburg (2005) elaborate on the theory of Information Ecology, originally developed by Davenport (1997). It is a comprehensive approach intended to fully capture the effects of ICTs on public administration and regional politics. The overall thesis guiding their approach is that local information and decision-making processes are increasingly intertwined with cross-national and even global information processing and thinking. As Bekkers and Homburg (2005) conclude, however, the next step should be to develop a comparative study of a set of similar organizations. This study picks up the "baton", as we can now carry out empirical analyses of the relation between ICT and patterns of contacts between institutions at local, regional, national, Nordic and European levels of governance.[1]

The *empirical data* are based on a survey of local politicians in the main cities and regions in the Nordic countries, i.e. executive committee members in Finland, Sweden and Norway. Each politician responding to the survey was asked a number of questions regarding their use of and experiences with a variety of ICTs. The number of responses is approximately 600 (185 in Finland, 279 in Sweden and 137 in Norway). The data collection was conducted between 2007 and 2009 (cf. Chapter 1 for further details of the survey).

Viewing Nordic E-Government Initiatives as an Information Ecosystem

The notion of *Information Ecology* (Davenport 1997, Bekkers and Homburg 2005) emphasizes both information diversity and information constraints. The information ecology perspective regards the informational space as an ecosystem: "An information ecology can be described as the evolving interactions and relations between a diversity of actors, their practice, values and technology within a specific and local (thus unique) environment. It is important to stress that social and technological aspects of an environment co-evolve" (Bekkers and Homburg 2005:10).

---

1   Although a small number of studies have previously compared Nordic public ICT innovations, they have primarily attended to the supply side (e.g. Baldersheim and Øgård 2008). Typically, ICT improvements are measured through development of web portals or access to broadband and computers in households (OECD 2006). Few – if any – studies have reported political experiences with ICTs on the demand side. Nor has empirical research contributed to answering key questions concerning cross-institutional ICT effects. These are somewhat surprising observations, given the vast attention "digital democracy" and "network society" have been given in recent e-government/e-democracy/e-service literature (Becker 1981, Tsagarousianou et al. 1998, Korac-Kacabadse and Korac-Kacabadse 1999, Hacker and van Dijk 2000, Hoff et al. 2000, Baldersheim et al. 2008, Haug 2007, 2009).

Viewing Nordic e-government initiatives as an "information ecosystem" thus emphasizes the relationship between the distribution of information and how political institutions both influence and are influenced by their *environments*. Local information "ecosystems" are thus set in a context of larger systems, even that of global information ecosystems (Davenport 1997). The most important global information ecosystem is the Internet, in particular e-mail and various networks on the World Wide Web.

Networks and ICTs facilitate acquiring knowledge, not only about innovations in distant places, but also how these may be implemented. James March (2008), for instance, applying a local learning perspective on networks, reminds us that institutions learn from what is known elsewhere: "Knowledge, information, practices, and beliefs that are known in one place are transferred to another place. Indeed, most of what we ordinarily describe as 'learning,' for example, through education, consists in such diffusion" (ibid: 280). The role of ICTs in generating knowledge, openness and contact patterns is also highlighted in a number of *diffusion and innovation studies* (Rogers 2003, Poole and Van de Ven 2004, Fagerberg et al. 2005). ICTs are, furthermore, considered important in the recently suggested paradigm shift *from government to governance* which positions government organizations (including politicians) in a complex network society (Castells 1996/2000, Salamon 2002).

To What Extent and in What Way Do Nordic Regional Politicians Use ICTs?

Looking at the empirical findings from the survey of Nordic politicians, Table 7.1 presents the use of ICTs by city and regional politicians in Finland, Sweden and Norway. Each politician was presented with several alternatives as to how he/she might use a computer to carry out different tasks during a typical month. Maximum score is five and the number of politicians answering the survey is just above 600. The survey captures what we label *digital competence* – i.e. ICT know-how and use. Note that the table is ranked according to the most frequent use of ICT.

One key observation is striking: Nordic politicians are eager consumers of ICTs. E-mail is, of course, a popular tool, followed by word processing and text editing. This is closely followed by reading news online. All three activities are more or less daily activities by the Nordic politicians. Next, carried out monthly or weekly, are tasks such as online banking services, scheduling meetings or surfing with no particular aim. The least popular tasks, done less than once a month or never, are involvement in organized online training (e-learning), as well as participating in online debates. The last point is perhaps surprising given the "deliberative" potential of ICTs. The findings are, however, supported by several studies on e-participation and deliberation (Haug 2007, 2008): ICTs are primarily used to collect political information rather than for interactivity and participation.

Although similarities are evident, more detailed factor analysis identifies two distinct groups (cf. Baldersheim and Øgård 2008): On the one hand, a group of

**Table 7.1   General use of ICTs: Nordic city and regional politicians
(average scores – typical month)***

	Finland	Sweden	Norway	*Total*
Electronic mail (e-mail)	4,81	4,90	4,84	*4,86*
Writing or text editing	4,61	4,57	4,37	*4,54*
Reading about news and events	4,18	4,52	4,43	4,39
Online banking services	3,69	3,14	3,35	*3,36*
Scheduling and calendar	2,85	3,19	3,26	*3,10*
Surfing (without a particular aim)	3,03	3,07	2,90	*3,02*
Accounting, spreadsheet or statistical analyses	2,89	2,62	2,47	2,67
Graphics, design, pictures or presentations	2,83	2,53	2,31	*2,57*
Participated in online debates	2,04	2,28	1,85	*2,11*
Organized tuitions/ training via Internet	1,63	1,42	1,41	*1,48*
Average score (scale: 1 = never, 5 = daily) (N)	*3,26* *(185)*	*3,22* *(279)*	*3,12* *(137)*	*3,21* *(601)*

* *Note*: the number of responses (N) varies slightly from question to question

local politicians who primarily use basic ICTs such as e-mail, word processing and reading news online. On the other hand, more advanced ICT users that also participate in online debates, e-learning activities and use analytical tools such as spreadsheets.

To summarize Table 7.1: Nordic local politicians are eager consumers of modern ICTs, even more than the population average (Baldersheim and Øgård 2008). Elementary ICT tools are those most frequently used. One group also uses more sophisticated ICTs (an ICT political elite?). Few variations are evident when comparing ICT utilization between local politicians across the Nordic states. This is not unexpected, due to a shared culture and the well-documented general Nordic ICT-maturity and a generally *high level of digital competence in Nordic societies*. A further question naturally emerges: given the frequent use of ICTs among city and regional politicians in the Nordic countries, can this also be traced in their various roles as local politicians? Does digital competence lead to greater capacities in the performance of the various duties of elected politicians and thus to their further *empowerment*?

New Technology in Old Political Roles: Empowered Politicians?

To answer the second question concerning the possible political effects of ICTs, the Nordic politicians were shown a list of statements about the way in which they considered ICTs to be useful in their work. Each statement measures different aspects of ICTs. The variables were later grouped according to four traditional political roles (indices): Ombudsman, Representative, Decision-Maker and Controller (cf. Offerdal 1992, Mouritzen and Svara 2002, Baldersheim and Øgård 2008). Below, each index is presented and discussed (Tables 7.2 to 7.5).

Two different information-seeking processes can be anticipated in this respect: localism and cosmopolitanism. Localism basically suggests that politicians choose to utilize ICTs to strengthen pre-established information-seeking processes, i.e. within local power bases as an ombudsman, a local party representative and for tasks related to controlling the local municipal administrative apparatus. These functions are related to features of "localism" as outlined by Merton (1968), (Merton primarily analysed reading patterns in newspapers). However, ICT also makes it easier for politicians to cross organizational, functional and territorial boundaries, i.e. information-seeking processes beyond the traditional local power bases; cf. the information ecological thesis presented above. Information seeking beyond the local community is the essence of the behaviour of "cosmopolitans" depicted by Merton (ibid.). Consequently, the impact of ICTs is generally hypothesized to be that of producing more cosmopolitans among urban and regional politicians.

Task 1: ICT and the Role of Ombudsman

The role as *ombudsman* primarily concerns general contact with and receiving information about citizens, non-governmental organizations, local businesses and industry. It includes taking care of individuals and group interests, e.g. interests concerning civil rights vis-à-vis the government. Communication might take place in different arenas, however, such as personal meetings, conferences, contributions in local newspapers, by telephone, local television and so forth. ICT is claimed to empower and support the role as ombudsman in several respects (Øgård 2008). In this study, the political role as ombudsman is operationally defined through four *assertions* to which the political representatives from Finland, Sweden and Norway have responded. As above, maximum score is five (wholly agree).

Looking at Table 7.2, the most important finding is that ICTs increase "direct" communication between citizens and politicians. Based on the index mean score, the role as ombudsman seems not significantly empowered by ICTs. The score close to three indicates a neutral effect. Direct requests from the e-citizens have, however, made it easier to receive complaints, suggestions and generally take care of individuals and group interests. The Internet has also supplemented traditional media as a source of information. Few politicians follow online debates on municipal homepages, or make use of mobile technology and text messages.

Table 7.2   ICT and the role of the *ombudsman*: Nordic city and regional politicians (2008–09). Mean scores. N=601

	Finland	Sweden	Norway	*Total*
ICTs generate more direct requests from citizens	3,45	3,90	3,75	*3,73*
I can equally well follow what is taking place in my community by Internet as by newspapers and radio/TV	3,23	3,53	2,56	*3,22*
I closely follow debates on my municipality's website	2,88	3,36	2,85	*3,10*
I receive equally many requests via text messages as via e-mail	2,21	1,38	1,88	*1,75*
Total mean score (max 5)	*2,94*	*3,04*	*2,76*	*2,95*

Note: Scale: 1=totally disagree, 5=totally agree

Analysing the table from a comparative perspective, similarities rather than differences are evident. Two exceptions are worth mentioning. The first exception concerns a weak, yet interesting tendency for Swedish politicians to more eagerly participate in online political communication compared to the Finns and the Norwegians. Second, Finnish politicians are more exposed to text messages than their colleagues in Norway and Sweden (perhaps a "Nokia effect"?). However, the key finding is that text messages – mobile technology – have not yet entered the political arena to the same extent as e-mail. The role as ombudsman, basically addressing general public contact, is not deeply affected by ICTs.

Task 2: ICT and the Role of Controller

Local politicians also have an important role as controllers, i.e. monitoring and supervising public administration and services. This task includes following up political decisions, public services, financial performance and results, as well as ensuring public effectiveness and efficiency. Lack of control causes challenges in terms of political legitimacy governance capacity and accountability. ICTs might enhance this role in various ways. Tools such as "total quality management" and balanced scorecards are widely used in this respect. Tangible aspects such as control over projects and investments are also important. Also, ICTs are supposed to compensate for organizational distance in decentralized governance structures: ICTs enhance the capacity of politicians to monitor the activities of decentralized agencies. ICTs bring transparency by helping to process more information and combine the information in new ways. This again opens up for new and more sophisticated way of control (Bekkers and Homburg 2005). Politicians' use of ICTs in the role as controller is measured as follows:

Table 7.3   ICT and the role of *controller*: Nordic city and regional politicians (2008–09). Mean scores. N=601

	Finland	Sweden	Norway	*Total*
Internet has provided me with a better overview of the municipal activities	3,68	4,21	4,01	*4,00*
Elected representatives' access to ICT has improved political control of the municipality	3,91	3,62	3,43	*3,66*
The elected representatives have sufficient control over the municipality's ICT efforts	2,66	3,09	2,96	*2,92*
Total mean score (max 5)	*3,41*	*3,64*	*3,47*	*3,53*

Table 7.3 illustrates that ICTs support the role as controller. This is particularly evident when it comes to providing a better overview of the various municipal activities. There are some variations between the three Nordic states, but generally ICTs are claimed to enhance the control capacity of politicians. This basically means that local politicians feel that they can do a better job with new technology, e.g. by ensuring that political decisions are implemented properly by the municipal apparatus. They do not, however, feel that they are in full control of ICT efforts and investments. ICT development seems to be a policy area in which politicians play a limited role.

Task 3: ICT and the Role of Representative

As representatives, politicians espouse the causes of political parties and political issues. ICTs can support the tasks of the party representative in several ways, e.g. through internal communication facilities such as e-mail lists, the intranet or text messages. ICTs might also better facilitate external communication, e.g. through party web presentations, information share points, electronic campaigning or various "social technologies" (Twitter, Facebook, etc). In addition, ICTs can be used as a tool to promote political individuals and programmes through online "streaming" of political meetings. Being a political representative, of course, also entails frequent collaboration with other representatives. A further aspect of the role of the representative is that of *issue* representation. Some causes are closer to the hearts of the politicians than others. With the emergence of e-government

Table 7.4   ICT and the role of *representative*: Nordic city and regional politicians (2008–09). Mean scores. N=601

	Finland	Sweden	Norway	*Total*
ICT has made it easier to consult party group members/party members ahead of political meetings	4,44	4,69	4,48	*4,56*
E-mail has resulted in an increase in requests from other municipal councillors in my own municipality	3,24	4,06	3,62	*3,71*
E-government is one of my areas of interest as a councillor	3,32	2,83	2,90	*3,00*
Total mean score (max 5)	*3,67*	*3,86*	*3,67*	*3,76*

as an important strategy for the modernization of government operations, it could be expected that the issue of e-government would be high on the list of causes prioritized by local representatives. Has e-government entered the set of issues espoused by local politicians?

In Table 7.4, a positive finding is evident. The overall mean score is 3.76. ICT is considered by the Nordic politicians to empower the role of representative. ICTs are particularly useful when consulting party colleagues before political meetings (average scores 4.56). This is an interesting finding, illustrating how ICT might reduce time- and space-related hurdles to consulting political colleagues. As mentioned above, Nordic city and regional politicians are by and large part-time politicians. Most of them have regular jobs and must often travel far to the city or meetings at County Hall. Being able to quickly consult party colleagues is an essential improvement. It is also interesting that e-mail has resulted in an increase in requests from other councillors within the municipality. ICTs are considered constructive ways of "consulting others" or of "being consulted". Given the positive effects experienced by local politicians, it seems rather paradoxical, however, that relatively few politicians take an interest in ICT strategy. Swedish and Norwegian city and regional politicians are particularly indifferent to ICT developments as an "area of interest". The Finns are slightly more enthusiastic. The fact that politicians do not play a major role in the shaping of e-government is well documented, however. Jæger (2005) states that the lack of politicians' involvement partly explains why e-government has had a limited focus, i.e. mainly on service delivery and less on the democratic potentials of ICTs.

Task 4: ICT and the Role of Decision-maker

What about the role as decision-maker? Has ICT made it easier to gather information from alternative sources? Is it possible to identify an increase in "rationality" due to the use of ICT as envisioned by Herbert Simon? Making decisions is a key assignment in day-to-day political work on city councils, executive committees and political panels. As mentioned above, local politicians are typically part-time workers. As such, they often depend on "cut-and-dried" information provided by the CEO and the larger municipal apparatus. The quality of the large "piles of paper" varies considerably, however. Information might be difficult to comprehend given the time available. Modern ICTs appear promising in this respect. And, as argued above, ICT might reduce "bounded rationality" hurdles related to information processing and analyses (Simon 1973, 1995). By means of modern decision support systems, e.g. electronic consultations or comparative data, benchmarking tools, quality management systems and so forth, local politicians might well find ICTs helpful. Technology might also stimulate political initiatives. The role as decision-maker is operationally defined by four statements to which the politicians have responded.

The empirical findings are interesting: more than any other political role, that of decision-maker is supported by ICTs. The average score for all four statements is 4.22. This score is exceptionally high given a maximum score of five. First, politicians agree that e-mail and ICTs has made it easier for them to collect

Table 7.5   ICT and the role of *decision-maker*: Nordic city and regional politicians (2008–09). Mean scores. N=601

	Finland	Sweden	Norway	*Total*
E-mail and ICTs have made it easier to collect information from other sources than documents supplied by the local administration relating to the cases	4,70	4,76	4,54	*4,69*
Access to e-mail and the Internet have made the work as a politician easier	4,64	4,58	4,57	*4,59*
E-mail and the Internet have made it easier to take political initiatives	4,08	4,37	4,12	*4,22*
I frequently search for information about other municipalities via the Internet (e.g. to compare our municipality with other municipalities)	2,98	3,78	3,04	*3,37*
Total mean score (max 5)	*4,10*	*4,37*	*4,07*	*4,22*

information from other sources than local case documents. This essentially means that local politicians may find it easier to oppose, compare, supplement or otherwise respond to propositions elaborated by the local administration. ICT seems to help politicians counterbalance an administrative information hegemony. Second, access to e-mail and the Internet is claimed to make the work as politician easier. ICT has also made it easier to initiate political proposals. Note that all three views are strongly supported by the respondents consistently across all three states. Fourth, although not as strongly, local politicians consider ICT useful in their search for information about other municipalities via the Internet (e.g. to compare and learn from other municipalities). This statement is particularly supported by Swedish local politicians, possibly indicating a more competitive, yet knowledge-oriented Swedish political decision-making culture.

Table 7.6 summarizes the key findings for all four political roles presented: ombudsman, controller, representative and decision-maker. The table is ranked according to the total mean score on each index. Clearly, the role considered the most empowered by ICTs is that of the decision-maker. This is an important finding, documenting the positive effects of ICTs in the service of democracy. If more, faster, better and alternative information generates more rationality in decision-making (Simon 1973, 1995), then ICTs contribute to this. The roles as representative and controller are also empowered by ICTs. Note that the single most positive impact of ICT in the representative role is an enhancement of the capacity "to consult party members ahead of political meetings" (see Table 7.4). This strengthens the argument above concerning a positive relation between rational decision-making and ICTs. The role as ombudsman is not as clearly affected by ICT, however. This may be surprising given the promises of ICTs in this respect (Tsagarousianou et al. 1998, Hacker and van Dijk 2000, Haug 2008, 2009, Øgård 2008).

ICTs seem first and foremost to strengthen cosmopolitan-oriented behaviour among politicians, i.e. the externally oriented search processes. In general, ICTs have made it easier to collect information from sources other than the local municipal setting. Access to e-mail and the Internet have made the work as politician easier. And when directly asked whether e-mail and the Internet have made it easier to take political initiatives, Nordic politicians' are unanimous in their support. The conclusion is thus that modern ICTs have made an important impact. The role of local politicians is empowered in several key dimensions. Nordic regional and city politicians are ardent users of modern information and communication technologies (cf. Table 7.1). And more importantly, they do find the new tools useful! Optimism and positive experiences – rather than pessimism and negative experiences – dominate the evaluations of ICT usage of Nordic city and regional politicians. The Finns take the lead in using ICTs in day-to-day operations, yet the Swedes appreciate the effects slightly more than do their Nordic colleagues. But the differences are minor. Similarity – rather than variance – is a key observation when studying ICT use among Nordic local and regional politicians. However, when relating ICT experience to different political categories (based on classical political

Table 7.6   **ICT in the service of democracy – impacts on role components; summary: Nordic city and regional politicians. Mean scores**

	Finland	Sweden	Norway	*Sum*
Decision-maker	4,10	4,37	4,07	*4,18*
Representative	3,67	3,86	3,67	*3,73*
Controller	3,41	3,64	3,47	*3,50*
Ombudsman	2,94	3,04	2,76	*2,91*
Total	*3,53*	*3,73*	*3,49*	*3,58*

roles), each role is not equally stimulated. Across all three states, the strongest effects of ICT seem to be on the decision-making role. Although a "localist" view of information gathering and processing is still evident, more externally oriented "cosmopolitan" search processes are rapidly emerging. Given the characteristics of e-mail and the Internet, this is not surprising and in accordance with the information ecology perspective presented above (Bekkers and Homburg 2005).

These are interesting findings, but are there downsides? An increase in communication is surely politically demanding as well as time-consuming. The most popular ICT tool is e-mail. Thus, we asked the politicians to consider whether widespread Internet access in the population had resulted in *too many e-mails*? Surprisingly, the Nordic city and regional politicians generally denied this. Although a few did find it challenging, in general, the majority did not. The average score in Finland was 2.08, in Sweden 2.75 and in Norway 2.82 on a scale from one to five. The main conclusion is thus that ICTs have made the work of city and regional politicians considerably easier. More importantly, perhaps, the potential for rationality has also improved as alternative developments strategies are more effortlessly accessed, ultimately making local politicians less dependent upon the local context and the municipal administrative apparatus.

The Relation between ICT Use and Wider Contact Patterns: Compensation, Reinforcement or Transformation?

The third question is whether widespread and positive experiences with ICTs among Nordic politicians have further institutional repercussions. Does ICT proficiency lead to more intense or far-flung patterns of networking? Below, three propositions are developed and tested in this respect: reinforcement, compensation and transformation. Note that all hypotheses are related to Granovetter's (1973) argument about "the strength of weak ties". If communication is not established between groups, enthusiasm for an idea or invention in one organization (or one "clique" in Granovetter's terms) would not spread to others, but would have to develop independently in each one (1973: 481ff.). To test the propositions, data on ICT use and experiences are related to data on the politicians' contact patterns.

Proposition 1: The Compensation Hypothesis

First, several influential theoretical contributions have argued that ICTs erode barriers related to "time and space". This is a key argument developed by Manuel Castells' work (and that of others) on "glocalism" and the emergent "network society" (1996/2000). The core of the network society approach is "informationalism": "a technological paradigm based on the augmentation of the human capacity of information processing and communication made possible by the revolutions in microelectronics, software, and genetic engineering" (Castells 2004: 9). Similar arguments, although not as radical, are evident in the work of Fountain in *Building the Virtual State* (2001) and *Governing by Networks* (Goldsmith and Eggers 2004). Rogers (2003: 215) likewise asked: "Can Internet messages serve a role in the innovation-decision process similar to that performed by interpersonal channels?" The Internet is a powerful communication channel – a means by which innovation messages get quickly from a source to a receiver by e-mail as well as the World Wide Web. Clearly, local politicians and others familiar with ICTs, and eager users of the World Wide Web, can benefit by "innovation surfing" as well as wider contacts. In fact, the Internet influences three important drivers of innovation in the Diffusion of Innovation theory: communication, networks and time. Consequently, the Internet is a means for municipalities to find ideas and inspiration, eventually obliterating physical barriers. This has potential implications beyond ICTs in a technical sense. The core premise is that ICTs will compensate for time- and space-related hurdles, which lead to the compensation hypothesis: the more regional policy-makers make use of modern ICTs, the more their patterns of communication will be characterized by dense and far-flung networks.

Proposition 2: The Reinforcement Hypothesis

Second, "social capital" might well determine patterns of contact. Social capital concerns "features of social organization, such as trust norms, and networks, that can improve the efficiency of society by facilitating coordinated actions" (Putnam 1993: 167). Applied to e-government (Fountain 2001: 71 ff.); "Social capital, like other forms of capital, accumulates when used productively" (ibid: 72). Trust can be defined as "the willingness to accept vulnerability based on positive expectations about another's intentions or behaviours" (McEvily et al. 2003: 92). But trust is not something that suddenly appears; it is created through time, through repeated cooperation and contacts and experiences (Axelrod 1984, Lorenz 1991, Fountain 2001, Provan and Kenis 2007). This might hamper ICT effects on long-distance communication patterns. The argument has empirical support: in the early URBIS project "Computers and Politics" by Danziger, Dutton, Kling and Kraemer (1982), the networking effects of ICTs on American local governments were examined. ICTs did not eliminate existing political/territorial constraints. The overall finding was that the use of ICTs primarily stimulated already well established patterns of communication. Based on substantial empirical research, early research essentially stated that ICT tended to extend and reinforce the prevailing biases of governmental structures and processes. However, this was the finding almost 30 years ago. It is nevertheless still an interesting premise, i.e. that use of ICTs will primarily reinforce and consolidate already existing patterns of communication. This is labelled a reinforcement hypothesis: the communication patterns of regional and urban policy-makers are expected to be mostly of a regional and local nature; the impact of ICTs will be to reinforce such local and regional patterns.

Proposition 3: The Transformation and Transparency Hypothesis

Overall, ICTs can help make the public sector more transparent and accessible to the general public – if there is a political will to make use of the available digital resources for this purpose. And many efforts are in fact made in this regard by public authorities. Providing politicians with digital equipment and training them in its use may be one step in this direction. Does an enhancement of the digital capacity of politicians lead to just more communications and contacts with other politicians and public bodies, or does it also lead to more community contacts, i.e. with business and industry, civic bodies and the media? In short, do digital capacities in politicians lead to an opening up of politics to more community interaction? The third hypothesis suggests that politicians' use of ICT will lead to this. Such a development would also be in keeping with suggestions that local politics is undergoing a transformation from "government" to "governance" (Salamon 2002, Kersbergen and Waarden 2004), with a growing emphasis on public action through public-private partnerships and networks.

To test the three hypotheses (compensation, reinforcement and transformation), a new index has been developed from the Nordic data set labelled "cross-institutional contact". It consists of a total of 16 different variables, each measuring how often Nordic local politicians are "in contact" with a variety of local/regional, private, national and European institutions (cf. Table 7.7). Accordingly, five indices are calculated to test the argument (see Appendix A for details). Next, each index is analysed against the two ICT indices presented in the first part of the chapter: uses of ICTs (digital competence) and impacts of ICT with regard to role components or capacities (digital empowerment). These are the independent variables of the subsequent analysis.[2] Our main interest is identifying possible

2   The two ICT indices are of course related. Pearson Correlation between ICT use (index 1) and ICT experiences (index 2) is as follows: Finland (.431**), Sweden (.435**) and Norway (324**).

correlations between the independent variables and wider collaboration patterns. In addition, four variables are included as control variables. When running regression analyses between the two ICT indices and wider contact patterns, several interesting findings emerged.

The most important finding in Table 7.7 is that there is (with some exceptions) a positive and strong connection between the digital competence and empowerment of politicians and various kinds of cross-institutional contact patterns (local/regional, community/civic, national, Nordic and European). On an aggregate level, it is not surprising that competence and personal resources are related to contact patterns and behaviour. What is surprising however, are the direction, strengths and the consistency of these connections.

The hypothesis that ICTs may expand patterns of contact is thus supported. National contact patterns are those most strongly boosted, but the sturdy and positive connection between Nordic and wider EU contact patterns and digital competence is also in accordance with the compensation hypothesis. Clearly, ICTs help politicians overcome physical distance. However, the internationalization effect seems to flow primarily from *digital competence*. The "empowerment index" yields a more complicated pattern, with no connections as to international

Table 7.7   **Regression analyses: ICT proficiency (use and experiences) and cross-institutional contact patterns. Nordic city and regional politicians (2006–08). Beta coefficients**

Model (std. beta coefficients)	Local/ regional Contact (pol/adm)	National Contact (pol/adm)	National Contact (NGO/ priv)	Nordic Contact	European Contact
(Constant)					
ICT competence of politicians	157***	.213***	.240***	.159***	.143***
ICT empowerment of politicians	.114***	.103**	.152***	.084	-.012
Region or regional city	-.162***	-.132***	.084*	-.069	-.142***
Age	.032	-.018	.032	.033	.016
Gender	.102***	.073	.109***	.090*	.012
Dummy: Finland	.195***	-.037	-.072	-.242***	.115*
Dummy: Sweden	.377***	-.077	.102*	-.076	.209***
Adjusted R Square (N=584)	.185	.082	.155	.075	.056

Note: *** Correlation is significant at the 0.01 level (2-tailed). § Cf, appendix for details

contacts. This is perhaps anti-intuitive and against the compensation hypothesis presented above. With regard to digital empowerment it is the proximity thesis that is supported; the reinforcement hypothesis. However, the connection between digital empowerment and local contact patterns is not as strong as the "national" one, which is somewhat against the reinforcement hypothesis. This is confusing, but we may return to the previous section for a possible answer, i.e. the lack of "localist" impacts found in Tables 7.2 to 7.5. For instance, the political role as "ombudsman" is not significantly stimulated by ICTs.

What about the transformation or governance-generating hypothesis, which posits a growth in relations between public bodies and the private/third sector as a result of the digitalization of local politics? Table 7.7 demonstrates that the more regional policy-makers make use of modern ICTs, the more their communications are characterized by private/third sector contact patterns. This is true of both ICT indices, thus the hypothesis is supported.

Conclusions

Does ICT influence the collaboration patterns of politicians? The answer to the question is clearly – yes! To recap, the research aims presented in the introduction were three-fold: (a) to identify and compare the use of ICT by Nordic regional and city politicians: (b) to investigate whether they consider ICT a useful tool and how they utilized ICT in different political roles, and (c) to test suggested relations between the utilization of ICTs and wider patterns of communication.

The key findings are as follows: information technology is used frequently by Nordic politicians, even more so than by the population at large. Variation is minimal between Finland, Norway and Sweden. Similarity rather than variation are key characteristics. When measuring experiences with ICTs, politicians are in general very satisfied with the new tools. With few exceptions, modern technologies bring positive effects to the Nordic politicians. Looking at political roles, however, variation is evident. First and foremost, ICTs stimulate the role of decision-maker, followed by the role as representative and controller. The role of "ombudsman" is less affected.

With regard to communication patterns, when analysing variation, the overall finding is that digital competence and as well as digital empowerment stimulate already well established patterns of communication. This survey thus confirms earlier empirical research essentially stating that ICT extends and reinforces prevailing biases of governmental structures and processes. However, a positive and rather strong correlation between the use of ICTs and various kinds of cross-institutional contact patterns supports the "compensation hypothesis". Wider national and international patterns are more easily maintained in the Information Society, and this seems to be related to politicians' digital competence. This is in accordance with the information ecology perspective presented by Bekkers and Homburg (2005). As argued by the authors, the evolving interactions and relations between a diversity of actors, their practices, values and technology, need to be interpreted within a specific and local (thus unique) environment. Social and technological aspects of the environment co-evolve. What we now can add to this general view is that past collaborations influence contemporary communication patterns – also in cyberspace.

The term "glocalism" might capture what we are witnessing through the Nordic survey: political communication is externally oriented – even globally as the Internet is frequently used as a means for information search, yet locally oriented when contact patterns are utilized and new ideas put into a competitive local political decision-making process.

Even though additional data are required to confirm these observations, one implication relevant to policy is that cities and regions must be prepared to handle more political initiatives as well as alternative development strategies presented by local politicians to City Hall. More and alternative information available to politicians during the executive process might be demanding, e.g. require *additional analytical system capacity*. But it will also add positive value to local and regional political decision-making processes and development.

Appendix

Table 7.A   Operational definitions of the dependent and independent variables of Table 7.7

Dependent variables (indices)	Coding	Source

Local/regional contact (political/administrative)
  a. Contact: CEOs in other municipalities in the County
  b. Contact: Mayors in other municipalities in the County
  f. Contact: County governor
  g. Contact: Other regional authorities
	Sum variable. Continues	Own survey of regional and urban politicians

National contact (political/administrative)
  h. Contact: Ministry, department,
  i. Contact: Government representatives
  j. Contact: Member of Parliament
	Sum variable. Continues	Own survey of regional and urban politicians

National contact (private/NGOs)
  c. Contact: Private business/industry representatives
  d. Contact: Third sector, volunteers
  e. Contact: Humanitarian/public foundations
  k. Contact: Municipal interest organizations
  l. Contact: Media
	Sum variable. Continues	Own survey of regional and urban politicians

Nordic contact
  m. Contact: representatives from municipalities or regions from other Nordic states
  n. Contact: Nordic institutions, e.g. the Nordic Council, Nordic Council of Ministers)
	Sum variable. Continues	Own survey of regional and urban politicians

European contact
  o. Contact: representatives from EU institutions and agencies
  p. Contact: Regional Committee
	Sum variable. Continues	Own survey of regional and urban politicians

Note: Letters refer to items in the original questionnaire

Table 7.A   (Continued)

Independent variables (and indices)	Coding	Source
ICT use – digital competence (politicians) (See table 7.1 for details)	Sum variable. General use of ICTs: Nordic city and regional politicians (typical month). Each variable is coded 1–5: 1 = Totally disagree 5 = Totally agree	Own survey of regional and urban politicians
ICT role impacts – digital empowerment (politicians) (see Tables 7.2–7.5 for details)	Sum variable. Continues Each variable is coded 1–5: 1 = Totally disagree 5 = Totally agree	Own survey of regional and urban politicians
Age	Continues	Own survey of regional and urban politicians
Gender	1= Women 2= Men	Own survey of regional and urban politicians
Dummy: Finland	Dummy (Finland 1, else 0)	Own survey of regional and urban politicians
Dummy: Sweden	Dummy (Sweden 1, else 0)	Own survey of regional and urban politicians

Chapter 8

"The New Kid on the Block".
Faroese Foreign Affairs –
between Hierarchy and Network

Joan Ólavsdóttir, Jens Christian Svabo Justinussen and
Beinta í Jákupsstovu[1]

Introduction

One intriguing political innovation increasingly evident this century is the appearance of non-sovereign states in the international political arena. For example, several of Canada's provinces (Quebec, Ontario, Alberta and British Columbia) have their own international representations; as demonstrated in the previous chapters of this book Nordic and other European regions today also pursue their own version of a foreign policy through international collaboration and networks. Within the larger context set by the superpowers such as USA, China, India, and Russia, there is an emerging mosaic of smaller states, microstates, provinces, dependent territories and regions all participating in the international arena and pursuing their own interests. These may be offshoots of larger phenomena such as globalization and/or the end of the Cold War but nevertheless create many new constellations in international politics. One such offshoot is the development of Faroese foreign affairs. This chapter outlines some of the strategies and constraints the Faroes face in their endeavours.

The Faroe Islands (*Føroyar*) are a group of 17 inhabited islands, with a total land area of 1,400 square km. They are located in the North Atlantic, 285 km north of the Shetland Islands and 450 km east of Iceland. There are 49,000 inhabitants, most of whom are descendants of the original Norwegian settlers. The national language, Faroese, is closely related to Old Norse. Dominion over the Faroes passed from the Norwegians to the Danes in 1380 and they are now a self-governing unit within the Danish kingdom.

The Faroes elects two representatives to the Danish parliament in Copenhagen, 1,350 km away, and the Danish government has control over Faroese monetary policy, defence and other key areas. The Faroese parliament (*Løgting*) is located in the capital, Tórshavn, and has extensive, though restricted, powers to pass domestic

1   Thanks to Árni Ólafsson for helpful comments on earlier drafts to this paper and to Are Vegard Haug for inspirational help with the data analysis.

laws, impose local taxes, administer local health and educational services and so on. The Faroese government consists of the prime minister's office and seven ministries. In January 2008, the newest ministry was created when the ministry of foreign affairs was made separate from the prime minister's office.

On the municipal level, a process of amalgamation is taking place: in 2009, there were 30 municipalities. Tórshavn is the largest one with nearly 20,000 inhabitants in 2009. 95 per cent of export consists of fish products. Today, however, only 16 per cent of the labour force are fishermen or fish-farm workers. The employment rate is very high, 92 per cent for men and 87 per cent for women; and the unemployment rate, in spite of the global finance crisis, was less than 4 per cent in July 2009. In 2008 GDP was DKK 12,474 mill., or DKK 256,733 per inhabitant.

In 2006, subsidies from the Danish state to the Faroese government amounted to DKK 870 mill. (DKK 615,5 mill. in a block grant, the rest to finance the expenses of institutions still under Danish administration, for example the police, the Church etc.). The grant amounted to 12.4 per cent of public income.

The Faroes and the Danish State

Regional and microstate governments are challenged by the extent to which they possess the formal authority to organize intergovernmental and international networks, as well as their ability and capacity to utilize the opportunities within such networks. Complicating matters, the Faroes are neither a microstate, nor an ordinary region within the Kingdom of Denmark; this creates a state of limbo for the Faroese government in international relations. However, the Danish state has taken a pragmatic approach to the Faroes and their status within the Danish state structure, allowing for the gradual involvement of the Faroes in their own foreign affairs. For many years, the Faroese government has thus developed international networks partly or wholly autonomously of the Danish state, but with its acceptance. This is especially true of policy issues of special Faroese interest, particularly fisheries policies. However, the Faroese government's investment in a separate governmental body for general foreign affairs as well as Faroese missions abroad is still relatively new and developing.

In 1969 a Faroese trade representative was stationed at the Danish Embassy in Rome. In 1973 he was moved to Copenhagen, and in 1979 his office became a Faroese government office. In 2002, a Faroese mission to the EU was established in Brussels. The same year, a Faroese office was opened in London, replacing the trade representation which had existed in Aberdeen since WWII.[2] Most recently, in 2007, a Faroese representation was established in Reykjavik.

---

2   Árni Ólafsson 11.08.09.

The Evolution of Greater Independence in International Affairs

The Faroes used to be a regional part of the Kingdom of Denmark but, throughout WWII, the Faroes were occupied by British forces while Denmark was occupied by Germany. During this period the cleavage between the Faroes and Denmark grew and, in 1946, a Faroese referendum voted by majority to establish a sovereign Faroese state. The subsequent negotiations with the Danish state lead to the Home Rule Act of 1948, granting specific powers to the Faroese Home Rule authorities, the *Løgting* (parliament) and *Landsstýri* (the executive, or the Home Rule government). Legislative and administrative powers in a number of areas could be assumed by the Faroese Home Rule authorities, provided they undertook to finance them. The remaining areas were Danish or joint Faroese/Danish responsibilities. For example, the financing of the health, social and educational sectors was shared and so the Faroese and Danish governments cooperated in the policymaking processes. In addition, the more direct control functions of the Danish state were significantly reduced. In 1988, a number of burden-sharing arrangements were replaced by a fixed block grant from the Danish government. As the Danish government was no longer involved in the details of the spending of the subsidies, the nature of the Danish/Faroese relationship gradually changed. In 2002, the Faroese government reduced the amount requested in subsidies from Denmark, and since then the amount has been frozen at DKK 615,500,000. Two of the main goals of the coalition of the pro-independence Faroese parties were to be financially independent and to establish *yvirtøkulógin* ("take-over law") and *heimildarlógin* ("authority law") which combined would give the Faroe Islands increased authority, also in foreign affairs.

The Faroese and Danish governments adopted the two laws in 2005, formalizing the developments that had been evolving over the years. *Yvirtøkulógin* gave the Faroese Home Rule government the option of taking charge of legislative and executive power in all areas except those regarding the constitution, citizenship, foreign, security and defence policy as well as money and monetary policy. *Uttanríkispolitiska heimildarlógin* gave the Faroese government the authority to negotiate and conclude international agreements in areas in the charge of the Faroese government, such as fisheries. Faroese home rule has some limitations. The Faroes are still a part of the Danish state. The Home Rule Act in principle does not allow the Faroes to pursue an independent foreign policy. The Faroes and Denmark do not always have identical interests in the international arena and this has mostly been respected by the Danish government.

The Faroes chose not to join the EU while Denmark joined the EEC in 1973. Since the Faroes (and later also Greenland) are exempt from Denmark's EU membership, alternative avenues for contact with the EU must be developed. Likewise, in areas under full EU exclusive competence, where the EU – not its members states – takes part in international organizations, the interests of the Faroes and of Greenland are taken care of by specific membership of "Denmark in respect of the Faroes and Greenland" (DFG).[3] Before 2005, negotiations on agreements regarding relations between the Faroes and a third country were conducted either by representatives of the Danish government assisted by Faroese government representative or vice versa. According to the 2005 laws, the Faroes now have the authority to negotiate with foreign countries and multilateral organizations on areas which have been assumed by the Faroese government. According to the law, these agreements can be overruled by the Danish authorities if they deem it necessary to protect the greater interests of the Danish realm: the Danish government must also be informed about possible negotiations, the process and result of such and the suspension of such. These constraints signalize that the Faroes remain a part of the Danish state; however, there are significant opportunities for the Faroes to conduct an independent policy in the international arena.

With a new political coalition taking office in February 2008, the Faroese Ministry of Foreign Affairs was established on 15 February 2008. By virtue of a Faroese Ministry of Foreign Affairs, the Faroese government can now, better than before, be an active and, to some degree, controlling part in the pursuit of Faroese interests in the international arena. In that sense, the Faroes can be seen as "the new kid on the block" having to learn to look out for itself, find friends, establish contacts and so forth. In short: the Faroes have to find their place in the hierarchy, figure out what the room for manoeuvre is, and perhaps even climb that hierarchy. And constantly network to explore the possibilities that might exist within the current position.

But how do these new governmental bodies for foreign affairs help the Faroes to be an active partner in the international political arena? And how active are the Faroese politicians in this relatively new field in Faroese politics? Furthermore, how satisfied are the politicians with their participation in international affairs so far?

First, we present the theoretical framework for our analysis of Faroese international relations, institutions, hierarchy and network; we then scrutinize the legal framework enabling the Faroes to implement their own foreign policy.

International Relations and Institutions

The theory of realism is a dominant position in the study of international relations. It states that international politics is basically an anarchy: every sovereign state sees itself as the ultimate authority and does not recognize any higher power (cf. e.g. Mingst 2008). Under such conditions, it is rational for a state to compete for power and security. However, globalization has made such a position less relevant because of the growing interdependence between states. International relations are partly an outcome of the power balance between countries, but international relations are also organized by institutions: as a result, states to some extent follow

---

3   Árni Ólafsson 11.08.09.

certain procedures and rules for international interaction. These international institutions give space for units such as the Faroes in the international arena.[4]

Institutions can be both formal and informal. A formal institution is constructed through laws and contracts. An informal institution has been created through tradition, continuous interaction and common procedures. The structure of an institution partly forms and organizes the actor and his/her behaviour; however, the actor also influences the structure (Giddens 1984). One of the purposes of an institution is to group actors with common interests and goals and thus ease relations and cooperation between actors. Therefore, institutions create a stronger front where actors act with a common attitude and a common understanding.

Institutions defined as either formal or informal norms and rules might be too general a concept to be useful as an analytic tool. But one can distinguish between three kinds of institutions: hierarchy, networks and markets. These can be placed on a continuum: hierarchy (the formal one), network (the hybrid one) and market (the free one). As international cooperation is compounded by different institutions, it is not simply a hierarchy, network or market, but a mixture of all three. For example, cooperation between the Faroes and Denmark and between the Faroes and the European Union is organized hierarchically through networks and by the market. However, in this analysis we focus on hierarchy and networks.

Hierarchy Theories

To explain the formation of the Faroese Ministry of Foreign Affairs and its capabilities in the international political arena, we have chosen to draw on theories of hierarchies and networks. Hierarchy is a formal way of organizing relations and cooperation between organizations, individuals, groups or institutions in a ranked or graded order. A hierarchy is a formal cooperation or relation founded on firm processes and concrete laws and contracts. Hierarchical relations are often governed by a contract that binds the parties involved. A hierarchy is a top-down organization: the actors act on orders from their superior. The chain of command in a hierarchy is vertical, from the top, down through the levels of the hierarchy (Scott 1995). However, horizontal contact can also occur between actors within a hierarchy, but only between actors on the same level of the hierarchy; in horizontal contacts there is no chain of command. If an actor within a hierarchy receives information, he will send it further up through the hierarchy; therefore the information does not circulate as widely as it would in a network (Rhodes et al. 2006). A hierarchy is thus more effective than a network in keeping a secret. Fukuyama maintains (1999) that the hierarchical structure is in no need of social capital or trust in order to function. Fukuyama also states that a hierarchy will

---

4   While larger countries might rely on their military and/or economic power to promote their interests, and ignore the institutional rules of the game, microstates and regions can only rely on the established institutional rules of the game and the space those institutions create for them.

often stop bad ideas that may come from the bottom because the idea has to travel through several layers of actors before it reaches the top; it can also be self-destructive because good ideas may not reach the right actor at the right time.

The Faroese government is subordinate to the Danish state and the Faroes are bound by law to do as its superior, the Danish state, instructs. Thus the chain of command within the hierarchy of the Danish state goes from the Danish state to the Faroese government. Consequently, information may not always flow freely within the hierarchy; information from the Faroes may be supressed by superior actors, resulting in some information being lost in the flow between actors. The fact that the Faroes are not the superiors of their own state makes it difficult for them to act independently in the hierachical international arena.

In summary, the hallmark of a hierarchy is as follows: 1) the actors within a hierarchy are ranked and the chain of command is vertical; 2) cooperation in a hierarchy is formal and based on laws and contracts; 3) information flows in a hierarchy go from several actors to a single, superior actor.

Network Theories

A network is in its purest form informal cooperation with no written laws, founded on common interests, traditions and recurring cooperation. Actors within a network are equals and not ranked in relation to each other (Koppenjan and Klijn 2004). Kontopoulus states (1993) that there must be at least three parties to form a network; network practice emphasizes several interactive dyadic networks. Consequently, there must be at least three different actors in a network; a triad. However, in most cases a network consists of several interactive links. Networks do not have a core but are intertwined nets of relations between different actors (Castells 2004).

Networks are formed through recurring relations when actors interact. They are more or less stable patterns of social relations between actors who have a common interest or policy problem. They are formed, maintained and changed through a series of "games" and interactions. But within these networks are several "arena rules" that provide the actors with a tool to analyse what sort of network and arena they are a part of. These rules depict situation, reality and subsidies: the social reality. There are also interactive rules that have a court-like ability, informing the actors what is allowed or not within the network. This rule modifies behaviour within the coherence of arena rules (Koppenjan and Klijn 2004).

A network stretches further than just the one network. This is what Granovetter (1983) calls weak ties; weak and strong ties are one definition of how a network is constructed. In interdependent relationships, a strong tie is a direct relationship in which the actors know each other. Weak ties are more fluid or intangible relationships between actors who do not have a regular relationship. In a strong tie relationship, the actors often have common interests and the information that spreads through these strong ties will often reinforce current interests or beliefs;

on the other hand, a weak tie can bring new information and ideas that may challenge the actor's beliefs, thus potentially making weak ties valuable in the flow of information in research and development.

A network is a link to the rest of the world and the knowledge that exists in the rest of the world. A network is good at gathering and spreading knowledge (Jackson and Wollinsky 1996). It may thus serve to enhance one's ability to compete in a world where research and technical developments are developing faster than ever. Trust and social capital are factors influencing network development by lowering transaction costs. If a transaction is made between two individuals, who have not had any previous encounters, there will be more administration from the transaction and thus the cost will be higher both in time and in capital (Granovetter 1983) than between actors who have a long track record of dealing with each other. Trust is therefore important for cooperations that are closer to the network than hierarchy. Trust strengthens the prognosis because it minimizes the risk in cooperations and transactions (Koppenjan and Klijn 2004).

Because of the small population of the Faroes, many of the inhabitants know each other or know of each other and this minimizes transaction cost. Logically, transaction cost will be lower in a country with relatively few inhabitants than in a country with many inhabitants. Similarly, transaction cost will be lower between neighbouring countries that share some common factor such as religious beliefs, history, traditions and language. Traditionally, the Faroese have mastered the Scandinavian languages to a greater extent than English. This has had a determining effect on which countries the Faroese have historically cooperated with. However, as the younger generation becomes more integrated into the global, English-speaking world, English-based networks may grow.

In summary, the hallmark of a network is as follows: 1) relations between actors within a network form horizontal links between equal partners; 2) cooperation between actors within a network is informal; 3) information flow within a network spreads from one actor to many actors.

Hierarchy or Network?

Hierarchy and a network are two different ways of structuring cooperation and relations between actors. Consequently, in some cases a hierarchy will be more effective while in other cases a network will be more effective. A hierarchy is a top-down structure and has firm processes and contracts that must be followed. Therefore, an actor within a hierarchy knows his place. Within the network, on the other hand, the actors are equals, not ranked; on that note a network can be harder to control or manage than a hierarchy. A hierarchy will thus be able to make quick decisions but a network relies on consensus which can be time-consuming in negotiations. A network is not bound by written laws, as a hierarchy is, but is founded on procedures that have been formed through recurring interactions; as a result, the actors have a more fluid position than do those in a hierarchy.

The informal cooperation within a network will be able to stretch further and will, in many situations, be more flexible than the formal cooperation of a hierarchy. All cooperation and relations are different, but hierarchical cooperation is based on control while network cooperation is founded on information. A hierarchy organizes cooperation through laws and formal procedures. A network is more fluid and does not have the same form of control over the cooperation (Jackson and Wollinsky 1996).

Because of the information flow from many actors to many others, it is easier for a network to get hold of new knowledge and further develop its knowledge. A hierarchy will, on the other hand, have more trouble participating in research and innovation because of the information flows from many actors to one, at the top of the hierarchy. Hierarchies are more homogeneous than networks because they do not reach much further than their own hierarchical structure. A network is better than a hierarchy at distributing information and commodities that are not distributed on the market, i.e. commodities that do not have a concrete capital value. A hierarchy is better than a network at holding on to information when it is important that the information does not spread; for example in the case of a new market commodity (Rhodes et al. 2006).

If we analyse Faroese foreign policy in a network context we may expect the Faroes, due to their small population, to be constrained by the capacity of individuals; the Faroes do not have enough human capacity to exploit all cooperations and relations to their full potential. For that reason, the extent of Faroese networks may be limited. A small country such as the Faroes could potentially compensate to some degree for its limited network capacity by taking advantage of weak ties in the pursuit of developing wider networks. In principle, weak ties would make it possible to stretch the networks further out in the world than they otherwise would do if they were primarily based on strong ties.

There is a critical difference between a hierarchy and a network institution. The framework of the cooperation is of great importance to the relationship and to its ability to work and develop. Hierarchical cooperation is tangible and has concrete laws and processes. Network cooperation is at the same time intangible and informal and is more easily developed as it is not founded solely on written laws. A network cooperation will thus be able to reach further than a hierarchical cooperation. However, foreign-policy cooperation is structured in a hierarchical manner and will affect networks in foreign policy, i.e. networks in foreign policy will be influenced by the hierarchical structure that is foreign policy. This means that it is most likely that foreign policy networks will unfold within an increasing hierarchy.

Faroese Foreign Policy in a Hierarchical Structure

The Faroes are subject to the Danish constitution which is therefore the highest law and all other laws in the Faroes must be compatible with it. The Faroes are structured by law in the hierarchy that is the Danish state.

Nevertheless, *Heimildarlógin* does give the Faroes the authority to expand governmental relations in foreign affairs. As early as 1948, the *Heimastýrislógin* (Article 8) gave the Faroese Home Rule government some guaranties of influence upon the way in which the Danish authorities would take care of the international interests of the Faroes. One of these stipulations gave the Faroese authorities the opportunity to place their own staff at Danish embassies with a view to taking care of Faroese commercial interests. *Heimildarlógin* broadens the scope by authorizing the Faroese authorities to place emissaries at Danish embassies where the Faroes have a particular political interest (*Heimildarlógin Article 3*). Neither of the two laws allows the establishing of separate Faroese embassies or diplomatic missions.[5] If the Faroes choose to establish their own separate representation, it cannot have diplomatic status because the Danish embassy is in fact the diplomatic representation of the Faroes. Not being a sovereign state, the Faroes cannot act in the international arena as if they were one. They cannot be at the top of the hierarchy in foreign policy.

In Reykjavík, however, a special construction was created in 2007: the Faroese government set up its own separate representation there that is not a part of the Danish embassy and therefore does not have official diplomatic status. But the head of the Faroese representation is simultaneously a counsellor at the Danish embassy in Reykjavík, which gives her diplomatic status.

There is, however, an interesting use of language within *heimildarlógin* that contributes to a constructed reality among the Faroese people. The word used in the Faroese version of *heimildarlógin* for the person sent abroad to represent Faroese interests is *sendimaður* or, in English, emissary. This is not the same as the word *sendiharri* (ambassador). One has to keep in mind that Faroese governmental bodies for foreign politics is a new phenomenon, thus the difference between the words *sendiharri* and *sendimaður* is not commonly known. The majority of the Faroese public apparently does not realize that the Faroese *sendimaður* is in fact not an ambassador but only an emissary. This constructs a reality in which the Faroese people believe in more possibilities and power than the *heimildarlóg* actually states.

The formal flow of information on foreign policy is bound by ancient rules of cooperation and interaction in the diplomatic sphere. The diplomatic laws and customs of interaction and cooperation are very hierarchical.The fact that the Faroese offices abroad do not have the status of an embassy, nor are the emissaries ambassadors could, in theory, hinder the representation in interacting with other embassies and ambassadors. The political course over the past few years has been to develop the Faroes with the intention of acting more like a state and less like a region. Former emissary in Brussels, Hákun Jógvanson Djurhuus, explains that, at the request of the Faroese, the Faroes mission to the EU has moved to a separate location from the Danish embassy; and that the Faroese request was met with a positive attitude by the Danes and has not affected the cooperation between

_____

5   Árni Ólafsson 11.08.09.

the Faroese mission and the Danish embassy. Formally, the Faroese emissary is still a counsellor at the Danish embassy. This also shows that the Faroes are interested in acting as, and in portraying themselves as, a more independent unit than a regional unit in the international arena.[6] This may have deprived the Faroese of some opportunities, unlike, for example, Greenland that to a greater extent takes advantage of the opportunities that lie in being a region. The Faroes have mostly, due to their status within the Danish state, been represented through Denmark in international organizations; therefore, the Faroes often cannot be a part of the decision-making process but may try to make some efforts in decision-*shaping*. Decision-shaping processes include influencing important flows of information and how this information is interpreted. By representing themselves in the international arena, the Faroes can promote their own interests in formal international cooperation.

Another reason the Faroes do not take full advantage of the opportunities that lie in being a region is that they have to prioritize their workforce – they do not have enough staff capacity. But first and foremost, the policy of the Ministry of Foreign Affairs is to "brand" the Faroes not as a region, but as a country.

Vibeke Kolderup (1999), in her comparison of the relations of the Faroes and the Åland Islands to their respective mainland states (Denmark and Finland), concludes that the Faroes chose not to receive any funds from the European Regional Fund. She explains that it seems that the Faroes have less vertical acting power, but greater autonomy, while the Åland Islands have gained vertical acting power, but have less autonomy (Kolderup 1999: 21). Her observations are substantiated by statements made by Høgni Hoydal, former minister of foreign affairs, and Árni Ólafsson, adviser on Faroese matters for the Danish ministry of foreign affairs, that the Faroes strongly prefer to develop cooperation where the Faroes can have an independent representation. The Faroes are moving from a primarily hierarchical model towards a network model in the international arena. On the other hand, the Åland Islands have moved from a network model towards a more hierarchical model. The opportunities to cooperate as a Danish region are not taken advantage of by the Faroes. Thus, many cooperative opportunities in Brussels are ruled out. It appears that the Faroes focus on leveraging information flows and on influencing possibilities that can benefit the Faroes as an autonomous unit in the foreign policy arena.

The flow of information in the relations and cooperations between actors will be influenced by their personal relationship; however, the flow of information will be limited because the actors are parts of a more comprehensive hierarchy (Castells 2004). Information will not flow freely from the Faroes to the top of the EU, but will be met by a row of impediments stemming from formal cooperations and rankings. Thus, the Faroese opportunities within the ranked system are ultimately decided by the Danish state. However, using networks, the Faroese emissary can through a good personal relationship with key actors help

---

6   Árni Olafsson 14.4.2008.

get important information to the right actor, though it is uncertain whether the information will get to the right actor at the right time. According to the former Faroese emissary in Brussels, Hákun Jógvanson Djurhuus, rank has not been a great issue. During his years in Brussels he managed to establish several formal and informal kinds of cooperation. This shows that individual actors also play a great part in influencing the pathways of cooperation.

Network Relations in Faroese Foreign Policy

Rank is not necessarily of great importance in network cooperation. Therefore, in a *pure* network cooperation, the Faroes will be the equals of the Danish state. However, the Faroes are ranked in the Danish state and are thus influenced by a more comprehensive hierarchy when in network cooperation with Danish authorities; this makes the actors less ranked than in a pure hierarchy but not equal as in a pure network.

Network cooperation unfolds differently than a hierarchy and has other methods of cooperation (Koppenjan and Klijn 2004). For countries that are not highly ranked in the international arena, it is of great importance to use network cooperation to develop relations and cooperation around the world. Globalization has strengthened the possibilities of the Faroes to develop their networks. The geographical position of a country is not as decisive a factor as earlier due to technological developments over recent years. As communication and cooperation through the Internet, satellite and affordable air travel have become more common, cooperation has become less formal. The emphasis is now on quick and effective contacts rather than on following procedures (Castells 2004). This informal manner of cooperation and communication has also made the actors more equal.

However, diplomatic cooperation is traditionally a highly hierarchical form of cooperation with ranked actors, even though networks are of great importance in foreign policy cooperation. As a result, actors may be both a part of a hierarchy and a network. However, for the most part network cooperation will be between actors of the same rank within the hierarchy for largely social reasons, although there may be exceptions.[7]

Nevertheless, through network cooperations the Faroes may have more access and influence on the decision-making process in the global foreign-policy arena. Networks will, in many cases, create a connection between actors built on mutual interests and trust. In some cases it can also lead to personal friendship between actors. However, the diplomatic manner of cooperation is hierarchical and the same actors that are a part of a network cooperation will thus also be a part of a larger hierarchy such as for example the WTO, EU or EFTA. The network will thus be influenced by the larger hierarchy.

Interviews with Danish and Faroese representatives in Brussels confirm that if actors are a part of an informal bond they will create a new network and thus expand

---

7   Herluf Sigvaldsson 15.01.2008.

the possibilities within the hierarchical international arena.[8] A senior diplomat at the Danish representation to the EU has for several years been in charge of handling EU matters relating to Greenland and the Faroes. As a representative of the Danish state, the diplomat explains that he gives the Faroes space to negotiate directly with the EU;[9] however, he claims that the EU often demands a Danish representative to be present to ensure the negotiations are consistent with the laws and policies of the Kingdom of Denmark. The EU is careful about not coming into conflict with the member state of Denmark by negotiating directly with the Faroes without a Danish representative present. The diplomat frames this by saying that this is not to be seen as a demand by the Danish state, but as a symbolic confirmation that the Danish state has given the Faroes the authority to negotiate on these matters.[10] The cooperation between the Danish diplomat and the former Faroese emissary to the EU was good and strengthened by their network relations.[11]

Networking is, of course, an important part of being an ambassador. But for Faroese emissaries it is even more important to network and use the advantages that a network has within the hierarchical international arena. As the Faroes are a subset of the Danish state in the international arena, the emissaries naturally network with Danish actors. However, when asked directly whether they mostly network directly with Danish actors or not, an interesting picture emerges. In Table 8.1 below, we see results from a survey conducted in January 2009 (Ólavsdóttir 2009).

As Table 8.1 shows, only the Faroese emissary in Copenhagen mostly networks with Danish actors.[12] The importance of having an arena for cooperation, stated by Koppenjan and Klijn (2004), is shown as the Faroese emissaries to a great extent creating their own network outside the Danish system. The emissary in London mostly networks with British actors on business agreements;[13] the Faroese emissary in Reykjavik largely networks with actors from Iceland and Norway.[14]

Table 8.1   Faroese emissaries' responses to the question: "Do you mostly network with Danish actors?"

	Yes	No
Copenhagen	x	
London		x
Brussels		x
Reykjavik		x

8   Herluf Sigvaldsson 15.01.2008 and Hákun J. Djurhuus 29.05.2008.
9   Ole Samsing 29.05.2008.
10   Ole Samsing 29.05.2008.
11   Hákun J. Djurhuus 29.05.2008.
12   Herálvur Joensen 08.01.2009.
13   Áki Johansen 08.01.2009.
14   Gunvør Balle 07.01.2009

The emissary in Brussels networks mostly with other Nordic nations that are not a part of the EU.[15] Consequently, the Faroese emissaries are networking with other actors or organizations with common interests and often common languages, potentially reducing the transaction cost of the relations (Granovetter 1983).

Asked whether there is a network strategy for his mission, the Faroese emissary in Brussels states that, partly due to his limited staff and limited networking options, his strategy is to network as high up in the hierarchy as possible, thereby gaining access to the most relevant and important knowledge available.

Faroese Politicians and Faroese Foreign Policy

We will now turn to the Faroese *politicians'* involvement in and views of international networking and analyse how these views compare with those of regions and cities in mainland Scandinavia in the light of the hybrid position of the Faroes between region and micro state. Faroese politicians were also covered by the survey of elected members of governing boards in Finland, Sweden, Denmark and Norway. In the Faroes, three sets of political bodies were covered by the survey: the parliament, the government and the municipal boards of the capital city of Torshavn and of the second largest town of Klaksvík. All politicians in office in 2008/09 were asked to contribute, and the response rate was 50 per cent for each body.

The first comparison to other Nordic regional and urban politicians concerns their actual participation in international projects (see Table 8.2).

Table 8.2 shows that the top politicians in the Faroes are (on average) somewhat more involved in cross-border contacts compared to other Nordic regional and urban politicians (sum means score is 1.37 for the Faroese and 1.25 for the Nordics). However, like the rest of the regional politicians, the Faroese politicians are not especially preoccupied with cross-border contacts (max score is 5 = almost daily).

Although they are not an EU member, the Faroes could establish contacts with DG Region, but as discussed above, the Faroese government has deliberately chosen to downgrade institutionalized regional cooperation through the EU. However, the Faroes do have formal cooperation with other EU institutions, the primary liaison bodies being DG Trade and DG Fish; and the DG for Research is now becoming a new important contact. Thus, the Faroes are not lagging behind the regions in the Nordic states. On the contrary, Faroese involvement in cross-border contacts among top politicians is widespread and vital compared to the other Nordic regional and urban politicians.

How satisfied are Faroese politicians with cross-border contacts compared to regional and urban politicians in Finland, Sweden, Denmark and Norway? The politicians were asked about their general satisfaction with the international

---

15　Jonhard Eliasen 07.01.2009.

Table 8.2 **Faroese politicians' involvement in cross-border contacts compared to East Nordic regional and urban politicians. Mean score***

	Faroese	Nordic
Participation in projects with regions/municipalities in other countries	**1,61**	1,29
Study visit to region/municipality in other countries	**1,81**	1,58
Participation at international conferences	**1,64**	1,44
Participation in collaboration in the West Nordic and /or Baltic Sea regions	**1,54**	1,20
Participation in other European regional collaboration	1,17	**1,22**
Participation at meetings of European regional associations	1,06	**1,14**
Contacts with DG Regional Policy (EU)	1,00	**1,08**
Contacts with other DGs (EU)	**1,22**	1,09
Contacts with other EU institutions	**1,25**	1,18
Mean score	**1,37**	1,25
(N)	*(35)*	*(812)*

Note: Scale: 1 = rarely/never; 5 = almost daily
*Q.: How often have you been involved in the following activities during the last year? 1: Rarely/never, 2: a couple of times, 3: almost monthly, 4: almost weekly, 5: almost daily

involvement of their respective institutions. As we can see in Table 8.3, Faroese politicians were on average less satisfied than politicians in the other countries.

Surprisingly, Faroese politicians' overall mean satisfaction with international involvements is the lowest in the Nordic regions (2.62). The difference is substantial, particularly compared to Norwegian city and regional politicians who are the most satisfied.

More detailed analysis (not included in the table) clearly indicates that almost 50 per cent of Faroese politicians are either completely (24 per cent) or mostly

Table 8.3 **Overall satisfaction with international involvement: Faroese politicians compared to Nordic colleagues. Mean scores**

	Mean	N
Norway	3,45	191
Denmark	3,33	205
Sweden	3,32	281
Finland	3,27	179
Faroese	**2,62**	**37**
Total	3,31	893

Note: Scale: 1= not satisfied at all, 5= very satisfied
Q.: Overall, are you satisfied with Faroese participation in international affairs?

dissatisfied (21 per cent) with the islands' international involvement. Compared to the other Nordic regions, this is unique. The formulation of the question does not offer any explanations for the Faroese politicians' dissatisfaction. It could be interpreted as an expression of higher ambitions, i.e. international participation efforts are too low, or the opposite, that the involvement and present investments in foreign policy are too high, pushing out other more urgent needs for public action.

However, a more detailed examination of the politicians' satisfaction with different types of regional and European collaborations shows higher satisfaction with these endeavours. In Table 8.4, we have compared the Faroese politicians' evaluation of specific arenas for international cooperation.

Table 8.4   Satisfaction with various regional/municipal collaborations: Faroese politicians compared to Nordic colleagues. Mean scores

	Faroese	Nordic
b) Satisfaction – *Nordic* regional/municipal collaboration	**4.32**	3.24
d) Satisfaction – *European* regional/municipal collaboration	**3.94**	3.22
e) Satisfaction – *European regional organizations*	**3.19**	3.16
Mean	3.82	3.21
(N)	*(35)*	*(788)*

Note: Scale: 1= not useful at all, 5= very useful

Q. 13: How do you value the benefits of Faroese participation in international affairs? Please tell us your opinion about the different ways of cooperation, i.e. if the cooperation is sufficiently beneficial, is "so-so", or is a waste of time. b) Cooperation with the Nordic countries d) Cooperation with other European countries e) Membership of European regional associations (for example Assembly of European regions, IULA).

When Faroese politicians are asked about their satisfaction with various regional/municipal collaborations, their assessment varies depending on the type of relation but is higher overall than that of the subnational politicians of the other Nordic countries. They are the group *most satisfied* with cross-border collaboration efforts with the Nordic countries (mean score 4.32). Also European regional/ municipal collaborations are considered useful (3.94).

A key question remaining concerns the Faroese top politicians' views of regional collaboration within the context of European integration. Table 8.5 presents the results from several *assertions* to which the political representatives from the Nordic countries have responded.

The average Faroese politician thinks that efforts in international relations will serve the Faroes, and more so than the average regional/city politicians in the other Nordic countries. To these politicians it is about time for each region to develop its own foreign policy (mean score 3.11 for the Faroese politicians compared to

Table 8.5   Faroese politicians' views of European collaborations compared to other Nordic regional and urban politicians. Mean scores

	Faroese	Nordic
Assertion: Regions have a lot to gain by European regional collaboration	4.26	3.73
Assertion: Nordic regional collaboration has been overrun by European collaboration	1.58	3.00
Assertion: Regions cannot have any independent position within the European Union	2.11	2.61
Assertion: European regional collaboration costs more than it's worth	2.28	2.66
Assertion: The Faroe Islands'/the regions' position should be strengthened in the European decision-making process	3.92	3.44
Assertion: It is about time that each region develops its own foreign policy	3.11	2.62
Assertion: Too many organizations represent the European regions	3.19	3.42
(N)	*(36)*	*(809)*

Note: Scale: 1= disagree completely, 5= agree completely
Q. "There are often many opinions when regional cooperation in Europe is considered. Please mark whether you agree or disagree with the statements below ..."

2.62 for the other Nordic politicians). However, mean scores may hide opposing views in the group. A more detailed picture emerges if we look more closely at the politicians' answers to the five options of each assertion. In Table 8.6, the full responses are revealed.

Table 8.6   "It is about time for each region to develop its own foreign policy". Per cent

	Faroese	Nordic
1. Disagree	19	29
2.	13	17
3. Difficult to say	25	23
4.	19	22
5. Agree	22	7
(N)	*(36)*	*(735)*

Compared to the Nordic average, Faroese politicians are more eager to develop an active foreign policy. However, Faroese politicians are also more equally divided into two opposing camps compared to the rest of Nordic politicians. In Table 8.7 we investigate to what degree the gap may be explained by the political cleavage in

Table 8.7   **"It is about time for each region to develop its own foreign policy". Respondents grouped according to their party's position on Faroese autonomy. Per cent**

	In favour of unaltered dependency on the Danish state	In favour of sovereignty / more autonomy to the Faroe Islands
1. Disagree	28	13
2.	28	4
3. Difficult to say	21	27
4.	14	22
5. Agree	7	31
Total	14	22
	100	100

Faroese politics between parties wanting more autonomy/a sovereign Faroese state, and parties who prefer the current position in the Danish state hierarchy.

Table 8.7 sheds light on the polarization in Faroese party politics in the politicians' attitudes to giving foreign policy higher priority. For those who want a sovereign Faroese state, a capability to work in the international arena is crucial. We see that politicians in favour of unaltered dependency on the Danish state are more reluctant to developing a distinctly regional foreign policy (21 per cent agree) than those in favour of greater autonomy and (55 per cent agree).[16] However, approximately one-fourth of all the politicians are in doubt. The ongoing investments, described in the introduction are allowing the Faroes to intensify their involvement in foreign policy. Table 8.7 reveals that there are divergent opinions *inside* the political fractions, as some belonging to the "extended autonomy parties" disagree with the emphasis on foreign policy, while others belonging to "Danish state hierarchy parties" do agree with such a priority. In Table 8.8 we also find that the municipal politicians, whom we may presume to be more concerned about local than international problems, are more reluctant to prioritize foreign policy than the politicians at the national level.

---

16   As mentioned above, all the members of Parliament and the Government as well as all the members of the municipal boards of Tórshavn and Klaksvík were asked to respond to the survey; the response rate was 50 per cent in each of the three groups.

Table 8.8   **"It is about time for each region to develop its own foreign policy". Per cent**

	Municipal politicians	National politicians*
1. Disagree	18	20
2.	18	12
3. Difficult to say	27	24
4.	27	16
5. Agree	9	28
Total	11	25
	100	100

Note: *Members of Løgting and Landsstýri

Conclusion

In this chapter we have analysed Faroese foreign policy from a hierarchy versus network perspective. The Faroes have used traditional hierarchichal structures to establish representations in Europe and have, in some cases, then moved on to establish expanded international networks. These networks leverage openings created by formal ties and can help to establish entirely new and important relationships. The survey showed that the Faroese top politicians are somewhat more active in cross-border contacts compared to other Nordic regional and urban politicians. Regional politicians, however, are not particularily preoccupied with cross-border contacts, and we find that among Faroese politicians opinions diverge as to the efforts to expand Faroese involvement in international relations. Even though the Faroese politicans are more active on average in their networking activities compared to those from the other Nordic countries, we also found that they are not very satisfied with their international networking activites. However, we do not know exactly what they are dissatisfied with. Is it the lack of status as a fully sovereign state (the hierarchical position of the Faroes in the international arena)? Or perhaps the opposite: do they fear an undermining of the present Danish-Faroese hierarchical structure? Are they simply not satisfied with the outcome of their networking activity? Do they not get enough in return for their investment (time, effort, money)?

Interestingly, they are more satisfied than other Nordic politicians with cooperation with the Nordic countries and less satisfied with contacts with the European Union. This finding is consistent with the theory of transaction costs. Since the Nordic countries are culturally and linguistically closer, interaction flows more easily – hence the greater satisfaction. This might suggest that the dissatisfaction expressed by the Faroese politicians is caused neither by the lack of status as a fully sovereign state, nor by a fear of undermining the present status as subject to the Danish state. Perhaps the Faroese are sceptical about the high threshold they must cross to gain access to the EU's political apparatus?

Sources

Websites

http://dk.nanoq.gl.
http://www.stm.dk/rigsombudet_a_1733.html.
www.grundlov.dk.
www.logir.fo.
www.logting.fo.
www.mfa.fo.
www.vestnordisk.is.

Laws

Circular note JTF. File No. 8.U.107, Copenhagen 7 November 2005.
Danmarks Riges Grundlov nr. 169 af 5. juni 1953.
Færø Amts Kundgørelse Nr. 11 af 31.03.1948 af Lov om Færøernes Hjemmestyre.
Lóg nr. 79 frá 12. mai 2005 um mál og málsøki føroyskra myndugleika at yvirtaka.
Lóg nr. 80 frá 14. mai 2005 um altjóðarættarligu sáttmálar Føroya Landsstýris at gera.

Interviews

Áki Johansen 08.01.2009.
Árni Ólafsson 14.04.2008; 11.08.2009.
Gunvør Balle 07.01.2009.
Hákun J. Djurhuus 29.05.2008.
Herálvur Joensen 08.01.2009.
Herluf Sigvaldsson 15.01.2008.
Jonhard Eliasen 07.01.2009.
Ole Samsing 29.05.2008.

Chapter 9

Building Learning Ecologies: What Works and How? The Examples of the County Councils of Telemark and Aust-Agder (Norway)

Jørgen Sande Lysa and Morten Øgård

Introduction

The purpose of this chapter is to analyse the processes of international collaboration of two regions to attain a better understanding of a) the forces motivating the international involvement of regions and b) factors that impinge on the effectiveness of such involvement.

Our approach reflects a learning perspective. Organizational learning is often defined as the capacity of organizations to change routines in response to information about goal achievement. Thus a learning capacity is vital for an organization's ability to adapt to a changing environment (Argyris and Schön 1978, March 1991, Easterby-Smith 1997, Boekema et al. 2000, Rutten and Boekema 2007). In our analysis of the two regions, we focus not only on the *outcomes* of organizational learning, i.e. the project-generating capacity of regions, but also on the *organization* of learning, i.e. regional learning ecologies. The organization of learning is about structuring information flows; in our cases this means information flows related to international activities. Our analysis revolves around three principally different patterns of information flows, which we term "the anarchic model", "the awareness model" and "the strategic model".

In the *anarchic model*, action is not necessarily based on a rational problem or target-based logic. Instead, we witness a kind of international orientation, or search, driven by a random character strongly linked to individuals' interest (enthusiast), faith and good intentions. The process could be described as a bottom-up driven process that is not characterized by systematic, supervision and strategic orientation. It may equally be solutions that are seeking problems as the reverse (March and Olsen 1976).

The *awareness model* is driven by a quest to spread information and international contacts, financing, legal information, institutional knowledge, opportunity structures, etc. The aim is general information accumulation. This indirectly may lead to knowledge development, an ability to recognize opportunity structures, as well as to develop an action capacity in relation to the environment.

The *strategic model* is structured and goal-oriented. Organizational capacity is gained by concentrating resources in a strategic unit. The idea is that professional project developers or network members scan the outside world looking for project ideas and new opportunities that may help realize the region's strategic priorities. The strategic goal and result-oriented search process is led by a pre-designed international plan related to specific regional wants or needs.

The data are based on written sources such as county council documents, plans and other information material. In addition, we have used documents from projects portfolios, collaborations and organizations. The choice of the two cases is pragmatic. Initially we were looking for cases with an international involvement and how they handled these types of activities. Given the research interest, we had to choose regions that were actually active. Both county councils had an international commitment. At the same time, they were, as neighbouring county councils, easily accessible.

The chapter divides international engagement into two dimensions: breadth and depth. Breadth of engagement measures how many projects and organizations and how much cooperation each county council is involved in. The chapter also addresses the thematic range of engagement. The depth dimension basically measures to what degree the engagement is emphasized within the county, e.g. the position of people involved in different projects, collaborations and organizations. Do the regions take on a leading role? And to what extent are leading personnel from the regions involved, e.g. key political or administrative figures?

Furthermore, in what sorts of functions do the regions engage in their international activities? Inspired by the work of Ole P. Kristensen (1984), we distinguish between the functions of organizer, financer (or sponsor) and producer. The *organizer role* determines who will produce the services, how much, the quality and for whom. The organizer is similar to the role of a facilitator. Examples include coordinating parties in projects, e.g. by organizing workshops or facilitating the dissemination of information. The *financer role*, as applied in our analysis, basically concerns sponsoring. This is no insignificant role as it involves the commitment of resources.

Beyond the various roles presented above, counties are engaged in different kinds of international relations. Three main forms are evident: bilateral friendship cooperation, formal membership of international policy organizations and project-based cooperation. *Bilateral friendship cooperation* is often a non-binding commitment where informal meetings and exchange programs are the main activities. *Membership of international organizations* is based on a specific agenda aimed at developing policy or exerting influence internationally, especially on European regional policy. *Project-based* cooperation typically consists of commitments related to European structural funds, such as the substantial Interreg program. These projects can be classified as "Infrastructure", "Education and

Research", "Agriculture/Land Development, Landscape", "Environment", "Arena for Exchanging Experience" and "Innovation/Business Development."

The International Involvement of Two County Councils – Telemark and Aust-Agder in Norway

The main focus of the cases presented below concerns the period from 2000 onwards. It is, however, necessary to briefly explain what took place before. The brief historical review highlights attempts at an early stage, some of which failed and some of which succeeded, which as such influenced contemporary international engagement.

The County Council of Telemark and its International Involvement Before 2000

Telemark's tradition of international engagement can be traced back to the early 1990s. It was initially problem-driven, related to a major problem with airborne acid rain from Europe. This could not be solved by Telemark alone, but called for international cooperation between countries bordering the North Sea Basin. The cooperation led to the County Council's later membership of the North Sea Commission (NSC) (1991), as well as membership of the Conference of Peripheral Maritime Regions of Europe (CPMR). Later, this engagement was oriented towards the Baltic States and membership of Baltic Sea-State sub-regional Cooperation (BSSSC). Telemark County Council also became a member of the Assembly of European Regions (AER) through a large public network in Eastern Norway (*Østlandssamarbeidet*). Today, Telemark remains a member of most of these multilateral collaborations. The County Council also attempted to initiate bilateral business-based cooperation with Russia and Germany. These were entirely commercial initiatives. The aim and motivation for the County was to increase trade and exports from Telemark. The County Council played an important role in both cases, mainly by coordinating and funding coordinating activities. A key commercial partner was Norsk Hydro ASA.[1] However, due to increasing scepticism about the return on investments, the commercial actor decided to pull out: the agreement collapsed. The attempt to establish relations with regions in Germany stalled due to a lack of interest from industry in Telemark.

In the 1990s, international operations were managed by an internal "Regional Office" within the county administration. The budget was approximately NOK 2 million and the staff consisted of 2.5 man-years. In this period international engagement became an integral part of the comprehensive County Plan. Mention of international involvement could also be found in other policy documents, such as the Action Plan for Education. Beyond this, international engagement was not highly profiled, and few people in the administration were involved.

---

1   Norsk Hydro is one of the largest intergrated aluminium companies worldwide.

In 2000, the County Council commissioned an *evaluation* of its international engagement. The report stated that the activity was poorly grounded in the political leadership and administration of the County Council and was also little known in municipalities and communities up and down the county. One of the main conclusions of the report was that the County Council's international activity lacked clear motivation and needed to be better integrated into its ongoing operations.

Beyond 2000 – Consolidation and Political Drive

Since 2000, Telemark County Council's international involvement has gained a more central role in the administrative apparatus. International activities are today managed by an international team of five persons. Furthermore, information related to international activities has increased dramatically in scope. A central guideline is to strengthen the regional level and increase its influence nationally and in Europe. This is to be achieved by intensifying cooperation with other regions in Europe. The County Council also arranges collaborative arenas where various local and regional partners are invited to take part, such as municipalities, educational institutions and businesses. As stated in the County Plan, the overall aim is to produce "an added value" through cross-institutional cooperation across regions, including supporting applications for projects and project development related to the EU. Topics that are prioritized include project development with local authorities and other bodies in Telemark, business development with an international perspective, infrastructure, education, participation in EU programmes and arenas. Telemark still maintains membership of and activities related to two organizations mentioned above, the NSC and the CPMR. The County Mayor currently holds the position as President of the NSC and is First Vice President of the CPMR.

Telemark County's Friendship Relations

The friendship relation with the Hubei region in China is an important ongoing collaboration. It differs from most other international activities in which the County Council is involved. It started out as purely bilateral educational cooperation. Later, several partners such as Innovation Norway, as well as state schools in Telemark, Gjøvik municipality and the regional University College have joined in, as have equivalent developmental and educational institutions in the Hubei region. A friendship agreement between the two regions was signed in 2006 and has resulted in a Hubei-Norway week, first hosted in 2007 by the city of Wuhan. The delegation from Norway included local contractors and businessmen, as well as public employees and non-governmental organizations. The current aim of the collaboration is to develop and improve business opportunities between China and Norway, while promoting cultural exchange. Telemark County Council initiated a study of the two regions to determine areas of cooperation. Five areas were chosen: environment and energy, new materials, shipping and construction, health and biotechnology and Trade. For a more detailed description see (www.norway-hubei.net).

Telemark County Council sponsors a wide range of international activities by business and civic organizations. Some of these funds go to the development of EU Interreg programmes, while others support projects outside the existing structures. Examples of the latter include student exchange programmes and cultural study tours. Altogether, in 2008, the County Council supported 21 different projects with a total of NOK 522,715 in international grants, ranging from NOK 4,000 to 50,000. Table 9.1 lists Telemark's international activities.

Summary of the International Effort of the County Council of Telemark

Telemark's international commitments range from informal friendship cooperation to project-based activities. The friendship cooperation with the Hubei region breaks with the rest of the commitments. This is the only partnership in which one of the participating regions is outside Europe. It has been developed from a classical educational exchange programme towards a multidimensional, cross-continental and cultural collaboration.

Beyond this, most commitments are associated with the EU and Interreg. The County Council of Telemark demonstrates a will to take a lead in the projects and organizations in which it participates. Many projects are organized as arenas for exchanging experience. The dominant objectives in these projects concern coordination and cooperation in the areas where the cooperating regions have shared problems and see common opportunities. This is why the facilitator role is maintained to be important by the County of Telemark.

Through participation in the various organizations and forums, Telemark County Council develops its expertise in managing European projects. The producer role in the various projects is largely taken care of by local partners. This may be municipalities or public or private agencies. The role as facilitator is normally most evident in an early project phase. Because Norwegian regions and municipalities cannot propose projects to the Interreg without the participation of regions in EU member states, the Norwegians face a particular challenge. Telemark has tackled this by utilizing established networks to actively seek partners. Another important approach is the LIFT analysis, which systematically and strategically seeks to identify areas in which local businesses or municipalities have a potential to develop internationally. Then, by using forums, arenas and organizations in which the County Council participates, they try to find other regions/municipalities facing the same challenges. They also link the initiative to pre-existing international projects.

Table 9.1 Telemark County Council's international involvement ca. 2000–08*

Title	Theme	Purpose	Roles	International partners
North Sea Commission (NSC)	Interest promotion	Promote regional interests.	Leading role. Presidency and secretariat function	154 regions
Baltic Sea-State sub-regional Cooperation	Interest promotion	Promote regional interests.	Membership	157 regions
Conference of Peripheral Maritime Regions of Europe (CPMR)	Interest promotion	Promote regional interests.	Membership and Vice President	154 regions
Assembly of European Regions (AER)	Interest promotion	Promote regional interests.	Membership	270 regions
StratMos motorways of the sea (2008–11)	Infrastructure	Developing an effective, safe and sustainable freight transport.	Facilitate local project	Norway, Denmark, Germany, the Netherlands, England and Scotland
Nordic Transport political Network (NTN) (2003–05)	Infrastructure	Promote a transport corridor from South Norway and western Sweden to Central Europe.	Facilitate local project	Norway, Denmark, Germany and Sweden
Farmers for Nature (F4N) (2004–08)	Cultivated landscapes	Protect nature, the landscape and cultural identity in rural areas.	Facilitate local project	Netherlands, Belgium, England, Shetland and Germany
Canal Link (2003–06)	Agricultural/ landscape	How canals, rivers and lakes in the North Sea region could be developed so that the cultural and environmental heritage was safeguarded.	Producer/partner and facilitator for local projects	Netherlands, Belgium, England, Scotland, Sweden and Germany
Water City International (2002–06)	Agricultural/ landscape	Develop and promote cities where water is an important resource.	Facilitate local projects	Netherlands, Sweden, Germany and Denmark
Forum Skagerrak (2003–07)	Arenas for experience exchange	Creating an organization that would protect the interests of the area around Skagerrak.	Membership	Norway, Sweden and Denmark

Project	Category	Description	Role	Countries
Greenport	Arenas for experience exchange	Putting in place a system for handling waste from ships.	Lead Partner	Norway, Denmark, Netherlands and United Kingdom
Euromountains.net (2004–07)	Arenas for experience exchange	Shared challenges in regions with mountainous areas.	Producer/partner and facilitator for local projects	Norway, Spain, Italy, France, Britain and Portugal
VNE-Inland Waterways of Europe (2005–07)	Arenas for experience exchange	Developing waterways, such as canals, rivers and lakes where the cultural heritage is safeguarded.	Lead partner	United Kingdom, Belgium, Spain the Netherlands, Italy, Germany, Sweden, Hungary, and France
PIPE project (1999–2003)	Arenas for experience exchange	How to create innovation and new ideas to exploit peripheral regions' resources and opportunities.	Facilitate local projects	Norway, Sweden, Latvia, Estonia, Lithuania, Finland and Russia
Innovation Circle	Arenas for experience exchange	Continuation of the PIPE project.	Facilitate local projects	Norway, Sweden, Latvia, Estonia, Lithuania, Finland and Russia
SuPortNet II (1999–2004)	Arenas for experience exchange	Boat tourism and the challenges involved.	Facilitator and information disseminator	Sweden, Germany, Poland, Lithuania, Latvia and Estonia
BESST	Innovation/business development	Stimulating economic growth in rural areas by focusing on the specificity of each region.	Facilitate local projects	Norway, Sweden, Germany, Finland, Denmark, the Netherlands
Connect Baltic Sea Region (CBSR)	Innovation/business development	Connecting entrepreneurs, capital and expertise.	Sponsor and facilitator	Norway, Sweden, Germany, Finland, Denmark and the Baltic countries
Gateway to Guidance (2005–07)	Education	Long-term unemployed back to work.	Lead Partner and facilitator	Norway, Denmark, Ireland, Slovakia and the United Kingdom
GLOCAL–Global Education Business Partnership (2003–06)	Education	Better education for young people so that they were better equipped to take up a position in business after ending their education.	Sponsor and facilitator	Norway, Britain, Finland, Sweden, Denmark, Spain and Estonia

Note: * For a more detailed review of the various projects, see Sande Lysa and Øgård (2009)

After such a "link" is established, the County Council reduces its direct participation. But usually a Council employee is available to support and nurture the project. Two people have unique positions as employees of the North Sea Commission Secretariat. Other people linked to international involvement, such as those associated with the various thematic groups in the NSC, are usually there by virtue of their expertise in the field (functionally organized). Others are involved because they are related directly to the projects. These may be municipal employees in Telemark County or people in key positions at other participating institutions.

Overall, the County Council's international involvement must be characterized as relatively broad and deep. The projects and the organization build on a broad thematic platform and initiatives by the County Council are anchored both in its own administration and in surrounding municipalities, voluntary organizations and private companies. There is also a distinct developmental pattern to the County Council's international engagement. Modest and uncoordinated initiatives were taken during the 1990s. From 2000 onwards, the County's international engagement moved to focus on networking and forums for discussing joint problems, solutions and for exchanging experience. Cooperation between Telemark and Hubei stands as an example of the County Council using an pre-established point of contact to find new themes for collaboration. What started out as a friendship-based cooperation between two colleges became more of a thematically multidimensional partnership that is actively used to promote business cooperation and contacts. This has culminated in an annual meeting hosted alternate years in Telemark and Hubei respectively.

The development of international involvement does not seem to stop there. Telemark County Council has a large catalogue of possible future projects under consideration and several project proposals have been submitted to Interreg for review. The focus on international contacts seems to be increasing.

The County Council of Aust-Agder: Friendship and Solidarity

The history of the international involvement of Aust-Agder County Council differs from Telemark's. It is shorter and less comprehensive and Aust-Agder did not have a distinct international profile before 2000. Two events changed this: the first was the establishment of the Southern Norway European Office in 2005. Two years later, a joint international secretariat for the County Councils of Aust- and Vest-Agder was established. The secretariat was a result of the desire for better coordination of the international engagements of the two neighbouring counties of Agder. Until then, the international engagement of the County Council of Aust-Agder was characterized by random initiatives and unclear organization.

Among the earlier activities, we may find friendship cooperation with Viborg County in Denmark and an agreement with the municipality of Rezekne in Latvia. The friendship relation with Viborg was based on an agreement concluded in 1988 and activities largely consisted of mutual visits and exchanges of administrative staff and politicians. Cooperation with Rezekne was a solidarity project managed by the municipality of Arendal. The County Council of Aust-Agder joined the NSC in 1991 and thereby became a member of CPMR. Aust-Agder also cooperated with other regions in the Skagerrak Partnership in the cultural sector. In the mid-1990s, these four overarching initiatives were the entirety of the County Council's international engagements. The County Council as such had few international projects. For example, the international involvement of schools, civic organizations or businesses was seen as valuable activities, but not as the immediate responsibility of the County Council (FT-case 62/97, FT-Paper No. 18/98).

From May 1996, the EU adopted a new Community Initiative, Interreg IIC, which was of importance for the development of international involvement in Aust-Agder. During the preparation of the North Sea Programme, the County Council was increasingly drawn into more comprehensive projects with multiple participants, including the North Sea Circuit and SEAGIS. Interreg IIC was closed down in 2001, but replaced by Interreg IIIB and through their participation in the NSC, Aust-Agder wanted to take a more active role in promoting projects and programmes (County Plan 2000–03: Chapter 3).

By the year 2001, their international engagement had increased considerably. This in turn led to a need to develop a more comprehensive strategy. The CEO of the County Council prepared a proposal. The strategy's main objectives were increased understanding and friendship across national borders, more sustainable development and increased knowledge and new ideas that might benefit the county's population. Discussions of the strategy by the County Council emphasized the need for clarification of the political objectives as well as greater practical utility. The Council wanted the strategy to highlight democratic values, increase the competence of international relations, especially among young people, and spread information about Aust-Agder beyond its borders, ensuring biodiversity and social security and to increase competence, self-development and trade relations in business. With these amendments, the strategy was unanimously adopted (FT-case 27.01).

Aust-Agder's Friendship Relations

As briefly mentioned above, the friendship collaboration with Viborg was established in 1988. The formal agreement included Aust-Agder and Viborg, but the County Council of Vest-Agder has also taken part on study tours. The cooperation does not have its own defined objectives, however. The actual activity primarily consists of information exchange and exchanging experience, e.g. concerning the Danish structural reform of 2004.

Table 9.2   Aust-Agder County Council's international involvement ca. 2000–09*

Title	Theme	Purpose	Roles	International partners
North Sea Commission (NSC)	Interest promotion	Promote regional interests.	Membership	154 regions
Baltic Sea-State sub-regional Cooperation	Interest promotion	Promote regional interests.	Membership	157 regions
Conference of Peripheral Maritime Regions of Europe (CPMR)	Interest promotion	Promote regional interests.	Membership	154 regions
Southern European Office	Interest promotion	Develop a more international business and community leaders to exploit opportunities in Europe.	Owner	West-Agder County, municipalities of Kristiansand and Arendal
Norwegian Information Office of Southern Norway	Information	Working for increased cooperation in the Nordic and Baltic countries.	Sponsor role	
Nordic Transport political Network (NTN) (2003–05)	Infrastructure	Promote a transport corridor from South Norway and western Sweden to Central Europe.	Facilitator	Norway, Denmark, Germany and Sweden
Sustainable Development in Coastal Tourist Areas (SDTA) (1991–)	Agricultural landscape	Ensure the protection of vulnerable coastal areas from environmental damage caused by tourism.	Facilitator	Britain and the Netherlands
Forum Skagerrak (2003–07)	Arenas for experience exchange	Creating an organization that would protect the interests of the area around Skagerrak.	Membership	Norway, Sweden and Denmark
The North Sea Circuit	Arenas for experience exchange	Develop safe, good and continuous bike trails around the North Sea.	Facilitate local projects	Belgium, Netherlands, Germany, Denmark, Sweden, Norway, Scotland and England

The Scandinavian Triangle	Arenas for experience exchange	Business Development, IT/correspondence courses, culture and Nordic Link.	Sponsor and facilitator	Norway, Sweden, Denmark
Women in Business (WIB) (2009–11)	Innovation/ Industry Development	Stimulating innovation, development and sustainable growth in small and medium enterprises run by women in the Skagerrak region.	Lead partner	Norway, Sweden, Denmark
Creative interaction in the workplace (KIA)	Innovation/ Industry Development	Utilizing the creative force in the cultural sector to enhance the competitive situation of Skagerrak.	Facilitator	Norway, Sweden, Denmark
LEONARDO projects	Education	Promoting education and friendship cooperation.	Producer and sponsor	16 schools have projects with other schools in European countries, Zimbabwe and the United States

Note: * For a more detailed review of the various projects, see Sande Lysa and Øgård (2009)

Cooperation with the Latvian region of Rezekne initially started as collaboration between the municipalities of Arendal and Rezekne. In 1996 Aust-Agder County Council joined the agreement. Since then, the agreement has been revised several times. In practice, collaboration has mostly revolved around aid from Norway to the Latvian region, where the main activity has been social assistance of various kinds. This is also reflected in the fact that the cooperation has largely been voluntary with employees investing their own time and resources. Without this voluntary element, the cooperation would most likely have stranded. The cooperation has recently been given clearer objectives and strategies. Democracy and urban and regional development have gained greater importance. More concrete targets have been launched, including procuring equipment for and offering financial support to schools, hospitals, social centres and the like. For instance, a project was initiated to improve and upgrade the water supply network of the city of Rezekne. Another example is student exchange programmes. Other interests have gradually been drawn into the cooperation, private as well as public. In 1994, Friendship Society Arendal-Rezekne was founded. This is a private foundation that supports the operation of the institutions with direct financial aid. Southern Hospitals Health Authority in Norway has a partnership with the hospital in Rezekne, built around substance abuse and treating addiction. Until 2004, large parts of the projects were funded with the support of the Ministry of Foreign Affairs in Norway. Later, the County Council has been forced to find new funding. The answer was to apply for funds from the European Economic Area Mechanism,[2] which meant that Norway had to pay to establish a new EEA agreement. Approximately NOK 425 million was given to Latvia. Rezekne prioritized projects within the framework of the new treaty, such as health, reducing and preventing lifestyle-related diseases, helping children with special needs and conserving European cultural heritage. None of the projects Rezekne applied for was granted funding after the first application round. Despite this, the agreement was last revised in late 2007, when it was extended to 2011. Based on the economic development in Rezekne and the access to funding programmes through Latvia's EU membership, the cooperation could focus on projects beyond emergency relief. Greater attention was given to cooperation of mutual benefit within areas such as energy, sustainable development, industrial development, culture and education. The aid element was not wholly removed from the deal, as the County Council of Aust-Agder recognized that there was still a need for support, especially for the poorest part of the population that had not participated in the economic growth.

Table 9.2 lists key projects in the international engagement of the County of Aust-Agder.

---

2   The three members of the European Economic Area – Norway, Iceland and Lichtenstein – pay for their access to the EU's inner market through the European Economic Area Mechanism, which funds developmental projects in the poorer EU countries, which after 2004 have mostly meant the new member countries to the East.

Summary of the International Involvement of Aust-Agder County Council

The County Council's international involvement is characterized by fewer international projects and less extensive participation in international organizations than that of the County Council of Telemark. Friendship cooperation, however, is more vibrant, maintained over many years with both Rezekne and Viborg. Aust-Agder County Council takes no special leadership roles in organizations or projects in which it participates. Its role is limited to partnerships and memberships in organizations. A passive facilitator role covers most of the projects. It seems reluctant to tie up resources, both financial and staff, in international work. The project "Women in Business" (WIB) is an exception. WIB is relatively new, as is Creative Alliances. This may suggest more commitment is underway. The County Council has stepped up its activities and several applications have been sent to the new Interreg IVA Programme, which targets Øresund and the Kattegat. The County Council of Aust-Agder seems to lack individuals who stand out as movers in its international engagement. In 2001 the County Council estimated using half a man-year in the central staff office for its international efforts, the regional department about one man-year and the departments responsible for training, health and social services about three months each. Two structural factors that modify the overall picture given above are the establishment of the Southern Norway European Office and the Joint International Secretariat of Vest-Agder and Aust-Agder. Both the Secretariat and the European Office have employees who work full-time on international affairs for Aust-Agder.

This may explain why there are no employees within the County Council itself to perform such a role. An *external private company approach* has been chosen in Aust-Agder, whereas an *in-house approach* has been chosen in Telemark.

It is difficult to identify dominant themes in Aust-Agder's international activities as there are so few projects. Culture, business and arenas for exchanging experience are recurrent themes for international collaboration. Schools are also extensively involved in international activities.

Comparison of the International Involvement of the Two County Councils and its Organization

When comparing systematically the two county councils' international involvement, several interesting differences emerge. Telemark County Council's engagement is broad and more comprehensive. There are a number of projects of broad thematic spread. Telemark has in particular established a series of "Arenas for Exchanging Experience". Participation is high on the agenda for both counties, but Telemark County Council has gone one step further. Telemark is working in a more project-oriented fashion and seems to stand out as more developmental on behalf of its district; it also tries harder to involve the municipalities in the county. Aust-Agder County Council has managed to maintain bilateral collaborations, while Telemark has failed. Aust-Agder County Council has maintained a good working relationship with both Rezekne and Viborg, while Telemark County Council's bilateral attempt with German and Russian regions failed. Telemark, in turn, tried early on to attain concrete results for business cooperation. The private actors dropped out, however and the collaborations ended. One successful partnership Telemark does operate today is with Hubei in China. Interestingly, this was initiated by a high-school friendship initiative and has in later stages developed into close and promising business cooperation crossing institutional, linguistic and cultural boundaries.

Telemark County Council also appears to have a "deeper" involvement. This is marked by the County Council's willingness to take on leading positions in projects and organizations. They also appear more focused on certain thematic key areas, especially the "Arenas for Exchanging Experience". Both counties emphasize participation by local partners so that sustainable projects can be developed. Aust-Agder seems to have a better ability to mobilize its schools compared to Telemark. Telemark County Council in turn relies on its role as sponsor to activate other institutions more broadly.

The County Council of Telemark is conscious about its role as facilitator. Production is left to the municipalities after the partners have been linked. The County Council also uses its resources to disseminate information and arrange meetings and gatherings. Such an arrangement can be a success factor because the County Council will take the pressure and workload from the municipalities so they can concentrate more on implementing the projects. It also improves information flow and connects problems with the right people and thus prevents coincidences and uncertainties in the decision-making processes concerning the engagement.

Contrasting Organizational Patterns: The In-house Cell and the External Agency

Organizationally and managerially, Telemark and Aust-Agder County Councils represent two different organizational patterns in the structuring and positioning of their international involvement. Telemark County Council has chosen an organizational and managerial solution with all key functions of international work organized *in-house*. The County Council has developed a strategic centre or cell within its own administrative organization. This cell does not only "guide" international efforts; it also appears as a hub for initiatives and projects. Through this strategy, Telemark manages to develop and operate projects "at a distance" by using other actors in the region (for example, business firms, local authorities, voluntary associations, etc.). The hub is managed by a handful of experienced advisers who, in addition to being members of the County Council's international team, are located in various organizations and projects. Each project is defined by the County Council as being of strategic importance. The activities are supported by and anchored in the top political leadership. Key representatives from the political and senior administrative management have taken on strategically important positions in organizations and projects in the European arena.

Aust-Agder County Council has entrusted roles, tasks and initiatives in the management of international involvement to *external agencies*. The Southern Norway European Office is especially important in this respect, established jointly by the municipalities of Arendal, Kristiansand and the County Councils of Aust- and Vest-Agder. This means that functions, roles and tasks related to the international involvement of the County Council are performed by an organization located and operated outside its own organization. In this case, a limited company responsible for handling, interpreting, supporting and responding to opportunities in the European and international arenas.

Both organizational patterns represent strengths and weaknesses as means of developing the County Council's learning and development capacity. The *in-house* pattern stands out as giving the County Council authority and legitimacy to act on behalf of the region. It also provides legitimacy within the internal governing structure, so that local expertise and networks are better mobilized and utilized. This is a positive effect of the in-house model.

The challenge, however, is the risk of running operations for the team's own self interests, benefits and internal status. To avoid this, the facilitator role emerges as very important; creating opportunity structures by opening up network and international project/opportunities for the region as a whole. So far, the County Council of Telemark has taken important steps in the right direction in this respect.

The strength of the *agency* pattern is that it provides opportunities to design and develop a wider, even more specialized, knowledge-related platform for information and initiatives. It is also more accessible to regional businesses and municipalities, as well as promoting more coordinated advances on behalf of a region. Importantly, the agency pattern also makes it possible for the region to concentrate resources that might otherwise be scattered between the different actors.

There are several challenges related to the agency pattern as well. First, the distance from various international actors/interest can be problematic. Second, initiatives and projects might be loosely coupled to the municipalities and businesses in the region. Third, the agency model represents an organizing principle in which skills and learning capacities concerning international relation, organizations and projects are externalized (outsourced). Finally, the model suffers from a democratic deficit.

The Learning Ecologies of Telemark and Aust-Agder

In the introduction to this chapter, a learning approach was presented to analyse the effectiveness of the international involvement of the two regions. "Effectiveness" was defined as the capacity to mobilize other regional actors and to develop internationally orientated projects. Three learning models were outlined: the anarchic model, the awareness model and the strategic model. First of all, which of these learning models is most characteristic of the respective regions? Are international activities mainly driven bottom-up by local enthusiasts with elements of randomness? Have such bottom-up initiatives been supplemented by an overarching policy of information dissemination? Have international initiatives been related to the County Councils' general goals and strategies and are initiatives selected with such goals and strategies in mind? Analysing the patterns of international activities and the way these initiatives are managed with these questions in mind, we reached the conclusions outlined in Table 9.3.

Table 9.3   **The learning ecologies of Telemark and Aust-Agder County Councils**

TIME	Learning Model	Telemark County Council	Aust-Agder County Council
↓	Anarchic	XX	XX
	Awareness	X	XXX
	Strategic	XXX	(X)

When applying the three models to the two cases, both similarities and differences appear. An interesting similarity is that both seem to have started with the characteristics of the *anarchic* model with bottom-up processes and no systematic, strategic approach. While an unsystematic solidarity and friendship approach dominate until the mid-2000s in Aust-Agder, by the 1990s a shift towards a more systematic and strategically oriented approach is emerging in Telemark County Council. This was largely initiated by a problem related to acid rain, along with a political desire to support and stimulate the business sector in the region in their efforts to go international. It turns out that the private sector cannot, or does not want to, follow up on the initiatives and that these strategies eventually failed. The development of cooperation between Telemark and the region of Hubei demonstrates an interesting combination of anarchic and strategic features when a secondary school in Telemark initiates cooperation with a secondary school in Hubei. In the second phase of cooperation, the friendship cooperation expands to encompass commercial and cultural projects with participation from the private, voluntary and public sectors.

The turning point in Aust-Agder County Council took place with the establishment of the Southern Norway European Office in 2005. This was initially a project funded by the County Councils of Aust- and Vest-Agder with the municipalities of Arendal and Kristiansand. In 2009 this office was reorganized as a limited company with permanent representation in Brussels and Kristiansand. In many ways it influences and gives direction to the international orientation of the County Council of Aust-Agder today. The change from 2005 onwards involved the professionalization of international activities and a shift in learning approach.

The new approach largely conforms to the *awareness* model. The Southern Norway European Office appears to be a communicator of information, contacts and opportunity structures in the EU system. However, the establishment of a home office in Kristiansand may signal a new phase concentrating resources and expertise allowing steps towards a more active and strategically oriented model.

At an early stage, Telemark County Council shifted its international engagements towards a problem-driven strategic model. This emphasis was reinforced after 2000. An important evaluation was conducted of the County Council's international engagement. As a result, a shift in emphasis was evident: an enhanced information aspect (preparing its own information materials) and a professionalization and anchoring of the international work in the administrative body through the establishment of the international team. Objectives were outlined for certain strategic areas. The aim of all activities is to stimulate the development of projects. To this end, a flexible network organization was established (the in-house cell or "hub") to support and facilitate work across organizational, municipal, regional and national boundaries. Interestingly, this organizing principle seeks to maintain flexibility while encouraging a strategic orientation and clear foundation in the political and administrative leadership. One should perhaps not exaggerate the strategic aspect of Telemark County Council's international orientation. It is, however, interesting to note how strategically the county appears to act when key politicians assume important positions in organizations such as NSC. At the same time, representatives from the region actively seek out leading position in international projects that have been defined as of special interest to the County Council and the municipalities in the Telemark region.

Summary and Conclusion

The in-house cell pattern as it appears in Telemark County Council provides a higher impact on both the breadth and depth dimension of international involvement compared to Aust-Agder County Council's external agency organization. When it comes to models for organizing learning, Telemark County Council most clearly conforms to the strategic model and the Council has also managed to establish the greatest number of projects. Aust-Agder County Council relies, through its membership of the Southern Norway European Office, more on the awareness model and has generated relatively few developmental projects. The conclusion seems to be that Telemark's in-house cell pattern is more effective in establishing a vibrant ecology of regional learning compared to the achievements of the external agency of Aust-Agder. This conclusion should be drawn cautiously, however. With only two cases, our material has a limited scope. Furthermore, the external agency of which Aust-Agder is a member has been in operation for a relatively short period and may be able to demonstrate more achievements in project generation as it becomes more firmly established.

Chapter 10

International Cooperation of the New Danish Regions: Lifeline or Last Rites? The Case of Southern Denmark

Niels Ejersbo

Introduction

The Danish level of regional government underwent a major change on January 1 2007 following the Local Government Reform (cf. Chapter 2). The 14 existing counties were dissolved and replaced by five new regions. This change was more than a mere adjustment of formal boundaries; the reform fundamentally reorganized the portfolio of tasks of the regional government level, including the financing of these tasks. The regions are now responsible for health care (mainly hospitals), operating institutions in the social sector and special education and regional development. Unlike the former counties, the regions do not have the authority to collect taxes; therefore, their activities are now entirely financed by state subsidies and by activity-specific local government subsidies. The members of the regional council are still democratically elected, but they do not have the same level of influence as the former county council members. Overall, the new regions have lost influence and significance in the Danish public sector. Though the regions operate hospitals, their mandate to exercise independent governance and decision-making is quite limited. The state subsidies usually target specific activities and do not allow for resource reallocation across these activities. As a consequence of the reforms at the regional level, international activities are now mainly in health and regional development.

In today's regions, international cooperation is often closely linked to the internationalization activities of the former counties. Several analyses and studies of the internationalization of the Danish counties (Jensen 1995, Klausen 1996, Baldersheim and Ståhlberg 1999) show that this was closely linked to European integration after 1986. They also show that there was great variation in the international involvement of the counties and that many different models of international cooperation existed. Danish Regions, which is the interest organization of the regions, has established an international committee responsible for stimulating the international cooperation of the regions. However, this is not a formal cooperation between the Danish regions, but rather ad hoc in relation, for example, to the North Sea Commission. It is neither structured nor formalized.

Networks and International Cooperation

The network approach to understanding public policies denotes a move away from a narrow hierarchical reasoning, in which decision-making was seen to take place within the frames of a hierarchy, to attending to networks and cooperative relations. What motivates this move is the argument that the policy challenges of modern society are far too complex to fit the models of traditional public organization (Sandstrøm and Carlsson 2008: 497). This means that public organizations depend on their cooperative relations with actors outside the organizational hierarchy. These may be other public organizations within the same country, private actors, representatives of charitable organizations and representatives of the public and private organizations in other countries. On the one hand, the consequence is that more actors participate, resulting in increased independence and the spreading of responsibility. On the other hand, this requires increased coordination to ensure collective action which is the precondition for solving pressing policy issues (Blom-Hansen 1997).

Networks may have different aims and characteristics (Marsh 1998). They vary as to the number of participants, focus and interest, frequency of cooperation, time limit, the degree of unity within the network, resource allocation and the forum for decision-making.

The network provides an opportunity to solve complex policy challenges in a world characterized by increased globalization and transnational issues. However, this is not entirely effortless. Governing this type of network with many different actors is very complex and demands leadership strategies which differ from the more traditional approaches (Klijn 2008: 508).

The network approach is an obvious angle when discussing internationalization in the Danish regions. First, motives of international cooperation are often linked to policy challenges which are characterized by being complex and cross-national. Second, the organization of the international cooperation of the regions is often similar to networks. Therefore, by taking our point of departure in a network approach, we will study the organization, extent, structure and task fulfilment of cooperative arrangements.

What is to be expected of the new Danish regions in international activities? Against the background of the reduced status and limited responsibilities of the new regions, it would not be surprising to find a waning interest in international cooperation in the regions. With a highly task-specific portfolio of functions and limited financial opportunities, regional politicians may see little point in pursuing internationally oriented development strategies that almost by definition entail high levels of risk and uncertainty. And the compartmentalized institutional structure of the regions may make it very hard to follow up development initiatives encountered at the international level. At most, regional actors may try to maintain some of the task-specific international activities that may be of obvious benefit to their present responsibilities and even these may fade away after a while, at least as political concerns. In other words, international activities may appear as *the last rites* of the peculiar creatures that are the Danish regions.

However, international cooperation may also evolve as a *lifeline* to the new regions. This is suggested in particular by the network perspective. First, participation in international networks may provide a breathing space for constrained political actors by opening up arenas where political skills are in demand. Second, through networks, resources may become available for the pursuit of political priorities that are blocked by the constraints on regional funding imposed by national regulations (e.g. the lack of taxation powers or a general budget for regions). As a whole, the totality of the international networks of a region may evolve into a comprehensive developmental arena which may vitalize not only development processes but also regional identity and politics. If, of course, regional politicians are interested in trying out such opportunities.

Internationalization in the Region of Southern Denmark

The Region of Southern Denmark has 1.2 million inhabitants and is therefore the third-largest region in Denmark. The region is composed of the former Ribe, South Jutland and Funen Counties and parts of Vejle County. The region is governed by a regional council with 41 elected members. The first such council was elected on November 15 2005 and sits for four years. The head politician is the regional council chair who is elected by and from the members of the council.

In 2007, the Region of Southern Denmark adopted a strategy of international cooperation for the region, whereby it hoped to be able to meet the challenges of internationalization. The aim of the strategy was to incorporate the international dimension into strategies and plans within the region's areas of responsibility. The strategy formulated three aims: 1) to increase the international dimension of the cooperation between public and private actors; 2) to communicate knowledge to and involve the citizens, local governments, businesses and educational institutions of the region; and 3) to communicate knowledge to and involve the politicians and employees of the region in the international cooperation.

This strategy was applied to a number of focus areas and specific activities that were implemented to fulfil the aim of the internationalization strategy and that constitute the content of the internationalization strategies of the region.

Internationalization is the responsibility of a separate organizational unit consisting of three employees in the department of regional development; of the three employees, one is located in Brussels. The employees coordinate the international activities and encourage participation in international networks as well as ensuring that all employees incorporate the international perspective in their work.

Focus Areas of the Internationalization Strategy of the
Region of Southern Denmark

Below is a short description of the most significant international activities of
the Region of Southern Denmark as they are outlined in the internationalization
strategy documents.

Cross-national cooperation is considered the most significant activity
of internationalization in the Region of Southern Denmark. This is the result of
several factors. First, it is rooted in the former counties. Especially, the County
of Southern Jutland has – not surprisingly – strong ties to Germany and, in particular
with Schleswig-Holstein, a strong tradition of cooperation. Second, cross-national
cooperation is a key element within health care which is, indisputably, the most
important task of the Danish regions. Third, it comprises activities of immediate
consequence to the region's citizens and involve the employees of the region most
immediately.

The capacity problems within cancer treatment at the regional hospitals and
issues of waiting lists have resulted in cooperation with the hospitals in Flensburg.
This has also led to professional cooperation between the cancer doctors of the
region and German doctors treating Danish patients. The University Hospital in Kiel
and the University Hospital of Southern Denmark cooperate on highly specialized
treatments. This cooperation also includes other Danish regions, whereby they,
through the Region of Southern Denmark, are able to use the hospital in Kiel to
relieve capacity problems.

In addition to the cooperation with the German hospitals in terms of capacity
problems, a number of cooperation projects regarding health information
technology and welfare technology have been initiated. One example is a project
on radiology and related expert knowledge across Europe.

The Region of Southern Denmark also enters into cross-national cooperation
within other areas, such as regional development. Naturally, this does not have
the same significance and extent as the cooperation in the health area. Regional
development includes branding the region much like the Oresund Region, which
has become a well-known brand. In the words of the region, there is "no reason
why the southern part of Denmark or the northern part of Germany should feel
like end stations when there are strong opportunities for a beneficial cooperation
across the border".

At expert level, the cross-national cooperation concerning capacity and
waiting list issues within healthcare is situational and related to solving some very
specific tasks. It is also characterized by a high degree of stability based on many
years of previous cooperation. At management level, there is a mix of a situational
approach and a development-oriented perspective, which to a great extent includes
the long-term development opportunities for the different actors. It is also at
management level that the mainstay of the decisions is made. The political level
is only included when the decisions will have large financial consequences for
the region. The additional cross-national cooperation has a mainly development-

oriented approach and focuses on exchanging ideas and information. This form of cooperation is also characterized by a lower degree of formality and formal decision-making structures.

Another focus area is the cooperation with growing regions in specific countries. The Region of Southern Denmark cooperates with the Guangdong province in China, Olomouc in the Czech Republic and the Malopolska region in Poland.

The cooperation with the Guangdong province is an extension of a cooperation agreement with the former Funen County and was renewed in June 2007. The Guangdon province is characterized by major financial growth and therefore represents great export opportunities for the businesses in the region. The core of the agreement is the cooperation within the health area, particularly including the development and commercialization of herbal-based medicine, but also projects within energy and the environment.

The agreements with Olomouc in the Czech Republic and Malopolska in Poland have emerged from earlier cooperation agreements with Vejle County and Funen County respectively. These agreements are wide-ranging and embrace many areas and projects. Previously, these two cooperation agreements targeted developing democracy in Eastern Europe, whereas, today, they aim at promoting export and development in general. The cooperation with the Czech and Polish regions also provides better opportunities for EU applications, as the EU wishes to spread its policy and initiatives to the eastern part of Europe.

The agreements with the three growth regions primarily target developing new opportunities for cooperation for the businesses and institutions of the region, but also include more specific projects such as the development of herbal medicine. This project is also an example of how one area of international cooperation supports another focus area in the region. Within its regional development strategy, the Region of Southern Denmark concentrates on "the healthy life" of which the cooperation in the health area with the Guangdon province is an element. The foundation of the cooperation with all the regions consists of formal agreements, but it seems that the relation to the Chinese Guangdon province is more formalized with the cooperation entailing set frames.

Like other regions in Denmark, the Region of Southern Denmark is a member of several European networks and organizations. It is a member of the Assembly of European Regions, which aims to increase influence in the EU. Through the membership of the European organization for lifelong learning and innovation, the region has the opportunity to acquire information about current issues at the European level and activities in other regions. The region estimates that participating in this type of network enables the interaction of knowledge and thereby furthers the region's own activities. The region is also a member of the North Sea Commission and the Baltic Sea Commission, which aim at creating synergy in the region's industrial development strategy. Furthermore, the region is a member of Sustainable Regions and the Nordic Transport Policy Network.

The argument for participating in the various networks is partly the opportunity to influence decision-making within the EU and partly to obtain knowledge and information about activities and development tendencies at the European level. The degree of formalization and decision-making structure vary according to the type of network and the focus area.

With the local governments and the Regional Growth Forums, the Region of Southern Denmark contributes to the Southern Denmark European Office which offers international counselling and support for companies and informs them about their possibility of participating in EU projects. The region is represented on the board of the Regional Growth Forums which recommends the regional council for funding. The region has entered into a result-oriented contract with the Southern Denmark European Office, which commits the office to try to involve as many of the region's businesses as possible in EU projects. The development activities related to the office in Brussels are also connected to the business development strategy of the region.

The last of the chosen focus areas is the dissemination of information about the EU. The European Commission has a network of information offices in Denmark – Europe Direct. In the Region of Southern Denmark, the region and county libraries cooperate in three of the cities in the region. The purpose is to supply information about the EU and about initiatives, legislation and opportunities for subsidies.

In addition to the five focus areas mentioned, the internationalization strategy of the region also comprises a number of focus areas primarily targeting development projects and an overall internationalization of the region. Several of the other focus areas mentioned in the strategy are linked in some way to the five core areas.

Conclusions

The international cooperation of the Region of Southern Denmark includes a number of different activities. Some originate from specific problems, such as hospital capacity, whereas others primarily have a developmental aim or focus on informing about international opportunities – especially related to the EU. The strategy of internationalization tries to link the international dimension to the region's main tasks and incorporate it into the strategies within these areas. The most extensive and specific area is, not surprisingly, the activities within the health area, as these are linked to the immediate supply of services to the citizens of the region, but there are also other examples where the international dimension is linked more directly to the main tasks of the region.

What are the future outlooks of the internationalization of Danish regions – lifeline or last rites to unsustainable institutions? In the case of Southern Denmark, many international activities are clearly path-dependent – they represent a continuation of activities initiated by the former counties of which the region was composed. Or the activities have grown out of the needs of the highly specific tasks with which the region is charged; a prime example of this last point is the search for solutions to capacity problems in hospitals in cooperation with hospitals in Germany. These collaborative arrangements mostly take place at the level of technical experts and do not usually involve politicians. Such ventures will probably continue as and when technical needs dictate but do not amount to a lifeline for regional construction as such. However, there are also more overarching, internationally oriented initiatives, such as the adoption of an international strategy seeking to integrate the various task-specific functions of the region. The region also has dedicated personnel for international functions through its European Office, which also includes representation in Brussels. So international activities have, after all, the potential to become a lifeline to the region of Southern Denmark.

Chapter 11

Cultural Policies as Development Strategies in Nordic Regions – A Comparison of Two Projects

Aase Marthe J. Horrigmo

Introduction

This chapter examines the emergence of two initiatives in the field of arts and culture or creative enterprises and their interaction with local and regional politics: the Quart Festival and Film i Väst (FiV).

When the *Quadrardur Musical* was arranged in Kristiansand Square in 1991, few people could have imagined that what was to become Norway's largest rock festival would take place there, perhaps the heart of Norway's Bible Belt; indeed, as late as the 1970s, the city had refused to have even a theatre. Likewise, the industrial town of Trollhättan – famous for SAAB, aircraft engines and the energy company Vattenfall – seemed an unlikely location for great film producers and stars such as Nicole Kidman and Lauren Bacall, yet the town would achieve a solid market share in the Swedish film industry.

American researchers such as Richard Florida and Terry N. Clark have formulated theories on culture and cultural services as a driving force for urban development (Clark 2004a, 2004b, Florida 2002, 2007). The idea of local cultural initiatives as a possible strategy for regional development has not only become a popular research topic; discourse on "culture and industry", as well as the instrumental use of culture, have also become widespread in public administration and politics at all levels: nationally, regionally as well as locally. An example of this may be seen in the White Paper on "Culture and Industry" presented to the Norwegian Parliament in 2005 (White Paper 22 – 2005).

This chapter will focus on local and regional authorities as actors in the new field of cultural policies. By investigating the processes behind the emergence of Film i Väst and the Quart Festival, the chapter will seek to uncover the factors that combined to produce these cultural initiatives in these two rather unlikely settings.

Origins of the Two Initiatives

Film i Väst (FiV)

Sweden's largest contemporary film producer, FiV, is located in Trollhättan. Västernfilm, FiV's predecessor, was established in 1992 as an initiative to stimulate local film activities. Västernfilm was originally situated in the municipality of Alingås, but relocated to Trollhätten in 1996/97. Concurrent with the move, FiV was granted status as a regional resource centre for films and videos, along with seventeen other media establishments in Sweden (Bill Proposition 2005/06: 3). Accordingly, FiV was granted state subsidies for the very first time.

In 1997, FiV started to make feature films, aiming to co-produce four feature films annually. This goal was rapidly achieved. In 1998, the successful film "Fucking Åmål" was released and viewed by 860,000 people in Sweden and over 2.1 million people in Europe (Film database Lumiere). In 1999 another 11 feature films were made with FiV as co-producer. In 2000, FiV was granted status as a regional film-producing centre along with Filmpool Nord and Film i Skåne (Bill Proposition 1998/99: 13). For the very first time, subsidies would be received from the *Svenska Filminstitutet* (The Swedish Film Institute) for feature-film making. Concurrently, international film productions started to be produced at FiV's studio in Trollhätten in 2002, including the film "Dogville" starring actors such as Nicole Kidman and Lauren Bacall. An increasing number of feature films has been produced each year since 2004. The same year, FiV opened Scandinavia's second largest film studio, Studio Fares, built and owned by the municipality of Trollhätten.

Since 1998, FiV has been wholly owned by Region Västra Götaland. With the formation of this region in 1998, FiV went from being under the administration of the Culture Manager at Älvsborg County Council to becoming a limited company under the Regional Council. Their employers and head financiers are both the region's Regional Development Board and Board of Culture.

The Quart Festival

The Quart Festival was launched by the Office of Cultural Affairs in the municipality of Kristiansand in 1992. The festival was held there until its insolvency in 2008.[1] It was based on a youth event arranged during Kristiansand's jubilee (350 years old) in 1991. In 1994, the festival acquired its name, the Quart Festival. This was also the year that the Office of the Director of Culture ceased organizing the festival. The festival attracted 10,000 visitors in 1994 and the rapid growth in audiences made it clear that the municipality did not have the expertise or the capability

---

1   After insolvency in 2008, the Quart Festival's name was bought by local businessmen who arranged a new festival in 2009, which also went bankrupt. This event, however, is not included in the period of study on which this chapter is based.

to arrange another festival of this magnitude. When the municipality withdrew from the festival in 1994, the Quart Festival Foundation was established under the auspices of Kristiansand Music Committee. The festival was awarded an annual subsidy from the municipality of NOK 150,000 each year.

The festival became a success from early on, reflected by the size of the audiences it attracted. Twenty-five thousand people were registered at the event in 1996 and by 2002, 79,000 visitors attended (Danielsen et al. 2005). Quart had become the largest festival in Norway.

The driving force behind the festival and its manager, Toffen Gunnufsen, resigned in the autumn of 2006 to become involved in starting a new festival in the region. At this point, the festival had already been struggling financially for a number of years with losses in their millions. However, with financial support from the municipality, the bankruptcy court was avoided. Nevertheless, in the autumn of 2007 the festival had a deficit of approximately NOK 16 million and in June 2008 the festival was declared bankrupt.

Culture and Regional Politics – A Theoretical Background

A new type of regionalism has evolved in Europe (Keating 1997, 2002). Whereas regional policy previously focused on the redistribution of resources from financially strong regions to weaker ones (Keating 1997), regional competitive power is now the objective (Pastor, Lester and Scoggins 2009). Regional and local leaders increasingly seek to connect their regions to the global economy by developing their comparative advantage (Clarke and Gaile 1998).This leads to the state being pressured from below; from regions that want to take over tasks linked to regional development with the state functioning as a facilitator (ibid.). The result is a new territorial dimension in national politics with regions functioning as political entities in an area that was previously reserved for the state (Keating 1997, Keating 2002). These tendencies are also prevalent in Norway and Sweden. This trend has later been additionally emphasized in national discussions of the role of county councils as an economic development entity and entrepreneur (White Paper No. 12 2006–07). In Sweden, the *Landstingsforbundet* (The Swedish Association of Local Authorities and Regions) has demanded increased autonomy in such areas as business and industrial policy, in addition to cultural policy (Blomgren 2007: 84). Regarding cultural policy, it was argued that this should not be defined as an independent arts policy, but as part of the regional development policy (ibid.). But why is this relevant to studies such as this?

Research into the regional development issues has increasingly incorporated what Clarke and Gaile (1998) term innovation policy. An example of this is an increased emphasis on cultural policy as a method for city and regional development. The idea of culture as a regional driving force attracted many followers after Florida's (2002) book, *The Rise of the Creative Class*, was published. He pointed out that culture and "organic and indigenous street-level culture" (2002: 182) were vital factors for a region that wanted to attract creative and knowledgeable workers – the so-called creative class. According to Florida (2002, 2007), this class is crucial to regions that want to increase their competitive power.

Clark (2004) has taken this idea further. He argues that the traditional growth models, which understand culture as a subordinate explanation of the localization of production and work, are incorrect, and that the cause and effect relationship should be reversed: "… consumption, amenities, and culture [should be recognized] as drivers of urban policy" (Clark 2004: 2). The reason for the argument is that cultural services help attract human capital necessary for economic growth. This entails local and regional public entities being able to create a role for themselves not just as development entities, but as supportive collaborators for an active cultural policy beyond the activity that is required by the state, for example, schools of culture and libraries.

How is a Policy Window Created?

Using new regionalism as a point of departure, this chapter will apply Kingdon's (1995) theory on decision-making processes to establish a theoretical framework to explain the emergence of the two cases studied here. Kingdon describes decisions as the result of the coupling between three streams: problems, policies or solutions and politics. The first stream, problems or problem recognition, deals with policy problems which a decision maker or a number of decision makers want to solve. The second stream concerns policy or solutions. In this context, Kingdon (1995: 87) identifies various policy communities or networks comprising specialists in fields such as bureaucracy, planning, academia and interest groups, who generate solutions to policy problems. The third stream focuses on politics and incorporates the changes in political alignments, interest group campaigns, election results and changes in administration.

The coupling of the various streams is a decisive factor in decision-making. The coupling occurs when a policy window or window of opportunity opens. A policy window represents "… an opportunity for advocates of proposals to push their pet solutions, or to push attention to their special problems" (Kingdon 1995: 165). A window opens and remains open for short periods of time and represents the opportunity to act so that an area of policy can be added to the agenda of decisions. However, even if a window opens, it cannot be taken for granted that a decision or choice of policy will be the outcome. But the likelihood of a decision being made increases if all the three streams can be coupled together.

> … the key to understanding agenda and policy change is their coupling: The separate streams come together at critical times. A problem is recognized, a solution is available, the political climate makes the time right for change, and the constraints do not prohibit actions. (Kingdon 1995: 88)

Policy entrepreneurs are crucial in order to understand how the three streams are coupled together. Policy entrepreneurs are advocates of certain solutions who are willing to invest time, their reputation and money in the hope of profiting from the investment in the future (1995: 122). Policy entrepreneurs are often campaigners for a pet solution in addition to "being power brokers and manipulators of problematic preferences and unclear technology" (Zahariadis 2007: 74). Kingdon points out how an entrepreneur works:

> If a policy entrepreneur is attaching a proposal to a change in the political stream, for example, a problem is also found for which the proposal is a solution, thus linking problem, policy, and politics. (Kingdon 1995: 182)

By following their own favourite solutions, the role of the entrepreneurs is to function as the "couplers" of the various streams so that not only the problem and solution fit together, but so the coupling also finds support in the political stream.

If Kingdon's model describes these policy processes, a policy window should be identifiable. But what created this policy window? The aim is to examine and identify which factors helped create a policy window for the cultural initiatives studied here. To identify policy windows, the chapter discusses three possible approaches. First, the chapter will examine the extent to which local conditions or challenges within the music/film community have been significant. Second, the roles of the municipal and county councils will be investigated; or more specifically, did public planning create a policy window? The third question is which role enthusiasts or policy entrepreneurs played in establishing this type of enterprise.

Case Selection, Design and Methodological Reflection

The approach selected is process tracing (George and Bennet 2005, Gerring 2007), which reconstructs the causal process which has occurred in a given context (Gerring 2007: 216). Process tracing means that different types of evidence have been used to support conclusions deduced from the material (Gerring 2007: 173). Furthermore, a process study involves examining the political and administrative processes which led to the formation of the two cases in order to identify critical junctions (Gerring 2007) or the events that were critical for the process. This makes the method particularly suitable since it corresponds well with the understanding of political decisions that Kingdon (1995) represents. His multiple streams framework stresses the importance of critical points or policy windows for the formation of a policy or modifications to an existing one. This means that identifying critical junctions will be tantamount to discovering a policy window.

Process tracing is combined here with a comparative or multi-case approach (Yin 2003), where the objective is to compare and examine which of the three factors above has been the most significant in creating a policy window. This involves comparing the three factors both within each case study and between the two cases.

The two cultural phenomena examined here have been selected based on their sharing a number of similarities in background variables, and because they were formed at the same time. The launches of the Quart Festival and Film i Väst took place in 1991, and in 1992 both were established within the framework of the Municipal Office of Cultural Affairs.

Driving Forces Behind the Processes

The following sections will try to identify the central driving forces behind the two processes which led to the formation of Film i Väst and the Quart Festival to explain why these undertakings emerged.

Film i Väst

Local Facilities for Film Production? FiV, at that time called Västernfilm, was started under the management of the Älvsborg Regional Office of Cultural Affairs. FiV was a cultural policy measure. But why did the County Council start this measure? Did local conditions create a policy window for creating films?

When Västernfilm was formed early in the 1990s, it was a limited expense for the County Council. The media workshop was allocated SEK 100,000 to offer children and young people a facility to create something of their own related to films and television. A project manager was employed to assist in building up and maintaining a network linked to film making.

Film and television, which had not previously drawn the County Council's attention, appeared on the agenda when the County Council drew up a report focused on "new media". The report showed that the policy of the County Council was inadequate in this field and that there was a need to help make children and young people conscious of their relation to this media group. In addition, the development programme highlighted the County Council's lack of provision of facilities for children and young people to experiment and work creatively within film and television. At the same time, an evaluation of the County Council's cultural projects stated that knowledge that had been developed through earlier projects was not maintained by the organizations. The combination of these two factors led to the establishment of several media workshops in the region. The County Council decided to become a partner to Alingsås Media Workshop to support the further development of the workshop as a resource centre which could support the other media workshops. Tomas Ekilsson, who had headed the study, became project manager. The objective of the initiative was to offer a service to children and young people related to films and television.

However, rather than being a local resource pool for the subsequent launching of Västernfilm, Alingsås Media Workshop served to highlight the lack of local film-making resources, a gap which the county council's cultural office decided to fill.

Policy Windows Created by Public Planning?

The Region and the County Councils   Early in the 1990s when commitment to film creation was in the start-up phase, the County Council had no ambition to become one of Sweden's principal film producers. At this time, the County Council mainly talked of supporting pure art and culture (interview Quentzer 2009, Eskilsson 2008), and the role of films was to help make children and young people conscious of the new types of mass media. From the start, Älvsborg County took on the role of financier, but during the first year Bohus County also became a financier. From 1997, when FiV was awarded status as a regional resource centre for films, the County Council and later the Region, were obliged to support FiV financially. However, Blomgren and Blomgren (2003) show that the regional subsidy to FiV has substantially exceeded the requirements that accompanied participation in the network of the regional resource centre (Blomgren and Blomgren 2003: 11).

The size of the subsidy granted to FiV must be seen in connection with the County Council's gradual increase of its ambitions in industry and business policy. This could be seen for the first time when the County Council, along with FiV and the municipality of Trollhättan, applied to Fyrstad's Chancellery for money from the EU Structure Fund (Pettersen 1996). During the ensuing processes which involved forming a new region,[2] it became clear to the Region's management that FiV and film production could be a project used to profile a new region. This led to FiV also receiving financial support from the Regional Development Board. This shared financing has continued and in 2008 the Board of Culture awarded SEK 40 million and the Regional Development Board SEK 21 million. The division of finances has affected the assignments of FiV from Västra Götaland County. It is stressed that FiV "… shall in collaboration with industry and commerce participate in national and international networks on knowledge and competence development, as well as innovation and entrepreneurship to strengthen the competitiveness of the region's audio-visual sector" (assignment commissioned to Film i Väst 2009–11).

FiV has been a public undertaking from the very beginning, but for various reasons and with differing formats. The regional level has been an active collaborator, primarily the County Council at first, thereafter Västra Götaland Region, as owner, financier and employer. The reason why FiV is supported financially and gets assignments from the public authorities at the same time has changed in line its growth. At the beginning, Västernfilm's assignments were limited to working with children and young people, and the reason for this was

---

2   The new region of Vestra Götaland was formed in 1999 comprising the former county councils of Älvsborg, Skaraborg and Bohus and the City of Gothenburg.

linked to culture. When FiV wanted to produce films, the opportunity to create employment and have a policy on industry and commerce was stressed. This was linked to the area's EU funding being tied to the one-sided industrial structure of the region, but this type of argument was maintained even after the EU Structure Fund was no longer relevant. In this way, the contours of a policy window linked to the EU Structure Fund emerge.

At the same time, it is clear that FiV was part of a larger commitment to culture by Västra Götaland County. The region's subsidies for culture per citizen is double that of the national average of all the Swedish county councils and regions (The Culture Committee 2008): large sums of money are allocated to three central institutions in particular: Gothenburg Opera House, the Symphony Orchestra and Film i Väst.

The Municipality – Trollhättan as Facilitator   Trollhättan's committment to FiV dates back to 1995 when it participated in the application process for subsidies from the EU Structure Fund (Pettersson 1996). At that time, the large industrial companies in the city were experiencing hard times and unemployment was high. The administration of Trollhättan was thus open to new strategies and opportunities. For FiV this meant having an active municipal counterpart, something which according to FiV's management had not existed in the municipality of Alingsås, their previous location. When Västernfilm was formed, the municipality of Trollhättan had shown an interest in the media workshop and tried to have it located in the municipality, but without success. At the same time, a move to Trollhättan would enable FiV to apply for grants from the EU Structure Fund.

The municipality has also performed as a facilitator for film production. For example, granting permission to cordon off a street to film a scene was no trouble for the municipality, while the fire service would turn up to use its hoses to produce the effect of rain if needed. This attitude towards filming is also found in political circles in Trollhättan. Ordinary people, too, have on the whole been extremely positive towards FiV: "People are proud" was the usual comment made in interviews to explain why the citizens of Trollhättan were positive about supporting FiV.[3]

An examination of the municipality's role in relation to FiV indicates that Trollhättan chose to become involved in FiV for different reasons than the Region. While FiV has been a cultural commitment for the Region, for the municipality it has also involved a commitment to policy on industry and commerce with the aim of reducing high unemployment. In addition, FiV and film production are seen

---

3   The neighbouring municipality, Uddevalla, financially supported FiV earlier; however, this support was contested by one individual claiming that it was in breach of the Municipal Act. The complainant won. The same person also brought the region before the County Administrative Court for breaching the Municipal Act regarding support to FiV; however, the region won the case. As a result, Uddevalla stopped contributing money for a few years, but in 2008 it resumed its role as a provider of financial support.

as significant in establishing Trollhättan as a trademark (interview, Fredriksson 2009, Eksilsson 2008, Wennerblom 2008), although this was not a crucial factor in initiating a partnership with FiV back in the 1990s. The municipality of Trollhättan's vision for the future remains to be the further development of the city as a "leading technical and industrial municipality in Europe" (interview Andersson 2008). However, in this vision FiV is seen as receiving less business commitment from the municipality.

External Public Funding

The Region, the municipality of Trollhättan and three other municipalities provide financial support to FiV today. One event in particular triggered this support. The contours of a policy window appeared when Sweden became a member of the EU in January 1995. At this time, Sweden was experiencing an economic downturn and the areas of Trollhättan, Uddevalla, Vänersborg and Lysekil were severely affected. This area, called Fyrstad, had such high unemployment that it was classed as an objective-two area, thus it had the opportunity to apply for grants from the EU Structure Fund as a measure to change a one-sided business structure, as well as to increase the number of new enterprises formed (Brown 2000, www. ec.europa.eu). The objective-two programme was linked to the development of industry and commerce policy, not cultural policy. However, FiV was awarded over SEK 90 million from the EU fund between 1997 and 2005. How could a media workshop be granted such an amount?

In 1993, FiV started mapping the professional opportunities available in the area to produce films (Blomgren 2007: 67). The money from the EU had made this possible. From working primarily with children and young people, the organization was now going to create feature films, something which required a large staff and support network. This vision helped "sell in" a solution to help alleviate Fyrstad's hard times.

The economic downturn made it possible to get money, but to defend culture as a solution, the proposal needed to be linked to a policy on industry and commerce and employment. Tomas Eskilsson, FiV's Director, was a leading figure in this process. Along with other film collaborators, he wrote an article in the newspaper *Göteborgsposten* in 1996 in which he claimed: "Moreover, film production is the most important tool in developing the media industry in a region. Hence, a commitment to films is a crucial tool for increased employment" (Eskilsson et al. 1996, quote in Blomgren 2007: 69). This understanding of the way in which films could be a medium for industry and commerce policy formed the basis for the application to the Fyrstad Chancellery for structure fund grants, which was signed by FiV, the municipality of Trollhättan and Älvsborg County Administrative Court in 1996. Fyrstad Chancellery accepted the argument and granted subsidies to the project.

The original idea behind FiV, an emphasis on children and young people, was toned down in the application. Instead, the three applicants outlined the opportunities implied by a commitment to feature films and building up a skills centre in Trollhättan. These would be steps in establishing a "West Swedish film centre in Fyrstad" (Blomgren 2007, Dahlström et al. 2005, Pettersson 1996). It was stated that: "... by developing a film industry, the structure of industry and commerce in Fyrstad will be boosted. At the same time, the cultural structure of West Sweden will be strengthened" (Pettersson 1996: 1). The order of argumentation can be found in FiV's application to the same secretariat in 2000, when the objective of the project was to build an internationally strong film and media industry cluster (Film i Väst 2000). FiV's role as a cultural project did not, however, disappear completely, but was used instrumentally.

EU membership made the influx of "fresh money" from outside possible. At the same time, a requirement for receiving grants from the Structural Fund was that the Fund's share would amount to 16 per cent of the total support, and the regional and local partners would contribute the remainder of the funding. Payments to FiV from the County Council exceeded what the Structural Fund demanded in financial support (Blomgren and Blomgren 2003). This focus on film as an alternative business strategy fitted the Structural Fund's objective to increase the number of new enterprises formed in the area.

Policy Entrepreneur and Network Building

The process surrounding the structural fund application gives the impression that Eskilsson was a central collaborator in the coupling of film production and industrial and commercial policy. By referring to events in Europe, he helped establish an understanding that film production could be a means of regional development. His central role is underlined by all informants.

FiV worked actively to anchor the project in both the municipality and county and later in Region Västra Götaland. Eskilsson carried out this process with FiV's Financial Director among others, by standing up for FiV in communication with regional and local politicians. Early in the 1990s they travelled around and presented the project and their ambitions for FiV to different interest groups. FiV's strategy concerning the County and Region was based on broad argumentation, which could seem credible to both the right- and left-wing parties in regional politics. This was seen as a sound strategy in a county where the political majority was often replaced.

The promotional efforts continued after the 1990s and acquired renewed significance when Region Västra Götaland was formed by the three county councils of Älvsborg, Skaraborg and Bohus towards the end of the 1990s. According to Eskilsson, FiV had "the big EU money" during this period with SEK 18 million in annual subsidies from the Objective Two Secretariat. This provided the organization with a breathing space in which it could ensure its future existence by boosting human relations in the new region.

Although Eskilsson was the brains behind the coupling of films and industrial and commercial policy, he did not work alone. The importance of human relations was already present in the process involving EU money. Fyrstad Chancellery, which administered the money, was split regarding how positive it was to film production. But the highest political leader, Jonny Nilsson, supported Eskilsson's idea and this had consequences for Fyrstad Chancellery. This combination of support, not only from the County Council's management, but also from the cultural sector, and along with the minor ambitions present from the outset, formed the basis on which EU money was granted to FiV. And this allocation of money made it possible for FiV to continue anchoring its activities by building networks within the different levels of management, as well as among the region's inhabitants.

National Hindsight?

Up until the 1990s, financial support for feature-film production in Sweden was a national responsibility regulated by Swedish film agreements. The established network of agreements did not provide funding to regional film production and the majority of Swedish films were produced in the Stockholm area (Blomgren 2007). SOU (1995: 84) "Ny svensk filmpolitik" (National Public Report "New Swedish Film Policy") suggested for the first time offering financial support to the regional resource centre for films and videos. This status was awarded to FiV in 1997 and 17 other similar enterprises (Bill Proposition 2005/06: 3), but was accompanied by a reduction in subsidies (Bill Proposition 2005/06: 3). However, the national funding precipitated the granting of regional subsidies that at least equalled the amount issued by the state. The financial resources released could not be used for feature-film production. However, under certain circumstances, they could be used to produce documentaries and short films (Bill Proposition 1998/99: 131, p. 28).

This changed in 2000. SOU (1998: 142) (Swedish National Public Report) had already stated that in practice some regional production centres existed. In a proposal for a new film agreement for the year 2000, financial support for the regional production centres was proposed for the very first time. Grants amounting to SEK 3 million apportioned between Filmpool Nord, Film i Skåne and Film i Väst (Prop. 1998/99: 131) were awarded to the three regional enterprises that had already achieved some success. The awarding of grants marked a turning point in the way film production was looked upon in Sweden from a national and regional political point of view. In addition, films went from being a purely cultural affair and were supplemented with ambitions within industrial and commercial policy:

> The commitment to regional resource centres has also involved larger regional engagement for films as art and as a growth industry, which is presented in the regional development agreement that will be submitted to the government in April 1999. Several counties view regional film enterprise as a crucial factor in employment and growth. (Prop. 1998/99: 131 p. 28)

This change, however, has not been crucial to FiV's success. The wave of regionalism in Swedish film-making which FiV, Filmpool Nord and Film i Skåne represent, started before these changes at government level took place. FiV and Filmpool Nord had already started making feature films when they became regional resource centres and had already completed a number of successful projects when they received government subsidies for feature films in 2000. This is supported by Blomgren (2007) who understands national changes as a response to the film industry almost regionalizing itself on its own through regional, local and European subsidies.

The Quart Festival

Local Facilities for a Music Festival?

At the beginning of the 1990s, *Kristiansand Rockklubb* was the largest rock club in Norway and the initiative behind many concerts in Kristiansand. The city had good venues and an active concert-going audience, which made Kristiansand an important place to perform at this time (Brekke and Nordgård 2005: 77).

At the same time, however, the belief was prevalent at the Office of Cultural Affairs in the city that the municipality did not offer a proper service to those who were no longer children or teenagers or to people who did not benefit from the municipality's cultural services at that time, such as the symphony orchestra or Agder Theatre. In the autumn of 1990, the Office of Cultural Affairs employed a new Manager of Culture, who later became Director of Culture, and Toffen Gunnufsen as Cultural Executive. The same year, and for the very first time, the municipal departments were to draw up their own action plans as part of the introduction of a Goals and Results Management Programme in the municipal sector. During this work on the action plans, the idea of starting a festival was aired by several parties. When Kristiansand celebrated 350 years as a city in 1991, the idea was presented. The city jubilee did not have any events for young adults, and a festival targeting this group would compensate for this. The result was a festival in the city square for teenagers and young adults. During the planning stages of the festival, the municipal representatives visited *Kristiansand Rockklubb* to ask for some assistance, since this milieu was very large and vital to the festival. The club did not arrange the event on their own, but as collaboration between the Director of Culture's Office and the rock club (Strandberg et al. 2003, Danielsen et al. 2005). Thus, the municipality became responsible for arranging the concert whilst *Kristiansand Rockklubb* supplied people and equipment. This was the dawning of the Quart festival. The origin of the festival was formed as a supplement to a well-established local series of events. The start-up was also eased by the existence of a market for that type of music.

A Policy Window Created by Public Planning? The Role of the Municipality.

The pre-existing local facilities and services at *Kristiansand Rockklubb* were inadequate to start such marketing on their own, so the municipality of Kristiansand intervened. The role of the municipality has taken many forms, but can primarily be regarded as comprising two phases with different collaborators as the operators.

Phase one is linked to the establishment of the festival. At that time, it was widely believed by the political and the administrative management that the cultural services in Kristiansand was unsatisfactory and underdeveloped compared to the rest of the country. According to the political and administrative leaders, this made the city eager to increase the focus on culture. The primary factor in the first phase was the municipality's role as operator and owner of the festival, with the Director of Culture's Office as the central municipal entity. The principal goal of the municipality's involvement in the festival was an ambition to develop the city into a festival city, something which was concretized in the action plans for culture in the 1990s. This was supplemented with the idea that teenagers as a group should participate in the cultural life of the city, in addition to a desire to boost the existing rock environment in the city.

This phase came to an end after the festival in 1994 was held. The 1994 festival sold 10,000 tickets in all, but had ended up with a huge deficit and it was clear that the municipality did not have the capacity to arrange a festival of this magnitude. As a result, the festival was turned into a foundation from 1995 with *Kristiansand Musikkråd* (Kristiansand Music Committee) as the founder with the symbolic start capital of NOK 5000. The municipality transferred all rights associated with the festival to the foundation.

From 1995 onwards, the municipality of Kristiansand was no longer the owner of the festival although its association with it was not entirely terminated. First, the salary of the festival's Arts Manager, Toffen Gunnufsen, came from the municipality's budget for the first seven months of 1995. Second, the municipality retained its vision to develop Kristiansand into a festival city and the festival was placed in the culture budget to receive approximately NOK 160,000 in annual subsidies. Third, two municipal staff members were relieved of their regular duties to work on the festival when it was actually being held.

The next phase started in around 2003 after the Quart Festival had received a large amount of coverage in the newspaper *Dagbladet* in the summer, and the Office of Cultural Affairs was asked to assist in an investigation of the festival's organization. This resulted in a total reorganization of the festival and agreements with the suborganizations of the Quart Festival were terminated. The composition of the Board was also changed. No municipal representatives had been on the Board (Strandberg et al. 2003) until 2003, but from 2004 onwards, the municipality appointed several representatives to sit on the Board (Case Records Nomination and Remuneration Committee 27.10.04). The reason for appointing the board members was that the festival had fallen into financial despair after the

2004 festival had resulted in losses and the municipality paid NOK 3.7 million to support the festival (Case Records City Council Meeting 13.10.04). The reinstatement of the municipality's role as an active festival collaborator created an uproar in the festival organization, because some board members believed that the municipality was interfering inappropriately with the festival's business operations based on just a few incidents (Steen 2004).

The function of the municipality in this phase was to act as a guarantor for the debts incurred and assist with money towards a festival that at times faced great financial difficulties. The principal collaborators in this phase were first and foremost the political milieu and the Head of Administration and his staff, since the financial support that was granted to the festival was primarily awarded by the City Council and not from the usual budgets for the cultural sector. During this phase, the municipality of Kristiansand maintained its role as a facilitator associated with the infrastructure of the festival. In 2007, the Odderøya Amfi venue was completed, an outdoor concert stage with space for over 20,000 spectators.

As well as funding the festival through the City Council, the municipality of Kristiansand issued subsidies through two other organizations: the Cultiva Foundation, founded by the municipality to support art, culture and knowledge institutions in Kristiansand (www.cultiva.no/vedtekter) allocated NOK 17 million to the festival, and *Kristiansand Næringsselskap* (KNAS), which allocated 5.5 million. Up to 2007, the municipality has contributed over 31 million to the Quart Festival (City Council, Case No. 184/07).[4]

The financial contributions to the festival differed in the two phases. The earlier phase included a number of expenses linked to the festival, but it was first and foremost only after 2003 that the municipality allocated large sums to the festival. In the second phase, the idea of further developing Kristiansand into a city of culture became more vivid. However, this goal to create an image was supplemented by the term "industry and culture" as well as financial arguments. Wordings touching on employment and industry and commerce as areas of commitment within culture can be traced back to the Action Programme of the City of Kristiansand for the period 1993–96. One of the objectives of the programme was to help bring visitors to the city through events and festivals. This line of thought can be found in the Head of Administration's approach to the City Council concerning subsidies for the festival, in 2004:

> The Quart Festival is crucial to Kristiansand and Southern Norway when it comes to culture, finances, and its reputation at home and abroad ... It can be estimated that 20,000 visitors spend approx. 60 million kroner during the festival. The Quart Festival is therefore one of the strongest trademarks Kristiansand can offer. (Kristiansand City Council, Case No. 81/04)

---

4   The Festival produced a financial surplus most years, but had a deficit in 1996, 1997, 2003 and 2004 before it went bankrupt in 2007.

The quote indicates that the financial support to the Quart Festival was no longer based on providing culture to teenagers and young adults. On the contrary, financial profit and the building of a trademark are emphasized here. This suggests that what was originally a cultural measure had now become linked to Kristiansand's industrial and commercial policy.

Policy Entrepreneur and Network Building?

"But Toffen is the Quart Festival …", commented Håkon Moslet, Head of Music on the radio channel P3 when it was announced that Toffen Gunnufsen, the Festival Manager of the Quart at that time, was to resign (Olsbu 2006). This image of Gunnefsen is shared by the informants included in this study. In addition to his musical knowledge, Gunnufsen had remarkable communication skills. A previous municipal Head of Administration expressed it thus: "And we had, of course, Toffen's fantastic ability to communicate with everyone. He certainly had a countenance that could melt even supporters of KRF (The Norwegian Christian Democratic Party)".

Gunnufsen did not work independently on the Quart Festival. From the outset, he was well supported by the Director of Culture in Kristiansand and the Office of Cultural Affairs in general. This support continued after the festival became an independent foundation, because the festival meant so much to the staff at the Office of Cultural Affairs who had been involved since the beginning of the festival. As the festival became more professional, this collaboration was reduced, but the dialogue between the Quart Festival and the Director of Culture's Office was more tightly knitted than with the other collaborators.

Views of the festival were split in the political milieu and, in this regard, support from the mayor was very significant, according to a former municipal Head of Administration. On the Council Committee, as on the City Council, there was always disagreement about questions surrounding the Quart Festival. The Conservative and Labour parties both supported the festival, whilst the Christian Democratic Party and the Progressive Party opposed support to the festival. A former Head of the municipal administration attributes the support from the Conservative Party to the mayor:

> The crucial factor for the Quart Festival's survival in its first few years, one can say that without Toffen there would be no Quart and that Dagny was good support for Toffen, but the crucial factor for the survival of Quart was that we had a Mayor who had been Deputy Head at the lower secondary school and who was also a Conservative. If anyone else from the Conservative Party had been Mayor, the Quart would have died in the early days.

The mayor at that time also pointed out the significance of the political and administrative management agreeing on the continuation of the festival, even though it struggled financially at the beginning: "Many people wanted to close it down, but many people knew that this could turn into something". The role of the mayor as a supportive person was mentioned by all the informants. Gunnufsen, the Festival Manager, pointed out that the changes in the political and administrative management, with the hiring of a new Head of Administration and a Culture Manager, and the election of a new mayor, that occurred in the 1990s benefited the festival.

A new mayor was appointed after 2003 in Kristiansand, this time from the Christian Democratic, Party; at about the same time, a new municipal Head of Administration was employed. The financial support awarded to the festival at this time increased since the festival went through several financial crises from 2003 until its bankruptcy in 2008. The Quart Festival and Gunnufsen nevertheless felt that the new political management was less supportive than the previous one. At the same time, the former mayor said that she was not the only mayor who had supported the festival:[5] "My role was to be there when things got stuck, to try to find solutions ... Other mayors did this too".

External Opportunities? The Window that Slipped Away?

Despite the municipality investing relatively large amounts of money in the festival towards the end of its life, it could not prevent the festival closing down. But did other financial opportunities exist for the Quart Festival beyond the municipality of Kristiansand?

The festival received annual subsidies from the Norwegian Cultural Council, but this money ceased after 2004. Nevertheless, two other financial policy windows were evident to the Quart Festival at this time, but they had different outcomes. Locally, the Cultiva foundation was formed to help secure jobs and a good standard of living in Kristiansand by supporting the establishment of art, culture and knowledge institutions (www.cultiva.no/om). Cultiva was formed by the municipality and it quickly became one of the Quart Festival's most important financial contributors. This new financial channel came at a time when the festival was struggling with losses. The result for the festival in 2003 was a deficit of NOK 1.2 million and the year after NOK 1.5 million. Cultiva alone contributed NOK 5 million to the Quart Festival (Cultiva Records 2003). From 2003 to 2007, the foundation allocated over 17 million to the festival, but the money was not enough to pay creditors, with the exception of the support in 2006 to boost the equity in Quart (Cultiva Records 2007). As such, this was how Cultiva helped prevent the festival going bankrupt prior to 2008, but the festival was still not able to function independently.

---

5   During the Quart Festival's lifetime, Kristiansand had four mayors. Paul Otto Johnsen (Conservative) was mayor until 1991. From 1991 until 2003 Bjørg Wallevik (Conservative) was Mayor. Her successor was Jan Oddvar Skisland (Norwegian Christian Democratic Party) whose successor was Per Sigurd Sørensen (Conservative) in 2007.

Nationally, fresh opportunities for financial support appeared in the 2007 budget, presented by the Ministry of Culture and Church Affairs (Parliamentary Bill 1 2006–07). The budget had an entry for *knutepunktstatus* (music hub status) as a rock festival. *Knutepunktstatus* implies recognition as a festival that has a leading position within its genre, and with a high standard of musical expertise and knowledge of developments within its field (White paper No. 10 2007–08). Perhaps more important than actual recognition was that *knutepunktstatus* implied permanent state subsidies provided the local and regional authorities matched these amounts. In 2006, the Quart Festival applied for such status; the municipality and the county council were guarantors for regional subsidies within a total financial framework of NOK 5 million in combined public authority subsidies, to be shared between the government and the regional and municipal authorities (Vest Agder County, Meeting Records 2006). However, the Quart Festival was not granted such status and instead the Øya Festival in Oslo became the music hub for rock festivals in Norway.

Film I Väst vs the Quart Festival – What Can be Learnt from the Two Cases?

The two processes studied demonstrate a number of similar characteristics in their emergence as two expressions of cultural policy. Both started internally within the county and municipality respectively, with some members of staff as the driving force. The processes also show that after some years of operation, they transformed considerably in their organization, budgets and scope.

Local facilities have played different roles in the two cases. In Kristiansand, an active music milieu already existed which the municipality was able to build on in its desire to start a festival. Despite this milieu, there was a widespread belief that "young adults" did not receive satisfactory services from the municipality. Both the former mayor and the former municipal Head of Administration stressed the lack of cultural services in Kristiansand as a way to motivate more spending on culture. In light of a pre-existing and well functioning rock milieu in the city, it is interesting that the lack of services was stressed. The lack of services for children and young people was also central in the creation of Film i Väst. The County did not have a definite policy on new media, especially for children and young people. Additionally, no active film or television milieu existed in the area. At the same time, this was a period when media workshops were growing under the auspices of municipalities and counties throughout Sweden. In both cases, the involvement of the public authorities during the start-up phases was driven by an understanding that the lack of services from the county and municipality was problematic, and the two enterprises represented an attempt to expand local and regional cultural policy. Put in a context where culture during the same period of time was also seen as a development strategy, (Florida 2002, 2007, Clark 2004) a policy expansion was not unexpected. FiV and other regional film production centres in Sweden have, through their growth, contributed to changing the government's film policy in favour of a regionalized model, with the majority of Swedish films now produced outside Stockholm. This is in line with observations made by Keating (2002) and Clarke and Gaile (1998).

Public authorities such as the respective municipalities and counties were central agents in the start-up phases of FiV and the Quart Festival. In both cases, the administrative organizations of the public entities were responsible for the idea, for the implementation and completion of the undertakings, but supported by the political milieu, particularly the top political level. The support from the political milieu is clearly seen in the case of FiV. When they started making plans to produce films, a strong partner was found in the political leaders of the region. And the support from both the municipality of Trollhättan and Älvsborg County Council, as well as Region Västra Götaland, has been strong throughout the period. The political picture is more complex in Kristiansand. The political majority has supported the festival throughout, including the political leadership. However, the City Council has been divided in its support. The interviews in Kristiansand emphasized the conflict and disagreement surrounding the Quart Festival; however, in Region Västra Götaland and the municipality of Trollhättan conflict and disagreement were not mentioned; on the contrary, agreement and support for subsidies for FiV was communicated. However, the financial subsidies from Region Västra Götaland and the municipality of Uddevalla have still been the subject of judicial review following protests by citizens.

Both cases show that local enthusiasts have been crucial. FiV had Tomas Eskilsson and the Quart Festival Toffen Gunnufsen. These two have been central driving forces behind the implementation and further operation of the two phenomena. FiV's manager has excelled as a primary coupler and policy entrepreneur ahead of FiV's commitment to producing films, but also in promoting FiV to the political and administrative sections of Region Västra Götaland, when the Region being established. During the onset of film production, he was a key figure in selling the idea of linking industrial and commercial ambitions to film production and thereby created an opportunity for FiV to apply for grants from the EU Structure Fund. The Quart Festival's musical manager of many years has been vital in selling the festival to the political leadership in the municipality of Kristiansand. His success, however, has not equalled Eskilsson's when measured in financial support, but this is also linked to the Quart Festival gradually reducing its association with the municipality.

The two enthusiasts have not worked alone in promoting their organizations. The study shows that the two processes have been assisted by a number of supportive people. In Kristiansand the municipal cultural sector was a clear supporter, but the Head of Administration and the mayor recognized the value of the Quart Festival and wanted to help the festival further. Also in the case of FiV, it is evident that in addition to a visible front figure, there has been a network of politicians and administrative employees who have been advocates of the idea of film production in the region. A former Governor of Älvsborg is one of these, but also the former Manager of Culture in Älvsborg and Region Västra Götaland, the Regional Council and Regional Culture Council have all been important collaborators.

The different contexts have provided contrasting outcomes. FiV's financial frameworks have throughout been more predictable than the Quart Festival's. Except for the first few years when the festival was under municipal control, the Quart Festival has received NOK 160,000 in annual subsidies from the municipality and some subsidies from the County Council, in addition to money from the state via the Norwegian Culture Council. In comparison, FiV has received SEK 2.5 million annually since 1996 from one municipality alone, as well as funding from the Structure Fund, regional funding, state funding and contributions from other municipalities. This has helped FiV to have an immense commitment to producing feature films, while taking risks and forming bonds with new and unknown film directors. The Quart Festival has depended on good weather each July to secure further income from high sales of tickets and drinks. Some years have produced poor ticket sales, with bad weather leading to financial loss, which a festival with 5,000 kroner in equity has been unable to tackle. FiV, on the other hand, has handled the fluctuations in audience attendance of their productions with the large sums of public money guaranteeing the bottom line.

FiV experienced a significant policy window when Sweden became a member of the EU and the collaborators involved were able to take advantage of this opportunity. After the Norwegian referendum of 1994 that rejected EU membership there was, of course, no EU window for Norwegian regions and municipalities. However, Kristiansand and the Quart Festival also had less success in obtaining national funding and the festival was increasingly cut loose by the city administration. This difference highlights Tomas Eskilsson's capacity as an operator: his coupling of acultural initiative with industrial development schemes makes him emerge as a successful policy entrepreneur. Toffen Gunnufsen at the Quart Festival, however, was much lauded as musically skilled and a good communicator, but he does not demonstrate as much success as a "coupler". The process surrounding the Quart Festival also shows that the festival was dependent on certain types of people since the festival went through hard times when Gunnufsen left the festival. FiV, unlike the Quart Festival, has become more institutionalized, employs more staff and has a stabile organization with a clear internal division of work. This makes the organization less dependent on specific persons although Eskilsson is also considered a principal figure in the roles that FiV will play in the future.

What can be learnt from these two cases? First, the comparison shows that good local start-up resources do not necessarily lead to success. Second, enthusiastic individuals have played crucial roles. However, the role of enthusiastic individuals is played out through policy networks (Marsh and Rhodes 1992) that provide political and financial support. External events (EU membership) have been very significant in creating policy windows in the Swedish case, although the application as such was the result of local and regional public planning and coalition building.

A network of supportive people is also evident in Kristiansand, but they did not succeed in generating the type of support that FiV received.

Sources

Public Documents

Cultiva, Protokoll styremøte (Board Meeting Records) 16 December 2003.
Cultiva, Protokoll styremøte (Board Meeting Records) 6 November 2007.
Danielsen, Aage, Kallevik, T., Finsnes, E. and Kvanes, A. (2005) "Arbeidsgruppa for vurdering av organisasjonsmodell for Quart Festivalen m.v." (Working group for the evaluation of the organisation model for the Quart Festival, etc.).
European Commission "Sweden Fyrstad Objective 2" Sheet N° 95.15.13.005. Available at (July 2009): http://ec.europa.eu/regional_policy/reg_prog/po/prog_343.htm.
Filmdatabase-Lumiere. Available at (October 2008): http://lumiere.obs.coe.int/web/film_info/?id=8161.
Handlingsplan/Action Plan, "Kultur og Fritid" (Culture and Leisure), Kristiansand Kommune/The Municipality of Kristiansand 1993–96.
Handlingsplan/Action Plan: "Kultur og Fritid" (Culture and Leisure), Kristiansand Kommune/The Municipality of Kristiansand 1991–94.
KK-stiftelsen/The Knowledge Foundation: http://www.kks.se/templates/StandardPage.aspx?id=10234.
Kristiansand bystyre/Kristiansand City Council, saksnummer/case number 184/07 "Quartfestivalen – Refinansiering av Stiftelsen" (The Quart Festival – Refinancing the Foundation).
Kristiansand bystyre/Kristiansand City Council, saksnummer/case number 126/04 "Søknad fra Quart Festivalen om garantier/ lån / tilskudd" (Application from the Quart Festival concerning guarantees/loans/subsidies).
Kristiansand byutviklingsstyret/Kristiansand City Development Board, saksnummer/case number 312/06 "Utenomhusplan – Ny arrangementsarena på Odderøya"(Outdoor plans – New Event Arena at Odderøya).
Kristiansand Kommune/The Municipality of Kristiansand (2007), "Odderøya Amfi åpnet" (Odderøya Amfi has opened). Available at (March 2009): http://www.kristiansand.kommune.no/ncms.aspx?id=E1714F70-B643-48C7-B92A-FBA387528111&ax=center:6C02AFBA-4449-4FF8-AD89-6B6954947E1F,-1.
Kristiansand Kommune/The Municipality of Kristiansand, "Parkvesenet: Fakta om Odderøya Amfi". (Department of Parks and Recreation: Facts on Odderøya Amfi). Available at (June 2009): http://kristiansand.kommune.no/_bin/41A5A278-9BA0-405F-BD37-9ECAEAF4A8E0.pdf.
Kristiansand Valg og honorarkomite/Kristiansand Nomination and Remuneration Committee, saksnummer/case number 28/04 "Angående valg av nytt styre til Stiftelsen Quart Festivalen" (Concerning the nomination of a new board for the Foundation Quart Festival).

Kulturnämdens Uppdrag/Culture Board Assignment 2008, Film i Väst. Available at (March 2009): http://www.vgregion.se/upload/Regionkanslierna/Kultur/ Uppdrag_2008/filmivast_2008.pdf?epslanguage=en.

Kulturrådet/The Norwegian Culture Council (2008) "Kulturen i siffror" nr 7 (Culture in Figures No. 7). Available at (November 2009): http://www. kulturradet.se/Documents/publikationer/2008/kulturens%20finansiering/ kulturens_finansiering_2007.pdf.

Olsbu, E. 2006. Slutter som Quart-sjef (Resigns as Quart Manager) in Fædrelandsvennen 3 August. Available at (May 2009): http://www.fvn.no/ lokalt/kristiansand/article386479.ece?tipFriend=visible.

Prop./Bill Proposition 1998/99: 131 "Ny svensk filmpolitik" (New Swedish Film Policy).

Prop./Bill Proposition. 2005/06: 3. "Fokus på film – en ny svensk filmpolitik" (Focus on Film – A New Swedish Film Policy).

Riktlinjer och regelverk för Film i Västs samproducerandre verksamhet/Guidelines and Regulations for Film i Väst's Coproduction Activities: Långfilm/Feature Films. Available at (March 2009): http://www.filmivast.se/upload/FiV/FiV_ regelverk.pdf?epslanguage=sv.

Steen, K 2004. Quart-Uppstad: – Vi kan leve med kommunale føringer på repertoaret in Ballade 19.september. Available at (March 2009): http://www. mic.no/nmi.nsf/doc/art2004091711193433489127.

Vest-Agder Fylkeskommune/Vest Agder County, Fylkesutvalgets møteprotokoll 29.08.06 (County Committee Meeting Records 29.08.06).

Västra Götalandsregion 1999/Region Västra Götaland: Medel til "Långfilmssatsing" 1999. Beslut, Regionutveckling 22. Juni. Diarienurmmer RUN 612-1331-99 (Funding for Feature Films 1999. Decision, Regional Development 22 June. Registration No. RUN 612-1331-99).

Interviews

Agneta Mårdsjö. Regional Development Secretariat, Region Västra Götaland. May 2009.

Annika Wennerblom. Trollhättan Muncipal Director and Krister Olsson, Trollhättan Municipal Culture Manager. October 2008.

Arvid Dan Kvanes. Finance Manager, Employee under the Culture Director. June 2009.

Bjørg Wallevik. Former Mayoress of Kristiansand. August 2009.

Dagny Anker Gevelt. Former Municipal Culture Director in Kristiansand. April 2009.

Erling Valvik. Former Municipal Head of Administration in Kristiansand, currently Director of Administration in Cultiva. August 2009.

Jonny Nilsson. Chairman of the Board, Film i Väst. Telephone interview, June 2009.

Gert-Inge Andersson. Mayor of the Trollhättan Municipal Administration. October 2008.

Kent Johansson. Regional Council, RegionVästra Götaland. May 2009.

Kerstin Quentzer. Former Culture Manager, Region Västra Götaland/ County Administrative Court. May 2009.

Kirsten Kaalstad. Employee under the Culture Director. June 2009.

Stig Fredriksson. Former Municipal Director in Trollhättan. May 2009.

Tomas Eskilsson. VD Film i Väst. October 2008.

Torleif Gunnufsen. Former Festival Manager. September 2009.

Chapter 12

Conclusions:
The Policy Nexus in Network Governance

Harald Baldersheim, Are Vegard Haug and Morten Øgård

The point of departure for this book was the expectation that an ever accelerating process of globalization would be driving policy and institutional changes in sub-national regions, triggering policy learning, internationalization and cross-border contacts as ways of coping with changing environments. Regions with responsibilities as development agents would try to learn from each other through cross-border networks. Under conditions of growing uncertainty as to policy choices political skills would be in demand to create the levels of trust necessary for collective action. Consequently, political actors would be increasingly involved in cross-border activities.

A decade ago European integration was clearly driving cross-border networking and concomitant development efforts in Nordic regions. European integration has been and is largely motivated by pressures of globalization and the related competition emanating from other super-regions across the globe. Globalized pressures have hardly diminished in the 2000s, if anything, turbulence is more pronounced; the financial crisis of 2008/09 is a reminder of this and so are the budgetary and welfare cutbacks that most European states are implementing to cope with the aftermath of the crisis. Against this background regions could be expected to increase their networking activities to build ever more sophisticated learning ecologies.

The findings from the project do not fully confirm all of these expectations. In terms of territorial governance the Nordic countries have not continued on the course of enhanced regionalization that was observed a decade ago. Instead, there is uncertainty as to the future of regional governance. As outlined by Siv Sandberg in Chapter 2 the position of the regional level in the Nordic countries is becoming increasingly ambiguous. It appears that the internal regionalization of the Nordic countries has come to a standstill, maybe even a turning point has been reached. In Sweden and Norway, recent initiatives have aimed to create a stronger regional level with broader competencies and larger units. The theoretical arguments in favour of regionalization have met with little political enthusiasm. The Norwegian reform, although preserving directly elected county councils, contracted to a minimum of the intended reform. The bottom-up and gradual path to a new regional level in Sweden has not yet achieved any striking success and large-scale reforms seem unlikely. The Danish reform transformed the idea of regional self-government. The new Danish regions, although governed by directly elected councils, are creatures of the state, not self-governing institutions. In Finland, there is still no directly elected regional level of governance.

Although EU membership and European regional policy were important reasons for regional reforms in the 1990s, with the establishment of regional councils in Finland in 1994 and the regional experiments in Sweden from 1996 onwards, the EU as a driving force for regional action seems to have faded. The restructuring of regional government during the last few years has usually been motivated by domestic rather than international reasons. Since the Danish public sector reform, Denmark is viewed as one single region within the EU structural fund programmes. In the other countries, the direct connection between the regional authorities and structural fund programmes has diminished. Fewer Nordic regions are eligible for EU funds since the eastwards extension of the EU.

In terms of institutional patterns of regional governance the Nordic countries are drifting apart. Because of institutional asymmetries cross-border cooperation among regions in the Nordic area may become more difficult to organize in the future. This may also have negative repercussions for wider Nordic cooperation under the auspices of the Nordic Council and related bodies since regions have traditionally been important players on this field (Baldersheim and Ståhlberg 1999).

Nevertheless, regional development remains an important responsibility of the Nordic regions, perhaps somewhat less so in Denmark but arguably more important for Norwegian regions since they have lost other important functions. Consequently, elected politicians at the regional level can still be expected to be highly concerned about and sensitive to regional development problems. What are the policy preferences of politicians for regional development in a competitive world? And have these preferences changed much over a 10-year period? These questions were addressed in Chapter 3 by Harald Baldersheim. He found that policy preferences had remained remarkably stable over the decade. Information age types of policies are those most in favour among the politicians: more efforts regarding higher education, strategic alliances between regions and universities and channels of electronic communication. Urban and regional policy-makers clearly want their regions and cities to adapt to a knowledge-driven world. To highlight what this kind of development orientation is about Baldersheim introduces the term *knowledge brokerage* to denote the predominant development role of regions as it emerges from the policy choices of regional politicians. The paradigm entails natural roles for politicians in their capacity as brokers between different socio-economic spheres, a role in which trust-creating skills is at a premium. However, the politicians also have views regarding the institutions of territorial governance. The majority is clearly in support of larger and more powerful regions, but there are also cleavages, especially between cities and regions. Cities do not favour more powerful regions but are prepared to take over some of their tasks. The institutional developments outlined by Siv Sandberg indicate that the cities may have gained the upper hand in the struggle over institutions.

In Chapter 4 Baldersheim and Øgård analysed the extent to which regions actually engage in cross-border networks and what motivates them to do so. The networking urge has not subsided; but neither has there been any further surge of cross-border activities. The level of network participation is remarkably stable compared to a decade ago, and so are the patterns of cooperation and contact. Nevertheless, a fairly large proportion of politicians are involved in cross-border activities of one sort or another. Involvement goes beyond a small handful of top politicians. Political involvement may be taken to demonstrate that there is need of political skills in networks to cope with the uncertainty inherent in the development challenges and policy choices faced by regions. Cross-border networks have not become the routinized and bureaucratized affairs that one could also expect to happen over time. Through network involvement politicians establish a *learning ecology* that nurtures policy development in regions. Enhanced learning capacity is indicated by the finding that the politicians' perception of benefits of their involvement in cross-institutional and cross-border operation has become more positive since 1998.

The findings reported by Baldersheim in Chapter 5 show that policy-makers in Nordic regions (including the main cities) are still, 10 years on, decidedly in favour of and prepared to take on extended roles in European structures of decision-making on behalf of their regions. Integrative regionalism is the dominant attitude: taking part in European governance, and at the same time building regional networks between the Nordic countries, across the Baltic Sea or around the North Sea are not seen as competing regional projects. However, there are divergent positions: those of state-centred regionalism, extra-Nordic regionalism and plain competitive regionalism. The roles of regions in multi-level governance are divisive issues. With regard to integrative regionalism Swedish regions are clearly more enthusiastic than those of the other countries. However, views on multi-level governance were most clearly influenced by policy ideas and a background in cross-border networking, including familiarity with EU institutions. Policy shapes governance!

A further aspect of governance was studied by Baldersheim and Øgård in Chapter 6: strategies of transformation, i.e. how cities and regions seek to enhance how they relate to citizens through reforms of service provision and procedures for participation, information and communication. In adapting to new citizen expectations, the authors asked, would, patterns of change indicate more market-oriented, more communitarian or more neo-republican leanings? More concern with *choice*, *roots* or *virtue*? The findings demonstrate that cities and regions are growing in complexity. The particularly interesting finding is that growing communitarian and neo-republican concerns do not weaken the more individualized, NPM-oriented reform patterns that were observed 10 years ago. Instead, the authors find an overall trend where the learning and adaptive capacity of cities and regions is developed by adding new dimensions to the already existing structures. The outcome is more complex governance structures that may enable cities and regions to deal more effectively with a more complex and dynamic environment.

Analysis of transformation of governance was taken one step further in Chapter 7 where Are Vegard Haug highlighted how access to ICTs influences role formation among and communication patterns of politicians. The analysis was structured around the concept of *information ecology*, which identifies informational capacities as sources of political advantage. Would the high level of digitalization of government institutions in the Nordic countries contribute to internationalization of governance through new search and communication patterns of political actors? Digital resources, especially the Internet, serve two (inter-related) purposes: a source of information and an instrument for information searches and a channel of communication with the world. As a source of information and search instrument ICTs stimulate in particular councillors in their role as decision-maker, providing them with easy access to additional sources of information outside their own municipalities. ICTs thus trigger more cosmopolitan orientations among councillors. The roles of ombudsman, controller and representative were found to be less affected by ICTs. Nevertheless, contacts with civil society (associations, local businesses, media) were more vibrant among the digitally proficient councillors, helping to open up local and regional politics. The competitive advantage that ICTs bring to individual politicians is that of enhanced efficiency as decision-makers, closer relations with civic society and some edge in bridging long-distance relations. Thus, a city or region with an abundance of ICT-proficient politicians should be institutions with a competitive edge with regard to the quality of decision-making as well as acquiring international partners and mobilising civil society.

Chapter 8 takes us from quantitative analysis of network patterns to the dynamics of networking in the European arena. In this chapter Joan Ólavsdóttir, Jens Svabo Justinussen and Beinta í Jákupsstovu explain the formation of Faroese governmental bodies for foreign affairs and their capacities in the international political arena. To analyse their case they draw on hierarchy and network theories. Their analysis shows the importance and strength of weak ties and networks to the Faroes in the international arena. The Faroes have used the strength of strong ties to establish to promote their interests in Europe and have then moved on to use the strength of weak ties to establish their own networks in the international arena. The data show, however, that among Faroese politicians there are divergent opinions on the efforts to expand Faroese involvement in international relations. Therefore, further international involvement may depend upon political developments in the region.

In Chapter 9 Sande Lysa and Øgård compared the international engagement of two county councils in Norway. They observed, first of all, that the two county councils are extensively involved in a variety of cross-border networks. Second, the back-office functions of network involvement are managed more professionally than before. Sande Lysa and Øgård identify two different models of network management. One county council has chosen to organize back-office functions in-house by establishing its own international department run by county council staff. The other council has chosen to manage its international projects under a joint umbrella with a neighbouring county council setting up a separate international agency for the larger region of Southern Norway. While the professionalism of network management may be equal in the two cases, the former model, the in-house one, seems to lead to more involvement and commitment from politicians. If political learning is an objective, then the agency model seems to suffer from a handicap.

A Danish case was presented in Chapter 10 by Niels Ejersbo. His aim was to assess the effect of the structural reform in Denmark on regional internationalization strategies. Do cross-border networks represent a lifeline to struggling regions or the last rites at the end of the road? the author asks. The case study of the region of Southern Denmark shows that the region does maintain international relations even after the reform. These relations are structured by the region's remaining responsibilities. Hospitals are the chief function of the new regions, which is reflected in the cross-border partnerships. For the region of Southern Denmark this means that long-standing relations with hospitals in Northern Germany are carried on. These networks are highly specialized and are driven by a search for solutions to wicked problems (the treatment of cancer). They are dominated by professionals with very little involvement from politicians.

In Chapter 11, Aase Marthe Horrigmo has added an interesting new subject to the analysis of regional development strategies. Her interest is to study how initiatives in the field of culture can be used as a development strategy and she seeks to explain how two such radical innovations as "Film i Väst" and Quart Festivalen could emerge and become successes in two such initially unlikely places as Trollhättan and Kristiansand respectively. These are places that do not correspond well to the developmental preconditions outlined by the theories of the creative class, on which Horrigmo draws. Horrigmo compares the cases in the light of windows of opportunities created through policy entrepreneurship, local contexts, the municipalities as facilitators, and changing national contexts. This comparative case study shows how the idea of developing a cultural industry is getting accept even in the Nordic welfare state context. Horrigmo takes us into the dynamics of realising such strategies and identifies some of the challenges that this kind of thinking can meet outside the North-American world where the ideas were first developed.

The Urban Drift of Regional Policy and Governance

An analytical model consisting of three parts was presented in the introductory section (Figure 1.1): policy changes were expected to drive network activities, which were again expected to promote new patterns of governance. We found, first of all, that regional politicians do have strong policy views, which were summarized under the heading of knowledge brokerage and institutional re-tooling. They were more unanimous in their views on the former than they were with regard to the latter. We identified a cleavage between urban and regional politicians with regard to the distribution of functions and powers in the field of regional development policies. Partnerships necessary for the implementation of the favoured information age policies may therefore be hard to establish at the regional level although we can certainly point to examples to the contrary. It is, however, likely that the state will continue to be an important actor in the implementation of Triple Helix types of initiatives.

Second, the expected relationship between policy choices, network development and attitudes to governance did in fact emerge. Politicians with clear policy preferences were more likely to be deeply involved in networks of all kinds. The sum of networks form a learning ecology for regions and cities involved. The learning ecologies have matured over time, indicated by more satisfaction with network involvement now compared to 10 years ago.

Third, cities and regions demonstrate transformative capacities with regard to the pursuit of citizen-centred development strategies. Ten years ago transformation patterns were exhibiting traces of market oriented thinking (NPM) although democratic and community oriented initiatives were certainly also in evidence. User and market oriented trends are still there but they are complemented by stronger community and democratic measures, especially measures intended to enhance transparency and participation. Transformation is also in evidence as regards the roles of elected officers. Transformation is enhanced through the application of digital technologies that give a competitive edge to those who master the new technologies.

Finally, how can we relate the findings presented in this book to the wider changes in regional governance structures taking place in the Nordic countries as outlined in Chapter 2? Regional and urban policy-makers are more inclined to support enlargement of regions now than before. This means that many existing regions are seen as being too small for the ambitious policy options that are championed by many regions. The persistence of (too?) small regions may account for the absence of radical transfers of functions in all of the countries, with the exception of the two enlarged regions in Southern Sweden. The cleavage between cities and regions regarding institutional re-tooling may account for not only the defeat of the county councils in the recent Danish reform and the enfeebled version of regions that emerged out of it, but may also account for the watery regional reform that resulted in Norway and the reform on hold in Sweden. Cities seem on the ascendance in the Nordic countries in tune with population and migration trends. Triple Helix policies largely require urban locations. Creating attractive regions through cultural policies mostly means creating attractive cities. Regional governance structures that do not accord cities a prominent position may not be viable for long.

Bibliography

Agranoff, R. 2007. *Managing Within Networks. Adding Value to Public Organizations.* Washington, D.C.: Georgetown University Press.

Agranoff, R. and McGuire, M. 2003. *Collaborative Public Management. New Strategies for Local Governments.* Washington, D.C.: Georgetown University Press.

Airaksinen, J., Haveri, A., Pyykkönen, H. and Väisäinen, P. 2008. *Sinisistä ajatuksista moniin totuuksiin. Kainuun hallintokokeilun arviointi. Toinen väliraportti.* Helsinki: Valtiovarainministeriö.

Amin, A. and Thrift, N. (eds) 1994. *Globalization, Institutions and Regional Development in Europe.* Oxford: Oxford University Press.

Anderson, J., O'Dowd, L. and Wilson, T.M. (eds) 2003. *New Borders for a Changing Europe. Cross-Border Cooperation and Governance.* London: Frank Cass.

Ansell, C.K. 2000. The Networked Polity: Regional Development in Western Europe. *Governance* 13(3), 303–33.

Argyris, C. and Schön, D.A. 1978. *Organizational Learning: A Theory of Action Perspective.* Reading, MA: Addison-Wesley Publishing Company.

Argyris, C. and Schön, D.A. 1996. *Organizational Learning II: Theory, Method, and Practice.* New York: Addison-Wesley Publishing Company.

Aron, J.B. 1969. *The Quest for Regional Cooperation.* Berkeley: University of California Press.

Audretsch, D.B., Grimm, H. and Wessner, C.W. 2007. *Local Heroes in the Global Village.* New York: Springer.

Axelrod, R. 1984. *The Evolution of Cooperation.* New York: Basic Books.

Bache, I. and Flinders, M. 2004. *Multi-Level Governance.* Oxford: Oxford University Press.

Baldersheim, H. (ed.) 1990. *Fornyelse nedenfra. Desentraliseringen av den nordiske regionalpolitikken.* København: Nordrefo 1990: 5.

Baldersheim, H. 1997. Har fylkeskommunen ei framtid?, in *Kommunalt selvstyre i velferdsstaten*, edited by H. Baldersheim, J.F. Bernt, T. Kleven and J. Rattsø. Otta: Tano Aschehoug.

Baldersheim, H. 2003. Local Government Reforms in the Nordic Countries. Bringing Politics Back In, in *Reforming Local Government in Europe. Closing the Gap Between Democracy and Efficiency*, edited by N. Kersting and A. Vetter. Opladen: Leske + Budrich.

Baldersheim, H. 2004. Nordic Regions in a European Perspective, in *Nordic Politics. Comparative Perspective*, edited by H. Heidar. Oslo: Universitetsforlaget.

Baldersheim, H., Hansen, T., Ettersen, P.A. and Rose, L. 1990. *Publikums syn på kommunepolitikk og kommunale tjenester.* Bergen: LOS-senter rapport 90/2.

Baldersheim, H., Haug, A.V. and Øgård, M. 2008. *Mot den virtuelle kommunen. Studier i e-demokrati og e-forvaltning.* Bergen: Fagbokforlaget.

Baldersheim, H., Sandberg, S., Ståhlberg, K. and Øgård, M. 2001. *Norden i regionernas Europa.* Copehagen: Nordiska ministerrådet. Nord 2001: 18.

Baldersheim, H., Sandberg, S., Ståhlberg, K. and Øgård, M. 2001. Norden in Europe of the Regions. A Summary of Perspectives and Results, in *Social Sciences. The Nordic Countries and Europe*, edited by K. Ståhlberg. Copenhagen: Nord 2001: 23.

Baldersheim, H. and Ståhlberg, K. (eds) 1998. *Perspektiv på regioner i Norden.* Åbo: Åbo Akademi.

Baldersheim, H. and Ståhlberg, K. (eds) 1999. *Nordic Region-Building in a European Perspective.* Aldershot: Ashgate.

Baldersheim, H. and Øgård, M. 2008. La modernisation de l'administration locale scandinave: du mode réformateur à une écologie de l'apprentissage, in *Où en est la gestion locale? Annuaire 2008 des collectivité locales*, edited by G. Marcou and H. Wollmann, Paris: CNRS Éditions.

Baldersheim, H. and Øgård, M. 2008. Elektronisk kunnskapsforvaltning, maktforhold og partnerskap i lokalpolitikken: Folkevalgtes erfaringer med digitale ressurser i by – og fylkeskommuner, in *Mot den virtuelle kommunen. Studier i e-demokrati og e-forvaltning*, by H. Baldersheim, A.V. Haug and M. Øgård. Bergen: Fagbokforlaget.

Beck, U. 1997. *Was ist Globalisierung?* Berlin: Suhrkamp Verlag.

Becker, T. 1981. Teledemocracy: Power to the People. *The Futurist*. December, 6–0.

Bekkers, V. and Homburg, V. (eds) 2005. *The Information Ecology of E-Government. E-Government as Institutional and Technological Innovation in Public Administration.* Amsterdam: IOS Press.

Bell, D. 1993. *Communitarianism and its Critics.* Oxford: Oxford University Press.

Bellah, R., Madsen, R., Sullivan, W. and Swidler, A. 1985. *Habits of Heart. Individualism and Commitment in American Life.* New York: Harper and Row.

Bertelsmann Stiftung 1993. *Democracy and Efficiency in Local Government. Carl Bertelsmann Prize: Vol I. Documantation of the International Research.* Gütersloh: Bertelsmann Foundation Publishers.

Björklund, J.-Å. 2008. *Förändrad regional indelning. Redovisning av ett uppdrag att samordna diskussioner om förändrad regional indelning.* Stockholm: Regeringskansliet/ Finansdepartementet.

Blomgren, A.M. and Blomgren, R. 2003. Den svenska filmpolitikens regionalisering eller Varför går det så bra för Film i Väst. *Den første nordiske kulturpolitiske forskerkonferansen*. Århus 3. – 4 April. Available at: http://www.hum.au.dk/ckulturf/pages/news/papers/RogerBlomgren.pdf.

Blomgren, R. 2007. *Den onda, den goda och den nyttiga – Kulturindustrin, filmen och regionerna*. Research report: 2. Trollhättan: Høgskolan Väst (University West).

Blom-Hansen, J. 1997. A "New Institutional" Perspective on Policy Networks, in *Public Administration* 75(4): 669–93.

Blom-Hansen, J. 2004. Stordriftsfordele i den kommunale serviceproduktion? Skoleområdet som eksempel, in *Politisk ukorrekt*, edited by J. Blom-Hansen et al. Aarhus: Aarhus Universitet.

Blom-Hansen, J., Elklit, J. and Serritzlev, S. (eds) 2006. *Kommunalreformens konsekvenser*. Århus: Academica.

Boekema, F., Morgan, K., Bakkers, S. and Rutten, R. (eds) 2000. *Knowledge, Innovation and Economic Growth*. Cheltenham: Edward Elgar.

Borins, S. 1998. *Innovating with Integrity*. Washington, D.C.: Georgetown University Press.

Brekke, N. and Nordgård, D. 2005. *Hva hindrer Kristiansands kultur- liv?* Kristiansand: Høgskolen i Agder (University of Agder). Master thesis.

Brown, R. 2000. Clusters, Supply Chains and Local Embeddedness in Fyrstad, *European Urban and Regional Studies* 7(4): 291–305.

Brøndum, A. 2008. *Ville faglig bæredygtighed have været et centralt tema i den kommunale modernisering, hvis strukturreformen ikke var blevet til virkelighed?* Odense: Institut for Statskundskab, Syddansk Universitet. PhD Dissertation.

Buck, N., Gordon, I., Harding, A. and Turok, I. (eds) 2005. *Changing Cities. Rethinking Urban Competitiveness, Cohesion and Governance*. Houndsmill, Basingstoke: Palgrave.

Bäck, H. 2004. *Av de många ett. Västra Götalandsregionens politiker. Partipolitiska och territoriella skiljelinjer*. Göteborg: Förvaltningshögskolan vid Göteborgs universitet.

Bäck, H., Gjelstrup, G., Helgesen, M., Johansen, F. and Klausen, J.E. 2005. *Urban Political Decentralisation. Six Scandinavian Cities*. Wiesbaden: VS Verlag.

Bäck, H., Heinelt, H. and Magnier, A. (eds) 2006. *The European Mayor. Political Leaders in the Changing Context of Local Democracy*. Wiesbaden: VS Verlag für Sozialwissenschaften, Urban and Regional Research International Series.

Castells, M. 1996/2000. *The Rise of the Network Society*, 2nd edition. Oxford: Blackwell Publishing.

Castells, M. 1997/2000. *The Power of Identity*, 2nd edition. Oxford: Blackwell Publishing.

Castells, M. 1998/2000. *End of Millennium*, 2nd edition. Oxford: Blackwell Publishing.

Castells, M. 2004. Informationalism, Networks, and the Network Society: A Theoretical Blueprint, in *The Network Society*, edited by M. Castells. Northhampton, MA: Edward Elgar Publishing Inc.

Castells, M. (ed.) 2004. *The Network Society. A Cross-cultural Perspective.* Cheltenham: Edward Elgar Publishing Limited.

Chabal, P. and Daloz, J.-P. 2005. *Culture Troubles: Politics and the Interpretation of Meaning.* London: Hurst & Co.

Christaller, W. 1933. *Die zentralen Orte in Süddeutschland.* Jena: Gustav Fischer.

Christiansen, P.M. and Baggesen Klitgaard, M. 2008. *Den utænkelige reform. Strukturreformens tilblivelse 2002–2005.* Odense: Syddansk Universitetsforlag.

Clark, T.N. 2004a. Introduction: Taking Entertainment Seriously, in *The City as an Entertainment Machine*, edited by T.N. Clark. Oxford: Elsevier Ltd.

Clark, T.N. 2004b. Urban Amenities: Lakes, Opera, and Juice Bars. Do they Drive Development? in *The City as an Entertainment Machine*, edited by T.N. Clark. Oxford: Elsevier Ltd.

Clarke, S.E. 2003. Globalism and Cities: A North American Perspective. In *Globalism and Local Democracy: Challenge and Change in Europe and North America*, edited by R. Hambleton, H.V. Savitvh and M. Stewart. New York: Palgrave.

Clarke, S.E. and Gaile, G.L. 1998. *The Work of Cities.* Minneapolis: University of Minnesota Press.

Cohen, M.D., March, J.G. and Olsen, J.P. 1972. A Garbage Can Model of Organizational Choice, *Administrative Science Quarterly* 17(1): 1–25.

Cooke, P. and Piccaluga, A. 2006. *Regional Development in the Knowledge Economy.* London: Routledge.

Cyert, R.M. and March, J.G. 1963. *A Behavioral Theory of the Firm.* Englewood Cliffs, NJ: Prentice-Hall.

Dahlström, M. et al. 2005. Film och regional utveckling i Norden. Stockholm: Svenska Filminstitutet.

Danziger J.N., Dutton, W.H., Kling, R. and Kraemer, K.L. 1982. *Computers and Politics: High Technology in American Local Governments.* New York: Columbia University Press.

Davenport, T.H. 1997. *Information Ecology: Mastering the Information and Knowledge Environment.* Oxford: Oxford University Press.

Delaney, C.F. (ed.) 1994. *The Liberalism-Communitarianism Debate.* London: Rowan and Littlefield.

Delmaide, D. 1994. *The New Superregions of Europe.* New York: Dutton.

Donaldson, L. 2001. *The Contingency Theory of Organizations.* Thousand Oaks: Sage.

Dunford, M. and Kafkalas, G. 1992. The Global – Local Interplay, Corporate Geographies and Spatial Development Strategies in Europe, in *Cities and Regions in the New Europe*, edited by M. Dunford and G. Kafkalas. London: Belhaven Press.

Dunn, W.N. 2008. *Public Policy Analysis. An Introduction.* New Jersey: Prentice Hall. 4th edition.

Easterby-Smith, M. 1997. Disiplines of Organizational Learning: Contributions and Critiques, *Human Relations* 50(9): 1085–113.

Eriksen, E.O. and Weigard, J. 2004. *Understanding Habermas: Communicative Action and Deliberative Democracy.* London: Continuum International Publishing.

Etzkowitz, H. 2008. *The Triple Helix. University – Industry – Government Innovation in Action.* New York: Routledge.

Fagerberg, J., Mowery, D.C. and Nelson, R. 2005. *The Oxford Handbook of Innovation.* Oxford: Oxford University Press.

Feltenius, D. 2008. Från splittring till enighet. Om Sveriges Kommuner och Landstings ståndpunkt i regionfrågan. *Kommunal Ekonomi och Politik* 12(2), 37–65.

Florida, R. 2002. *The Rise of the Creative Class: And How it's Transforming Work, Leisure, Community and Everyday Life.* New York: Basic Books.

Florida, R. 2005. *The Flight of the Creative Class: The New Global Competition for Talent.* New York: HarperBusiness.

Fornahl, D. and Brenner, T. (eds) 2003. *Cooperation, Networks and Institutions in Regional Innovation Systems.* Cheltenham: Edward Elgar Publishing.

Fountain, J.E. 2001. *Building the Virtual State, Information Technology and Institutional Change.* Washington, D.C.: Bookings Institution Press.

Fukuyama, F. 1999. *The Great Disruption.* New York: The Free Press.

Gedde-Dahl, S., Hafstad, A. and Magnussen, A.E. 2008. *Korrupsjon i Norge.* Oslo: Kagge Forlag.

George, A. and Bennett, A. 2005. *Case Studies and Theory Development in the Social Sciences.* Cambridge: MIT Press.

Gerring, J. 2007. *Case Study Research.* Cambridge: Cambridge University Press.

Giddens, A. 1984. *The Constitution of Society: Outline of the Theory of Structuration.* Berkeley: University of California Press.

Gidlund, J. and Jerneck, M. (eds) 2000. *Local and Regional Governance in Europe. Evidence from Nordic Regions.* Cheltenham: Edward Elgar Publishing.

Goldsmith, M.J.F. and Klausen, K.K. (eds) 1997. *European Integration and Local Government.* Cheltenham: Edward Elgar Publishing.

Goldsmith, S. and Eggers, W.G. 2004. *Governing by Networks. The New Shape of the Public Sector.* Washington, D.C.: Brookings Institution Press.

Granovetter, M. 2004. The Strength of Weak Ties. In *Networks. Volume I*, edited by G. Grabher and W.W. Powell. Cheltenham: Edward Elgar Publishing Limited.

Gregersen, O. 1999. *Kommuner i front – organisationsudvikling blandt kommunale socialforvaltninger.* København: Socialforskningsinstituttet 99: 13.

Grindheim, J.E. and Trondal, J. 2007. *Europeisk integrasjon og regional endring.* Bergen: Fagbokforlaget.

Harbermas, J. 1981. *Theorie des kommunikativen Handelns. (Bd.1: Handlungsrationalität und gesellschaftliche Rationalisierung, Bd. 2: Zur Kritik der funktionalistischen Vernunft).* Frankfurt am Main: Suhrkamp.

Hacker, K.L. and van Dijk, J. 2000. *Digital Democracy, Issues of Theory & Practice.* London: Sage.

Hambleton, R. and Gross, J.S. (eds) 2007. *Governing Cities in a Global Era. Urban Innovation, Competition, and Democratic Reform.* New York: Palgrave.

Hambleton, R., Savitch, H.V. and Stewart, M. 2003. *Globalism and Local Democracy: Challenge and Change in Europe and North America.* New York: Palgrave.

Hannan, M.T. and Freeman, J. 1989. *Organizational Ecology.* Cambridge, MA: Harvard University Press.

Harris, M. and Kinney, R. (eds) 2003. *Innovation and Entrepreneurship in State and Local Governments.* Lanham, Maryland: Lexington Books.

Harvie, C. 1994. *The Rise of Regional Europe.* London: Routledge.

Haug, A.V. 2007. Local Democracy Online: Driven by Crisis, Legitimacy, Resources, or Communication Gaps? *Journal of Information Technology and Politics* 4(2): 79–99.

Haug, A.V. 2008a. Internett som kanal for politisk kommunikasjon: Hvordan kan det gjøres? Hvem er foregangskommunene? In *Mot den virtuelle kommunen. Studier i e-demokrati og e-forvaltning,* edited by H. Baldersheim, A.V. Haug and M. Øgård: Bergen: Fagbokforlaget.

Haug, A.V. 2008b. Hva slags demokrati i cyberspace? Behøver vi lenger valgte representanter? In *Mot den virtuelle kommunen. Studier i e-demokrati og e-forvaltning,* edited by H. Baldersheim, A.V. Haug and M. Øgård: Bergen: Fagbokforlaget.

Haug, A.V. 2009. *Lokaldemokratiet på nett og i nett.* Oslo: Faculty of Social Sciences, University of Oslo. Nr. 164/2009. PhD Dissertation.

Hobbs, H.H. 1994. *City Hall Goes Abroad. The Foreign Policy of Local Politics.* London: Sage.

Hoff, J., Horrocks, I. and Tops, P. 2000. *Democratic Governance and New Technology. Technologically Mediated Innovations in Political Practice in Western Europe.* London: Routledge.

Hooghe, L. and Marks, G. 2001. *Multi-Level Governance and European Integration.* Lanham: Rowman and Littlefield.

Hulst, R. and van Montfort, A. (eds) 2007. *Inter-Municipal Cooperation in Europe.* Dordrecht: Springer.

Indenrigs- og Sundhetsministeriet 2004. *Aftale om strukturreform.* København.

Inglehart, R. 1971. The Silent Revolution in Europe: Intergenerational Change in Post-industrial Societies. *American Political Science Review* 65(4): 991–1017.

Inglehart, R. 2008. Changing Values Among Western Publics from 1970 to 2006. *West European Politics* 31(1–2): 130–46.

Isard, W. 1956. *Location and Space-Economy: A General Theory Relating to Industrial Location, Market Areas, Land Use, Trade and Urban Structure.* Cambridge, Massachusetts: The MIT Press.

Isard, W. 1975. *Introduction to Regional Science.* New York: Prentice Hall.

Jackson, M.O. and Wolinsky, A. 1996. A Strategic Model of Social and Economic Networks, *Journal of Economic Theory* 71, 44–74.

Jacobsson, B., Lægreid, P. and Pedersen, O.K. (eds) 2001. *Europaveje. EU i de nordiske centralforvaltninger.* København: Jurist- og Økonomforbundets Forlag.

Jæger, B. 2005. Digital Visions – The Role of Politicians in Transition, in *The Information Ecology of E-Government. E-Government as Institutional and Technological Innovation in Public Administration*, edited by V. Beckers and V. Homburg. Amsterdam: IOS Press.

Janis, I.L. 1972. *Victims of Groupthink.* Boston: Houghton Mifflin.

Jensen, L.T. 1995. *Internationalisering og de danske amter.* Odense: Odense Universitetsforlag.

Jerneck, M. and Gidlund, J. 2001. *Komplex flernivåpolitik. Regional lobbying i Bryssel.* Malmö: Liber.

Jönsson, S., Rubinowitz, S. and Westerståhl, S. 1995. *Decentraliserad kommune. Eksempelet Göteborg.* Stockholm: SNS Förlag.

Keating, M. 1997. The Political Economy of Regionalism, in *The Political Economy of Regionalism*, edited by M. Keating and J. Loughlin. London: Frank Cass.

Keating, M. 2002. Territorial Politics and the New Regionalism, in *Developments in West European Politics*, edited by P. Heywood, E. Jones and M. Rhodes. London: Palgrave.

Keating, M. and Loughlin, J. (eds) 1997. *The Political Economy of Regionalism.* London: Frank Cass.

Kersbergen, K. and Waarden, F. 2004. "Governance" as a Bridge between Disciplines: Cross-disiplinary Inspiration Regarding Shifts in Governance and Problems of Governability, Accountability and Legitimacy, *European Journal of Political Research* 43: 143–71.

Kickert, W.J.M., Klijn, E.-H. and Koppenjan, J.F.M. (eds) 1997. *Managing Complex Networks. Strategies for the Public Sector.* London. Sage.

Kingdon, J.W. 1995/2003. *Agendas, Alternatives, and Public Policies.* 2nd Edition. New York: Longman.

Klausen, K.K. (ed.) 1996. *Erfaringer med Internationalisering i Amter og Kommuner.* Odense: Odense Universitetsforlag.

Klijn, E.H. 2005. Networks and Inter-organizational Management: Challenging Steering, Evaluation and the Role of Public Actors in Public Management, in *The Oxford Handbook of Public Management*, edited by E. Ferlie, L. Lynn, and C. Politt. Oxford: Oxford University Press.

Klijn, E.H. 2008. Governance and Governance Networks in Europe, *Public Management Review* 10(4): 505–25.

Kolderup, V. 1999. *En sammenligning av regional autonomi på Færøyene og Åland i lys av europeisk integrasjon.* Oslo: Department of Political Science, University of Oslo. Master Thesis.

Komninos, N. 1992. Science Parks in Europe: Flexible Production, Productive Disintegration and R&D, in *Cities and Regions in the New Europe*, edited by M. Dunford and G. Kafkalas. London: Belhaven Press.

Kontopoulos, K.M. 1993. *The Logics of Social Structure.* Cambridge: Cambridge University Press.

Koopenjan, J. and Klijn, E.-H. 2004. *Managing Uncertainties in Networks.* New York: Routledge.

Korac-Kakabadse, A. and Korac-Kakabadse, N. 1999. Information Technology's Impact on the Quality of Democracy – Reinventing the Democratic Vessel, in *Reinventing Government in the Information Age. International Practice in IT-enabled Public Sector Reform*, edited by R. Heeks. London: Routledge.

Krasner, S. 1988. Sovereignty. An Institutional Perspective. *Comparative Political Studies* 21(1): 66–94.

Kristensen, O.P. 1984. Privatisering – modernisering af den offentlige sektor eller ideologisk korstog? *Nordisk administrativt tidsskrift.* 96–117.

Landry, C. 2000. *The Creative City.* London: Earthscan.

Landstingsförbundet and Svenska Kommunförbundet 2003. *Nya samverkansorgan. Regionfrågans utveckling i landet 2003.* Stockholm: Landstingsförbundet and Svenska Kommunförbundet.

Larsen, H. 2002. Directly Elected Mayors: Democratic Revival or Constitutional Confusion?. In *Local Government at the Millennium*, edited by J. Caulfield and H.O. Larsen, H.O. Opladen: Leske + Budrich.

Lein-Mathisen, J. 2005. Nordic Lobbying in Brussels, in *The Nordic Regions and the European Union*, edited by S. Dosenrode and H. Halkier. Aldershot: Ashgate.

Leonardi, R. 1993. The Role of Sub-National Institutions in European Integration. *The Regions and the European Community*, edited by R. Leonardi. London: Frank Cass.

Levitt, B. and March, J.G. 1988. "Organizational Learning", *Annual Review of Sociology* 14(1988): 319–40.

Lorenz, E.H. 1991. Neither Friends nor Strangers: Informal Networks of Subcontracting in French Industry, in *Markets, Hierarchies and Networks. The Coordination of Social Life*, edited by G.J. Thompson, R. Frances, R. Levacic and J.C. Mitchell. London: Sage Publications.

Lowi, T. 1964. American Business, Public Policy, Case-studies and Political Theory. *World Politics* 16, 677–715.

Lundvall, B.A. 1992. *National Systems of Innovation: Towards a Theory of Innovation and Interactive Learning.* London: Pinter.

Magone, J.M. (ed.) 2003. *Regional Institutions and Governance in the European Union.* London: Praeger.

Mandell, M.P. 2001. *Getting Results Through Collaboration.* Westport: Qurom Books.

March, J.G. 1991. Exploration and Exploitation in Organizational Learning. *Organization Science* 2(1): 71–87.

March, J.G. 2008. *Explorations in Organizations.* Stanford, CA: Stanford University Press.

March, J.G. and Olsen, J.P. (eds) 1976. *Ambiguity and Choice in Organizations.* Bergen: Universitetsforlaget.

March, J.G. and Olsen, J.P. 1995. *Democratic Governance.* New York: Free Press.

Marks, G., Nielsen, F., Ray, L. and Salk, J. 1994. Competencies, Cracks, and Conflicts: Regional Mobilization in the European Union, in *Governance in the European Union*, edited by G. Marks et al. London: Sage.

Marks, G., Sharpf, F.W., Schmitter, P.H. and Streck, W. (eds) 1996. *Governance in the European Union.* London: Sage.

Marsh, D. 1998. The Development of the Policy Network Approach, in *Comparing Policy Networks*, edited by D. Marsh. London: Open University Press.

Marsh, D. and Rhodes, R.A.W. 1992. *Policy Networks in British Government.* Oxford: Clarendon Press.

Marshall, T.H. 1964. *Class, Citizenship and Social Development.* Garden City: Doubleday.

Martin, H.-P. and Schumann, H. 1996. *Die Globalisierungsfalle.* Hamburg: Rohwolt.

Matland, R. 1995. Synthesizing the Implementation Literature: The Ambiguity-Conflict Model of Policy Implementation. *Journal of Public Administration Research and Theory* 5(2): 145–74.

McEvily, B., Perrone, V. and Zaheer, A. 2003. Trust as an Organizing Principle. *Organization Science* 14(1): 91–103.

Merton, R. 1968. *Social Theory and Social Structure.* New York: Free Press.

Morgan, K. 1992. Innovating by Networking: New Models of Corporate and Regional Development, in *Cities and Regions in the New Europe*, edited by M. Dunford and A. Kafkalas. London: Belhaven Press.

Morgan, K. (ed.) 2002. *Regional Innovation Strategies: The Challenge for Less-Favoured Regions.* London: Routledge.

Mouritzen, P.E. 2006. *Stort er godt. Otte fortællinger om tilblivelsen af de nye kommuner.* Odense: Syddansk Universitetsforlag.

Mouritzen, P.E. and Svara, J. 2002. *Leadership at the Apex: Politicians and Administrators in Western Local Governments.* Pittsburgh: University of Pittsburgh Press.

Mydske, P.K. 1978. *Planlegging og forvaltning: makt og avmakt i den regionale planlegging.* Oslo: Norsk institutt for by- og regionforskning.

Mydske, P.K. (ed.) 2006. *Skandinaviske regioner – plass for politikk? Det regionale politiske demokrati i utvikling eller for avvikling?* Bergen: Fagbokforlaget.

Nilsson, L. (ed.) 2007. *Det våras för regionen. Västsverige 1998–2005.* Göteborg: SOM-instiutet, Göteborgs universitet.

Nonaka, I. and Teece, D.J. (eds) 2001. *Managing Industrial Knowledge: Creation, Transfer and Utilization.* London: Sage.

OECD 2006. *OECD E-government Studies. Norway.* Paris: OECD Publishing.

Offerdal, A. 1992. *Den politiske kommunen.* Oslo: Det norske samlaget.

Ólavsdóttir, J. 2009. Føroyar í uttanríkispolitikki. Masterritgerð, Søgu og samfelagsdeildin, Fróðskaparsetur Føroya.

Olson, M. Revised edition (ed.) 1971, 1965. *The Logic of Collective Action: Public Goods and the Theory of Groups.* Boston: Harvard University Press.

Osborne, D. and Gaebler, T. 1992. *Reinventing Government: How the Entrepreneurial Spirit is Transforming the Public Sector.* New York: A Plume Book, Penguin Group.

Ot.prp.nr 10 (2008–09) 2009. *Om lov om endringer forvaltningslovgivningen mv. (gjennomføring av forvaltningsreformen).* Oslo: Det kongelige kommunal- og regionaldepartementet.

Pastor, M., Lester, T.W. and Scoggins, J. 2009. "Why Regions? Why Now? Who Cares?", in *Journal of Urban Affairs* 31(3).

Petterson, A. 1996. Ansökan om medel ur EU:s strukturfonder (Application for Funding from the EU Structure Fund) 9 October. Diarienummer/Registration Number: Fy 24 1-54-96.

Pierre, J. and Peters, B.G. 2000. *Governance, Politics and the State.* London: Macmillan Press.

Poole S., and Van de Ven, A.H. (eds) 2004. *Handbook of Organizational Change and Innovation.* Oxford: Oxford University Press.

Porter, M. 1990. *The Competetive Advantage of Nations.* London: Macmillan Press.

Powell, W.W. 1991. Neither Market nor Hierarchy – Network Forms of Organization. In *Markets, Hierarchies and Networks. The Coordination of Social Life,* edited by G.J. Thompson, R. Frances, R. Levacic and J.C. Mitchell. London: Sage.

Provan, K.G. og P. Kenis 2007. Modes of Network Governance: Structure, Management, and Effectiveness. *Journal of Public Administration Research and Theory* 18, 229–52.

Putnam, R.D. 1993. *Making Democracy Work: Civic Traditions in Modern Italy.* Princeton, N.J.: Princeton University Press.

Putnam, R. 2001. *Bowling Alone: The Collapse and Revival of American Community.* New York: Simon and Schuster.

Reynolds, C. and Norman, R.V. (eds) 1988. *Community in America: The Challenge of Habits of the Heart.* Berkeley: University of California Press.

Rhodes, R.A.W., Binder, S.A. and Rockman, B.A. 2006. *The Oxford Handbook of Political Institutions.* Oxford, USA: Oxford University Press.

Rogers, E.M. Fifth edition 2003. *Diffusion of Innovations.* New York: Free Press.

Rokkan, S. 1975/1987. Dimensions of State Formation and Nation-building: A Possible Paradigm for Research on Variations within Europe, in *The Formation of National States in Europe*, edited by C. Tilly. Princeton: Princeton University Press.

Rokkan, S. and Urwin, D.W. 1983. *Economy, Territory, Identity: Politics of West European Peripheries*. London: Sage.

RP 155/2006. *Regeringens proposition till Riksdagen med förslag till lagar om en kommun- och servicestrukturreform samt om ändring av kommunindelningslagen och av lagen om överlåtelseskatt*. Helsingfors.

RP 59/2009. *Regeringens proposition med förslag till lagstiftning om revidering av regionförvaltningen*. Helsingfors.

Rutten, R. and Boekema, F. (2007). *The Learning Region: Foundations, State of the Art, Future*. Cheltenham: Edward Elgar.

Salamon, L.M. (ed.) 2002. *The Tools of Government: A Guide to the New Governance*. Oxford, USA: Oxford University Press.

Sandberg, S. 2004. Omöjliga vägval och framkomliga stigar. En granskning av beslut om den finländska lokal- och regionalförvaltningens struktur 1987–2003. *Nordisk Administrativt Tidsskrift 4/2004*, 242–60.

Sandberg, S. 2005. Den folkvalda regionala nivåns ställning i Norden, in *Självstyrelse på lokal och regional nivå*, edited by Pontus Tallberg. Malmö: Region Skåne and Västra Götalandsregionen.

Sandberg, S. 2007. En fråga om politisk logik: Om forsöken att försterka och omorganisera den regionale nivån i Finland och Sverige på 1990-talet, in *Federalism på svenska*, edited by N. Karlson and J. Santerius. Stockholm: Ratio.

Sandberg, S. 2010. Finnish Power-shift: The Defeat of the Periphery?, in *Territorial Choice – the Politics of Boundaries and Borders*, edited by H. Baldersheim and L.E. Rose. London: Palgrave MacMillan, 42–60.

Sandberg, S. and Ståhlberg, K. 2000. *Nordisk regionalförvaltning i förändring*. Åbo: Åbo Akademi.

Sande Lysa, J. and Øgård, M. 2010. Fylkeskommunalt internasjonalt engasjement: hvordan ser det faktisk ut? Eksemplene Telemark og Aust-Agder, in *The Rise of the Networking Region: The Challenges of Regional Collaboration in a Globalized World*, edited by H. Baldersheim, A.V. Haug and M. Øgård. Stockholm: NORDREGIO 2009: 10.

Sandström, A. and Carlsson, L. 2008. The Performance of Policy Networks: The Relation between Network Structure and Network Performance, in *The Policy Studies Journal* 36(4): 497–524.

Schepple, K.L. and Soltan, K.E. 1987. The Authority of Alternatives, in *Authority Revised: NOMUS XXIX*, edited by J.R. Pennock and J.W. Chapman. New York: New York University Press.

Schumpeter, J. 1942. *Capitalism, Socialism and Democracy*. New York: Harper & Row.

Scott, W.R. 1995. *Institutions and Organizations*. Thousand Oaks: Sage.

Scully, R. and Jones, R.W. 2010. Conclusion: Europe's Persisting Regions, in *Europe, Regions and European Regionalism*, edited by R. Scully and R.W. Jones. Houndmills: Palgrave Macmillan.

Simmie, J. (ed.) 1997. *Innovation, Networks and Learning Regions?* London: Jessica Kingsley Publishers.

Simon, H. 1973. *The Sciences of the Artificial.* Boston: The MIT Press.

Simon, H. 1995. *Administrative Behavior.* 4th ed. New York: Free Press.

Skinner, Q. 1981 *Machiavelli.* Oxford: Oxford University Press.

SOU 2003: 13. *Utvecklingskraft för hållbar välfärd. Ansvarskommitténs delbetänkande.* Stocholm: Statsrådsberedningen Näringsdepartementet.

SOU 2007: 10. *Hållbar samhällorganization med utvecklingskraft.* Stockholm: Fritzes.

SOU/Swedish National Public Records 1995: 84. "Kulturpolitikens inriktning" (Cultural Policy Alignment).

SOU/Swedish National Public Records 1998: 142. "Ny svensk filmpolitik – betänkande från Filmutredningen" (New Swedish Film Policy – Reflection on the Film Report).

SRR 9/2009. *Statsrådets redogörelse om kommun- och servicestrukturreformen.* Helsingfors.

St. prop./Parliamentary Bill Proposition 1 (2006–07) Kultur- og kirkedepartementet "For budjsettåret 2007" (The Ministry of Culture and Church Affairs: "For the Budget year 2007").

St.Meld.nr. 12 (2006–07): *Regionale fortrinn – regional framtid.* Oslo: Kommunal- og regionaldepartementet.

Statsrådsberedningen 2009. *Statsrådsberedningen, Utbildningsdepartementet, Socialdepartementet, 28 januari 2009: Regionfrågans framtida hantering presenterad.* [Online, 28 January] Available at www.regeringen.se.

Stewart, J. and Stoker, G. (eds) 1989. *The Future of Local Government.* London: Palgrave Macmillan.

Stigen, I.M. and Sandkjer Hanssen, G. 2007. *Enhetsfylke – et Columbi egg for organisering av regional forvaltning.* Oslo: Norsk institutt for by- og regionforskning, NIBR-rapport 2007: 19.

Stoker, G. 2007. *Why Politics Matters. Making Democracy Work.* New York: Palgrave.

Stoker, G. and Mossberger, K. 1994. Urban Regime Theory in Comparative Perspective.

Stone, C. 1989. *Regime Politics: Governing Atlanta 1946–1988.* Lawrence: University of Kansas Press.

Stortingsmelding nr./White Paper No. 10 (2007–08) "Knutepunkt" (Hub).

Stortingsmelding nr./White Paper No. 12 (2006–07) "Regionale fortrinn – regional framtid" (Regional Advantage – Regional Future).

Stortingsmelding nr./White Paper No. 22 (2005–06) "Kultur og næring" (Culture and Industry and Commerce).

Strandberg, B.E., Kvanes, A. and Aabelvik, T.J. 2004. "Gjennomgang av visse forhold rundt forvaltningen og driften av stiftelsen Quart Festivalen". Rapport til Stiftelsen Quart Festivalen (A review of certain conditions surrounding the administration and operations of the Foundation Quart Festival. Report for the Foundation Quart Festival).

Strukturkommissionen 2004. *Strukturkommissionens betænkning. Sammenfatning.* Betænkning nr. 1434. Köpenhamn.

Ståhlberg, K. 2001. Regionalism i Norden, in *Norden i regionernas Europa*, edited by H. Baldersheim, S. Sandberg, K. Ståhlberg and M. Øgård. København.: Nordisk Ministerråd. Nord 2001: 18.

Sullivan, H. and Skelcher, C. 2002. *Working Across Boundaries. Collaboration in Public Services.* Basingstoke: Palgrave Macmillan.

Thompson, J. 1967. *Organizations in Action.* New York: McGraw-Hill.

Tsagarousianou, R. 1998. *Cyberdemocracy, Technology, Cities and Civic Networks.* London: Routledge.

Tucker, R.C. 1981. *Politics as Leadership.* Columbia: University of Missouri Press.

Vazquez-Barquero, A. 2002. *Endogenous Development – Networking, Innovation, Institutions and Cities.* London: Routledge.

Von Dosenrode-Lynge, S.Z. and Halkier, H. 2004. *The Nordic Regions and the European Union.* Aldershot: Ashgate Publishing.

West, D.M. 2005. *Digital Government. Technology and Public Sector Performance.* Princeton: Princeton University Press.

Yin, R.K. 2003. *Case Study Research: Design and Methods.* London: Sage.

Zhariadis, N. 2007. The Multiple Streams Framework: Structure, Limitations, Prospects, in *Theories of the Policy Process*, edited by P. Sabatier. Boulder: Westview Press.

Øgård, M. 2001. Ombygging av de regionale institusjonene – demokrati og marked hånd i hånd? In: *Norden i regionernas Europa*, edited by H. Baldersheim, S. Sandberg, K. Ståhlberg and M. Øgård, København. Nordisk Ministerråd (Nord 21: 2001).

Øgård, M. 2002. *Forvaltningsinnovasjon i nordiske regioner og kommuner. I felles takt mot New Public Management?* Oslo: Dept. of Political Science. University of Oslo Ph.D. Dissertation.

Øgård, M. 2003. Is Local Democracy Under Pressure from New Public Management? Evidence from Norway. In *Political Leadership in a Global Age*, edited by H. Baldersheim and J.-P. Daloz. Aldershot: Ashgate.

Øgård, M. 2008a. Det lokaldemokratiske mulighetsrommet: Visjoner og eksempler, in *Mot den virtuelle kommunen. Studier i e-demokrati og e-forvaltning*, edited by H. Baldersheim, A.V. Haug and M. Øgård. Bergen: Fagbokforlaget.

Øgård, M. 2008b. IKT- prosjekt som iverksettingsprosess – eller hvorfor Bill Gates ikke behøvde å komme til byen, in *Mot den virtuelle kommunen. Studier i e-demokrati og e-forvaltning*, edited by H. Baldersheim, A.V. Haug and M. Øgård. Bergen: Fagbokforlaget.

Østergaard, U. 1992. *Europas ansigter. Nationale stater og politisk kulturer i en ny, gammel verden.* København: Rosinante.
Østerud, Ø. 1999. *Globaliseringen og nasjonalstaten.* Oslo: Gyldendal.

Index

Page numbers in *italic* refer to a table or figure. Page numbers followed by 'n' refer to a note.

Action Programme of the City of
    Kristiansand 154
addiction 126
Agder, Norway 9, *29*, 121–31, 152
agency model 129, 131, 169
aid 66, 126
Åland Islands *15*, 104
Alingsäs Media Workshop 146–7, 148
altruism 36, 45
Älvsborg 142, 146, 149, 158–9
anarchic model 115, 129, 130
Arendal municipality 123, 126, 129, 130
ASEAN (Association of South-East Asian
    Nations) 1
Assembly of European Regions (AER) 44,
    57, *109*, 117, *120*, 137
Aust-Agder, Norway 9, 122–31
awareness model 115–16, 129, 130, 131

Baltic region 36, 41, 42, *43*, 44, 49, 60,
    117, 167
Baltic Sea Commission 137
Baltic Sea Substate Council 56
Baltic Sea-State sub-regional Cooperation
    (BSSSC) 117, *120*, *124*
banking (online) 79, *80*
Barents Sea Council 56
BESST *121*
Board of Culture, Västra Götaland 142,
    147
Bohus County 147
branding 136, 148–9
business cooperation and development 22,
    89, 106, *125*
    Denmark 137, 138

and knowledge brokerage 4, 24, 25,
    26, 27, 28, *29*
Norway 117–31, 143, 154–5
Sweden 148–51, 158
businesses 28, 89, 91, 119, 126
    private sector 22, *68*, *93*, 130, 134,
        135
        and learning ecologies 119, 122,
            126, 127, 128
    state sector 14, 16, 17, 20, 28

Canada 95
Canal Link *120*
capacity-building 35–48
    Faroe Islands 96, 102, 104
    and health care 136, 138, 139
    and information and communications
        technologies 82, 83, 86, 89, 92
    learning capacity 115, 116, 129, 167
centrality 7t, 30, 32, *45*, 61, 62, *63*
children and young people 146, 147, 149,
    152, 153, 157
China 118–19, 128, 130, 137
choice, strategic 8, 65, *68*, 69, 72, 73
cities 7–8, 43
    and policy preferences 27, 30–32
    and regions 6–7, 9, *12*, 61, 62, *63*,
        65–75, 167, 170
        cleavages 166, 170
citizen orientation 65–75, 135, 167, 170
cleavages 2, 3, *31*, 97
    between cities and regions 7, *31*, 32,
        61–4, 166, 170
    ideological 17, 29–30, *31*, 32, 61–4,
        111

Cold War 95
collaboration, international 5, 47, 95, 115–31
Commission of the European Communities 50
Committee of the Regions 2, 51, 52, 60
Committee of Senior Officials for Regional Policy 56
communication patterns 77–94, 168
Communitarian Network 66n
communitarians and community involvement 65–7, *68*, 69–70, 71, 72, 73t, 74, 75, 167, 170
comparative framework 6–8, 61, 62, 64
compensation 87, 88, 89, 90, 91
competitive advantage 6, 77–94, 168, 170
competitive regionalism 2, 6–7, 65, 73, 74, 143, 144, 147, 165, 167
and integrative regionalism 49, 51, *59*, 60, 61, 64
complex governance *see* governance
Conference of Peripheral Maritime Regions of Europe (CPMR) 117, 118, *120*, 123, *124*
conferences, international *40*, 41, 42
Connect Baltic Sea Region (CBSR) *121*
consumer interests 65, 67
cooperation *see* business cooperation and development; cross-border cooperation; domestic cooperation; international cooperation; network cooperation
corruption 75
cosmopolitanism 81, 86, 87, 168
councillors *12*, 77, 84, 168
county councils 14, 21, 67–72, 143, 145, 165
Denmark *15*, 16, 170
Norway 11, *15*, 17–18, 21, *29*, 115–31, 165, 168, 170
Sweden *15*, 19, 20, 142, 147, 148, 150, 158
Creative Alliances 127
creative class 27, 35, 65, 67, 144, 169
Creative interaction in the workplace (KIA) *125*

cross-border cooperation 1, 35–48, 123, 134, 165, 167
Faroe Islands 107–8, 112
Nordic 52, 53m, 56, 58, *59*, 166
cross-border networking 1, 11, 35–48, 52, 107–8, 165, 167, 168–9
cross-institutional cooperation 35–48, 78n, 90, 118, 167
Cultiva Foundation *29*, 154, 156
culture 23, 24, *30*, *31*, *45*, *121*, 126, 169
cultural policies 4, 141–60, 170
cultural strategies 27, *31*, 32, 44, 46, 47
Culture and Industry White Paper 141
cycle paths 36
Czech Republic 137

debating (online) 79, 80, 82
decentralization 24–5, 82
decision-making, collective 5, 23, 49–51, 54–6, *59*, 60, 144–5, 167
and Denmark 133, 134, 137, 138
and Faroe Islands 104, 105, *110*
and information and communications technologies 85–7, 92, 168
democracy 13–15, 18, 21, 74, 86–7, 123, 126, 137, 170
Denmark *12*
business cooperation and development 137, 138
county councils *15*, 16, 170
and decision-making, collective 133, 134, 137, 138
development strategies 69, 70, 71–2, 75
education 14, 16, 21, 97, 133
EU membership 6, *7*, 32, 57, 97–8
and Faroe Islands 95, 96–107, 111
friendship relations 122, 123, 127, 128
health and hospital care 16, 20, 69n, 133, 136, 137, 138–9, 169
and integrative governance 52, 54–6, 58, 61
and international cooperation *43*, 44, *108*, 133–9

and regional development 3, 5, *9*, *31*,
165–6
and structural reform 13, 15–16, 22,
39, 57, 123, 133, 165–6, 170
responsibilities 14, 16, 20, 21,
69n, 169
dependency 36, 38, 44, 46, 111
development agents 1–2, 4, 5, 7–8, 22, 39,
77, 165
development strategies 11, 27, 67–73, 92,
134, 137, 138, 141–60, 169, 170
digital competance 77, 79, 80, 89, 90, 91,
94
digital empowerment 89, 90, 91, *94*
Director of Culture, Kristiansand 142,
152, 153, 155
Djurhuus, Hákun Jógvanson 103, 105
domestic cooperation 42, *45*, 46, 47

economic growth 21, 22, 73–4, 126,
143–4, 149
education 14, 17, 19, *26*, 27, 28, 166
Denmark 14, 16, 21, 97, 133
and international cooperation 118,
127, 128, 130
e-government 78–9, 83–4, 88
e-learning 79, 80
e-mail 79, 80, 82, 83, 84, 85, 86, 87
employment opportunities 24, 38, 49,
147–8, 149, 154, 156
endogenous development 4, 24, 25, 49
enthusiasts 130, 145, 159
environmental issues 4, 16
Eskilsson, Tomas 146, 149, 150, 158, 159
Euro-driven regional development 58, 165
Euromountains.net *121*
Europe Direct 138
Europe of the Regions 2, 13, 22
European Commission 36, 51, 138
European Economic Area Mechanism 126
European integration 2, 5, 10, 36, 38,
49–64, 109, 133, 165, 167
European Regional Fund 104
European Union (EU) 1, 20–22
DG policy 40, 41, 107, 108
EU Structure Fund 21–2, 147, 148,
149, 150, 158, 159
and Faroe Islands 104–5, 106–7, 111

and Finland 6, 13, 32, 52
Interreg 52–6, 116, 118, 123, 127
membership 6–7, 13, 21–2, 32, 38,
149, 150, 159–60, 166
and new member countries 2, 41,
126n, 166
non-membership 46, 97–8, 159
outsider/insider 6, 32, 62, 64
and network involvement 41, 42, 44,
46
and Sweden 6, 13, 52, 149, 150,
159–60
Euro-regionalism 57–8, 60
external agency 129, 131
external opportunities 156–7

Farmers for Nature *120*
Faroe Islands 3, *9*, 95–113, 168
Faroese Home Rule 97, 103
Faroese Ministry of Foreign Affairs 96,
98, 99, 104
film industry *see* Film i Väst (FiV)
Film i Skåne 142, 151
Film i Väst (FiV) 141, 142, 146–52,
157–60, 169
Filmpool Nord 142, 151, 152
Finland *12*
and European Union 6, 13, 32, 52
and information and communications
technologies *80*, 82, *83*, 84, 85,
86, 87, 91
integrative regionalism 52, 58, 61, 62
and international cooperation *43*, *108*
regional development 3, 5, *9*, 24–5,
31, 71, 73–4
regional self-government 13, 14, 22
structural reform 16–17, 20, 21, 166
Finnish model 14, *15*, 19–20
fishing industry 96, 97, 107
Flensburg, Denmark 136
Florida, R. 143–4
foreign policy 58, *59*, 60, 95, 96, 97,
102–12
Forum Skagerrak *120*, *124*
'free rider syndrome' 28, 36
friendship relations 116, 118–19, 122–3,
126, 127, 128, 130
Friendship Society Arendal-Rezekne 126

Funen County, Denmark 137
Fyrstad, Sweden 147, 149, 150–51

Gateway to Guidance *121*
Germany 117, 128, 136
globalization 1, 35–6, 38, 61, 77, 95, 98, 105, 165
GLOCAL-Global Education Business Partnership *121*
glocalism 88, 92
Goals and Results Management Programme 152
Gothenburg 66, 148
governance 16, 133
 complex governance 10, 75, 167
 and government 79, 89
 multi-level governance 2, 5, 50–51, 52, 64, 167
 reforming governance 51, 167
 strategies 2, 65–75, 167–8
 structures 49–64, 75, 82, 165–70
  patterns of governance 3, *4*, 5, 10, 52, 67, 169–70
Greenland 97–8, 104
Greenport *121*
growth forums 22, 56, 138
Guangdong, China 137
Gunnufsen, Toffen 143, 152, 153, 155–6, 158, 159

health care 14, 17, 19, 21, 22, 24, 97
 Denmark 133, 136, 137, 138–9
 Norway 17, 18, 126, 169
heimastýrislógin 102
heimildarlógin 97, 102, 103
herbal medicine 137
hierarchy theories 99–100, 101–2, 104, 105, 134, 168
home rule 3, 97, 103
hospital care 16, 17, 20, 21, 136, 169
Hubei region, China 118–19, 122, 128, 130

Iceland 106, 126n
identity 4, 24, 66, 135
industry *see* business cooperation and development; businesses; fishing industry

information age types of development 27, 32, 33, 44, 62, 166
 see also Triple Helix
information and communication technology (ICT) *26*, 27, 35–6, 77–94, 166, 168, 170
information dissemination 116, 128, 130, 138
information ecology 11, 78–9, 87, 91, 168
information ecosystem 78–9, 168
information flows 35–6, 42, 99, 100, 102, 103, 104, 115–16, 128
information society 3, 4, 91
informatization 6, 77–94
in-house cell 128–9, 131, 169
innovation 73, 79, 88, 95, 102, 143
Innovation Circle *121*
Innovation Norway 28, 118
institutional change 15–19, 165
institutional development 10, 13–22, 166
institutional dynamics 3, 95–112
institutional retooling 25–9, 30, *31*, 169–70
integrative regionalism 2, 5, 10, 36, 38, 49–64, 109, 133, 165, 167
 and competitive regionalism 49, 51, *59*, 60, 61, 64
international affairs 97–8, 108–9, 127
international cooperation 5, 42, 43, 47, 95, 108–10, 111, 115–31
 Denmark *43*, 44, *108*, 133–9
 and education 118, 127, 128, 130
 Finland *43*, *108*
 Norway *43*, 44, 106, *108*, 117–22
 Sweden *43*, *108*
international effort 119–22, 127, 128
international political arena 11, 24, 95, 98, 99, 168
international relations 42, 98–9, 116–22, 168
internationalization 11, 133–9, 165, 169
 and competitiveness 25, 27, 28, *30*, *31*
 and information and communications technologies 90, 168
 and learning ecologies 44, *45*, 46
Internet 67, 77, 79, 85t, 86, 88, 168
Interreg 52–6, 116, 118, 123, 127
 see also European Union (EU)

Joint International Secretariat of Vest-
Agder and Aust-Agder 127

Kainuu region 16–17, 20
Kingdon, J.W. 144–5
knowledge brokerage 23–33, 79, 101, 102,
137, 138, 166, 169–70
knowledge workers 25, 65, 144
knutepunktstatus 157
Kristiansand Music Committee 143, 153
Kristiansand Næingsselskap (KNAS) 154
Kristiansand, Norway 29, 130, 131, 142,
152–5, 157, 169

Landstingsforbundet 143
Latvia 122, 126, 127, 128
learning capacity 115, 167
learning ecologies 4, 37, 39–43, 129–31,
167, 170
learning outcomes 28, 46, 115
learning region 2, 4, 5, 28, 115, 131
LEONARDO projects *125*
lifestyle 4, 137
LIFT analysis 119
lobbying 5, 50, 52, 57
local authorities 14, 22, 38–9, 66, 67–72
Denmark 16, 21
Finland 17, 20, 21
Norway 118, 128
Sweden 19, 143
local government 14–19, 22, 54, 66, 67,
69, 74–5, 133, 135, 138
localism 81, 87, 91, 111

Malopolska, Poland 137
management of international involvement
129
market orientation *68*, 69, 70, 71–2, 73,
74, 99, 167, 170
mayors 67, 155–6
measuring international engagement
115–31, 168
mergers *see* municipalities
Ministry of Culture and Church Affairs,
Norway 157
Ministry of Foreign Affairs, Norway 126
multi-level governance *see* governance
municipalities 27, 67–72, 153–5

mergers 14, *26*, *30*, 44, *45*, 96
Denmark 16, 21, 74
Finland 17, 21
Norway 18, 29

nation-building 4, 23–4
neo-republican 66–7, 69–70, 72, 74, 75,
167, 170
network approach 134–5
network building 150–51, 155–6
network cooperation 102, 105
network involvement 3, 11, 168–9
and cleavages 2, 61, 62, *63*, 64
and learning ecologies 10, 36, 37,
38–48, 167, 170
network relations 105–7, 137
network society 88
network theories 95–113, 168
networking, cross-border 1, 11, 35–48, 52,
107–8, 165, 167, 168–9
New Public Management (NPM) 65, 70,
71–2, 74, 75, 167, 170
new technology *see* information and
communication technology (ICT)
news (online) 79, 80
Nilsson, Jonny 151
non-sovereign states 95–113
Nordic cooperation project 49
Nordic Council 2n, 52, 56, *93*, 166
Nordic Transport political Network (NTN)
120, 124, 137
Norsk Hydro ASA 117
North American Free Trade Agreement
(NAFTA) 1
North Sea Circuit 123, *124*
North Sea Commission (NSC) 36, 56
Denmark 133, 137
Norway 117, 118, *120*, 122, 123, *124*,
131
North Sea Programme 123
North Sea region 36, *40*, 41, 42, 60, 117,
120, 124, 167
Norway *12*, 115–31
business cooperation and development
117–31, 143, 154–5
county councils 11, *15*, 17–18, 21, *29*,
115–31, 165, 168, 170
cross-border networking 107, 168–9

cultural policies 141, 142–3, 152–60, 169
development strategies 69, 70, 71–2, 73, 74, 75, 141
friendship relations 118–19, 122, 123, 126, 128, 130
health and hospital care 17, 18, 20, 21, 22, 126, 169
and information and communications technologies *80*, 82, *83*, 84, 85, 87, 91
integrative regionalism 5, 57, 58, 61, 62, 64
international cooperation *43*, 44, 106, *108*, 117–22
and network involvement 44, *45*, 46, 47
and policy preferences *29*, *31*
and regional activism 6, 32
and regional development 143, 166
regional policy-making 3, *9*, 24, 25, 57, 58
regional self-government 13, 14, 21, 22
and structural reform 17–18, 39, 57, 74, 75, 165, 170
Norwegian Cultural Council 156, 159
Norwegian Information Office *124*

Odderøya Amfi venue 154
Office of Cultural Affairs, Kristiansand 152, 153, 155
Olomouc, Czech Republic 137
Opgavekommissionen 15–16
organizational learning 37, 115
organizational patterns 3, 128–9
Oslo 66, 157

peripheries 24, 38, 44, 46
PIPE project *121*
Poland 137
policy entrepreneurs 145, 147, 150–51, 155–6, 158, 159, 169
policy learning 38, 165
policy networks 3–5, 10, 61, 64, 102, 159
policy preferences 3, 10, 23–33, 144, 166
and network involvement 38, 44, *45*, 46, 47, 61–2, *63*, 64, 167, 170

policy windows 144–5, 147–8, 149, 153–5, 156–7, 159–60
political expertise 35–7
political ideology *12*, *45*, 45, 46, 47, 83, 150
cleavages 17, 29–30, *31*, 32, 61–4, 111
political mass mobilization 23, 24, 25
political meetings 83, 84, 86
political roles 39–43, 77–94
controller 77, 82–3, 86, *87*, 91, 168
decision-maker 77, 85–7, 91, 168
ombudsman 77, 81–2, 86, *87*, 91, 168
representative 77, 83–4, 86, *87*, 91, 168
process tracing 145–6
processes of international collaboration *see* collaboration, international
project development *40*, 41, 42, 56, 118
public debate 13–22
public planning 145, 147–8, 153–5, 160
public sector 6, 32, 65, 73–4, 89, 130, 134, 135
businesses 14, 16, 17, 20, 28
reform 13, 16, 21, 22, 166

Quart Festival 141, 142–3, 152–60, 169

redistribution 24, 27, 28, *31*, 44, *45*, 143
reforming governance *see* governance
regional activism 6, 32, 57, 58, 60
regional advantage 6, 77–94, 168, 170
regional development 16, 18–19, 23–33, 57–8, 126, 133, 135, 136, 143, 150
and culture 141, 143
funds 54, 56n
Regional Development Board 142, 147
regional development policies 3–4, 8, 10, 14–15, 22, 23–33, 68–9n, 143
strategies 11, 137, 141
regional learning 2, 4, 5, 28, 115, 131
regional planning 14, 16, 19
regional policy-makers 1, 6, 7, 8, 22, 23, 27, 49–64, 77–94, 170
and integrative governance 5, 10, 49–64, 166, 167
regional science 23
regional self-government 6–7, 17, 18, 19, 49, 58–62, 95, 166

Denmark 20, 32, 38–9, 61
Faroe Islands 104, 111
Finland 13, 14, 22, 32, 61
Norway 13, 14, 21, 22, 32, 38–9, 61
Sweden 13, 14, 21, 22, 32, 38–9, 61,
    143
regionalism, competitive *see* competitive
    regionalism
regionalism, extra-Nordic 60, 64, 167
regionalism, integrative *see* integrative
    regionalism
regionalism, new 141–61
regionalism, state-centred 57–64, 167
regionalization 21, 27, 28, *30*, 31n, 32,
    44, 165
regression analysis 30, 44, *45*, 61, *63*, 90
reinforcement hypothesis 72, 88–9, 91
Reykjavik 96, 103, 106
Rezekne, Latvia 122–3, 126, 127, 128
roots 65, 167
Russia 36, 95, 117, 128

Scandinavian model 14–15, 19–20
Scandinavian Triangle *125*
Schleswig-Holstein 136
service providers 5, *26*, 39, 66
settlement patterns 38
Skagerrak, Denmark *120*, 123, *124*, *125*
Skåne, Sweden 3, 18, 19
social capital 66, 88, 99, 101
social democrats 12, 17, 19
social networking 83, 100
social services 14, 16, 17, 97, 133
solidarity 36, 39, 46, 66, 122–3, 130
South Jutland 135–6
Southern Denmark European Office 138
Southern European Office *124*
Southern Hospitals Health Authority,
    Norway 126
Southern Norway European Office 122,
    127, 129, 130, 131
state functions 27, 28, *30*, *31*, 32, 44, 46,
    63, 143
state provinces 17
state/region relation 57
Stockholm 66
strategic model 115, 116, 129, 130, 131

StratMos motorways of the sea *120*
structural reform 15–19, 20–21, 38–9, 51,
    58, 74, 75
    Denmark 13, 15–16, 22, 39, 57, 123,
        133, 165–6, 170
    responsibilities 14, 16, 20, 21,
        69n, 169
    Finland 16–17, 20, 21, 166
    Norway 17–18, 39, 57, 74, 75, 165,
        170
    Sweden 18–19, 20, 39, 147, 165, 170
Studio Fares 142
study tours *40*, 41, 42, 119, 123
subsidization 24, 97, 133
    film industry 142, 147, 151, 152, 158
    music festivals 156–7, 159
super-regions 49, 165
SuPortNet II *121*
Sustainable Development in Coastal
    Tourist Areas *124*
Sustainable Regions 137
Svenska Filminstitutet 142
Sweden *12*
    business cooperation and development
        148–51, 158
    county councils *15*, 19, 20, 142, 147,
        148, 150, 158
    development strategies 69, 70, 71–2,
        73–4, 75
    and European Union 6, 13, 52, 149,
        150, 159–60
    film industry *see* Film i Väst (FiV)
    and information and communications
        technologies *80*, 82, *83*, 84, 85,
        86, 87, 91
    integrative regionalism 58, 61, 62, 64,
        167
    international cooperation *43*, *108*
    and regional policy-making 3, *9*, *31*
    regional self-government 6, 13, 14, 21,
        22, 32, 38–9, 61, 143
    structural reform 18–19, 20, 39, 147,
        165, 170
Swedish Association of Local Authorities
    and Regions 19, 143
symbolism 36, 106

taxation 14, 16, 20, 96, 133, 135
technological innovation *see* information and communication technology (ICT)
Telemark, Norway 117–22, 127–9, 131
territorial consolidation 23, 118
text messaging 82, 83
tourism 36, *124*
transaction costs 101, 107, 112
transformation and transparency hypothesis 89–91
transparency 66, *68*, 69, 70, 73t, 74, 75, 83, 89–91, 170
travel budgets *26*, 27
Triple Helix 4, 25, 27, *30*, *31*, 32, 44, *45*, 170
Trollhättan, Sweden 141, 142, 147, 148–9, 157, 169
trust 88, 101
twinning arrangements *40*, 43

Uddevalla, Sweden 148n, 158
universities 25, 27, 28, *29*
University College, Norway 118
University hospitals 136
urban development 126, 141, 144
urban drift 169–70

URBIS project 89
user orientation *68*, 69, 70, 71–2, 73, 74

value for money 66–7
Västernfilm *see* Film i Väst (FiV)
Västra Götaland 18, 19, 142, 147–8, 150, 158, 159
Vejle County, Denmark 137
Viborg, Denmark 122, 123, 127, 128
virtue 65, 66–7, 167
VNE-Inland Waterways of Europe *121*
voluntary bodies 14, *68*, *93*, 122, 126, 128, 130, 134

Warsaw Pact 2, 49
Water City International *120*
Westphalian state-building *see* nation-building
wicked problems 38, 44, 46, 169
Women in Business *125*, 127
World Wide Web 77, 79, 88

yvirtøkulógin 97

Øresund, Norway 127, 136
Østfold-Bohuslän/Dalsland 52, 53m
Øya Festival 157

THE INTERNATIONAL POLITICAL ECONOMY OF NEW REGIONALISMS SERIES

Other titles in the series

The Euro in the 21st Century
Economic Crisis and Financial Uproar
María Lorca-Susino

Crafting an African Security Architecture
Addressing Regional Peace and Conflict in
the 21st Century
Edited by Hany Besada

Comparative Regional Integration
Europe and Beyond
Edited by Finn Laursen

The Rise of China and the Capitalist
World Order
Edited by Li Xing

The EU and World Regionalism
The Makability of Regions in the
21st Century
*Edited by Philippe De Lombaerde and
Michael Schultz*

The Role of the European Union in Asia
China and India as Strategic Partners
*Edited by Bart Gaens, Juha Jokela and
Eija Limnell*

China and the Global Politics of
Regionalization
Edited by Emilian Kavalski

Clash or Cooperation of Civilizations?
Overlapping Integration and Identities
Edited by Wolfgang Zank

New Perspectives on Globalization and
Antiglobalization: Prospects for a New
World Order?
Edited by Henry Veltmeyer

Governing Regional Integration for
Development: Monitoring Experiences,
Methods and Prospects
*Edited by Philippe De Lombaerde,
Antoni Estevadeordal and Kati Suominen*

Europe-Asia Interregional Relations
A Decade of ASEM
Edited by Bart Gaens

Cruising in the Global Economy
Profits, Pleasure and Work at Sea
Christine B.N. Chin

Beyond Regionalism?
Regional Cooperation, Regionalism and
Regionalization in the Middle East
*Edited by Cilja Harders
and Matteo Legrenzi*

The EU-Russian Energy Dialogue
Europe's Future Energy Security
Edited by Pami Aalto

Regionalism, Globalisation and
International Order
Europe and Southeast Asia
Jens-Uwe Wunderlich

EU Development Policy and
Poverty Reduction
Enhancing Effectiveness
Edited by Wil Hout

An East Asian Model for Latin
American Success
The New Path
Anil Hira

European Union and New Regionalism:
Regional Actors and Global Governance
in a Post-Hegemonic Era.
Second Edition
Edited by Mario Telò

Regional Integration and Poverty
*Edited by Dirk Willem te Velde
and the Overseas Development Institute*

Redefining the Pacific?
Regionalism Past, Present and Future
*Edited by Jenny Bryant-Tokalau
and Ian Frazer*

The Limits of Regionalism
NAFTA's Labour Accord
Robert G. Finbow

Latin America's Quest for Globalization
The Role of Spanish Firms
*Edited by Félix E. Martín
and Pablo Toral*

Exchange Rate Crises in
Developing Countries
The Political Role of the Banking Sector
Michael G. Hall

Globalization and Antiglobalization
Dynamics of Change in the New
World Order
Edited by Henry Veltmeyer

Twisting Arms and Flexing Muscles
Humanitarian Intervention and
Peacebuilding in Perspective
*Edited by Natalie Mychajlyszyn and
Timothy M. Shaw*

Asia Pacific and Human Rights
A Global Political Economy Perspective
Paul Close and David Askew

Demilitarisation and Peace-Building
in Southern Africa
Volume III – The Role of the Military
in State Formation and Nation-Building
*Edited by Peter Batchelor, Kees Kingma
and Guy Lamb*

Demilitarisation and Peace-Building
in Southern Africa
Volume II – National and
Regional Experiences
*Edited by Peter Batchelor
and Kees Kingma*

Demilitarisation and Peace-Building
in Southern Africa
Volume I – Concepts and Processes
*Edited by Peter Batchelor and Kees
Kingma*

Reforging the Weakest Link
Global Political Economy and Post-Soviet
Change in Russia, Ukraine and Belarus
Edited by Neil Robinson

Persistent Permeability?
Regionalism, Localism, and Globalization
in the Middle East
*Edited by Bassel F. Salloukh
and Rex Brynen*

The New Political Economy of United
States-Caribbean Relations
The Apparel Industry and the Politics
of NAFTA Parity
Tony Heron

The Nordic Regions
and the European Union
*Edited by Søren Dosenrode
and Henrik Halkier*

The New Regionalism in Africa
*Edited by J. Andrew Grant
and Fredrik Söderbaum*

Comparative Regional Integration
Theoretical Perspectives
Edited by Finn Laursen

Japan and South Africa
in a Globalising World
A Distant Mirror
*Edited by Chris Alden and
Katsumi Hirano*

Development and Security
in Southeast Asia
Volume III: Globalization
Edited by David B. Dewitt
and Carolina G. Hernandez

Development and Security
in Southeast Asia
Volume II: The People
Edited by David B. Dewitt
and Carolina G. Hernandez

Development and Security
in Southeast Asia
Volume I: The Environment
Edited by David B. Dewitt
and Carolina G. Hernandez

Thailand, Indonesia and Burma in
Comparative Perspective
Priyambudi Sulistiyanto